First Books

First Books

~

The Printed Word
and
Cultural Formation in Early Alabama

Philip D. Beidler

THE UNIVERSITY OF ALABAMA PRESS
Tuscaloosa and London

Copyright © 1999
The University of Alabama Press
Tuscaloosa, Alabama 34587–0380
All rights reserved
Manufactured in the United States of America

1   2   3   4   5   6   7   8   9   •   07   06   05   04   02   01   00   99

∞
The paper on which this book is printed meets the minimum requirements of
American National Standard for Information Science–Permanence of Paper for
Printed Library Materials, ANSI Z39.48-1984.

Jacket design by Shari DeGraw

Library of Congress Cataloging-in-Publication Data

Beidler, Philip D.
First books : the printed word and cultural formation in early
Alabama / Philip D. Beidler.
p. cm.
Includes bibliographical references (p. 171) and index.

ISBN 0–8173–0985–3 (alk. paper)
1. American literature—Alabama—History and criticism.   2. American
literature—19th century—History and criticism.   3. Literature and
society—Alabama—History—19th century.   4. Literature publishing—
Alabama—History—19th century.   5. Printing—Alabama—History— 19th
century.   6. Alabama—Intellectual life.   7. Alabama—In literature.   I. Title.
PS266.A5 B45 1999
810.9′ 9761—dc21

99–6084

British Library Cataloguing-in-Publication Data available

In Memory of O. B. Emerson

Contents

~

Acknowledgments
ix

Introduction
Literature and Culture in Early Alabama
1

1. Satire in the Territories
Literature and the Art of Political Payback in an Early Alabama Classic
14

2. First Book
Henry Hitchcock's *Alabama Justice of the Peace*
23

3. "The First Production of the Kind, in the South"
A Backwoods Literary *Incognito* and His Attempt
at the Great American Novel
32

4. Belles Lettres in a New Country
47

5. Antebellum Alabama History in the Planter Style
The Example of Albert J. Pickett
63

6. A. B. Meek's Great American Epic Poem of 1855; or,
the Curious Career of *The Red Eagle*
76

7. Historicizing Alabama's Southwestern Humorists; or, How the
Times Were Served by Johnson J. Hooper and Joseph G. Baldwin
87

8. Caroline Lee Hentz's Anti-Abolitionist Double Feature and Augusta
Jane Evans's New and Improved Novel of Female Education
102

9. Alabama's Last First Book
The Example of Daniel Hundley
127

Notes
137

Works Cited
171

Index
177

Acknowledgments

~

I gratefully acknowledge the help of the following people: Salli Davis, Dwight Eddins, Bert Hitchcock, Fred Hobson, Jeff Jakeman, Malcolm MacDonald, Robert Phillips, Diane Roberts, Johanna Nicol Shields, and Hugh Terry. I would also like to thank especially the staff of The University of Alabama Special Collections Library for their expert bibliographic guidance and their wonderful collegiality in giving me access to their resources.

A University of Alabama faculty member revered by generations of students and renowned for his generosity to new arrivals in the English Department, my late colleague O. B. Emerson extended me the further scholarly benefit of sharing his vast knowledge of Alabama literature. He thereby awakened twenty-five years ago a career-long interest that I hope I have continued to honor in my scholarship. This book is dedicated in his memory.

Parts of this text have appeared in *Southern Literary Journal* 24, no. 2 (spring 1992): 106–24, and 30, no. 1 (fall 1997): 1–12; and *Mississippi Quarterly* 51, no. 3 (spring 1998): 275–90. Reprinted with permission.

First Books

Introduction

Literature and Culture in Early Alabama

The title of this book, I hope, truthfully advertises its subject. I mean *First Books* to be a case study in the forms and processes of cultural mythmaking. At the same time, focusing here on the idea of the production of literature in a new country, I also wish to draw attention to a peculiar instance of the phenomenon, related at once to the conditions of nineteenth-century American mass-print literacy and to the particular primacy placed during the early national era upon the word as an expression of the prospects and possibilities of early American democracy. To be specific, I wish to show how the literary and political culture of an early-nineteenth-century Deep South state created itself out of its first books.

A more concrete description of the relationship implied here would be that of literature and social ideology. Accordingly, as a case study in that relationship, *First Books* is meant to have a discrete value for what it tells us about the ideological character of specific literary productions, what we might call the political work of cultural formation within very specific contexts—in this case, contexts of gender, class, race, social ideology, and regional and national politics, with the chief among them, of course, quickly becoming the issue of chattel slavery. At the same time, in creating such a model of the relationship between literature and ideology in a particular early-nineteenth-century American culture, one wishes also to claim for a study of this kind, albeit with distinct allowances to Southern regionalism, a certain representative quality. Historically, that is, Alabama, among the burgeoning territories just beyond the boundaries of the original Republic once known as the Old Southwest and Old Northwest, emerged as part of the first significant constellation of post-Revolutionary states carving themselves out of the new country contained within the expanding national borders. Accordingly, in this case as a state formed in the crucial frontier period of early national consolidation, its own literature *as quickly* became a drama in regional microcosm of the larger record of the antebellum Republic—beginning with territorial life in the early national period, passing into the turbulences and unprecedented new political realignments of the Jacksonian era, and moving on through the agonizing decades of slavery debate toward the final crisis of Union.

To be sure, during the period in question, the production of a literary record corresponding to the processes of political evolution described is one that did not confine itself to a state or a region. Today the literature of the territorial and early statehood eras might surely provide Ohioans or Indianans, for instance, with analogous accounts of the ideological foundations of civic culture. Nor did the process cease with the Civil War. Today some Americans are Nebraskans and others are Oregonians, that is, precisely because they live in a country that still persists in suggesting that some identification with the culture of a given state has an important bearing on one's consciousness as a citizen of the larger nation.

At the same time, even among major pre–Civil War territories arriving at statehood in the early antebellum era, one is still struck here, as in few other instances, by the comparative plenitude and diversity of historical materials at hand, comprising in their totality something close to what one might call a fully embodied literary culture. To put this as a question: why, in terms of both the general richness and the relatively accomplished quality of materials, is not much easily made of an analogous literature of early Michigan, for instance, or of early Ohio, Illinois, Kentucky, Missouri, or Tennessee? Or, to return the matter to the declarative, especially given the benighted cultural reputation then and now of the lower South, it must surely strike us as ironic that the only local traditions of the era seeming to compare would be those of Louisiana and Mississippi. Yet to see the puzzle in just those terms is at the same time to begin to resolve it. For of course, what early Alabama found itself in possession of virtually overnight, as to a comparable degree did early Louisiana and early Mississippi, were the social, political, and economic conditions required to jumpstart a traditional literary culture in the old Anglo-European model: namely, a system of property-based class relationship founded on large concentrations of personal wealth, mainly landed and slaveowning, eventuating in the emergence of a planter elite, and quickly followed by the quick establishment of professional and merchant classes of similar social, political, educational, and literary predispositions. Further, such patterns of social development were abetted here by a characteristic nineteenth-century American print culture, arising at a number of identifiable publishing centers and quickly evolving into a widespread system of print production and distribution.[1] To be sure, it must remain one of the great and endlessly compounded tragic ironies of the early national era that, across the region described, such cultural flourishing in the traditional sense came about directly as a result of the removal of large, well-established, and for the most part peaceful populations of native inhabitants and the quick institution of an extremely profitable system of mass chattel slavery. Further, even for the beneficiaries of the system so described, the developments were hardly an easy ride, being constantly attended by the cataclysmic potential of boom and bust that marked the spectacular accumulations of wealth in the era. The flush times, for instance, of the early to mid-1830s, with their rampant borrowing and land, slave, and currency speculations, saw most of their wildfire profits evaporate in the Panic of 1837 and the ensuing bank crises of the 1840s; and the resurgence of the cotton economy of the 1850s, accompanied by a last, spectacular flourishing in profitability of the slave system, in turn proved but a prelude to the financial catastrophe of civil war.

Still, amidst frontier hubbub and tumult, and the riding of the waves of boom and bust speculation, the structures of traditional cultural relationship managed to institute themselves effectively in the Alabama of the early decades of statehood into the makings of a remarkably well configured society. A pattern of distinctive class relationship grew up, for instance, marked by various institutional definitions and assignments of status—as determined by property ownership, social and familial background, religious affiliation, educational opportunity, and access to general intellectual culture. In politics, the rise of a centralized government proceeded more or less smoothly, with a succession of strong chief executives including William Wyatt Bibb, Israel Pickens, Clement Comer Clay, and others, and a legislative branch vigorously exercising its functions in early capitals beginning with Huntsville, the seat of the 1819 constitutional convention, and then moving to Cahaba and Tuscaloosa before settling finally in Montgomery; and in the administration and codified interpretation of law, political stability was further ensured by the work of a judiciary including in its ranks a number of notably commanding and able figures, including such pioneers of the bench as Harry Toulmin, Henry Hitchcock, and Abner S. Lipscomb. More general political and economic developments also included the quick rise of a party system—with an early flourishing of political journalism abetted by a large complex of daily and weekly newspapers—and the chartering of a state bank, with the president and board of directors to be elected by joint session of the legislature. Established religion, among the ruling elites mainly Episcopalian, attempted to make its peace with rising new evangelical sects—Presbyterian, Methodist, and Baptist—of decidedly more populist orientation. Education, manifesting its institutional status in the early chartering and establishment of the state university, also took shape through the rise of local academies in the classical model; and by the 1850s the state had also passed an act making formal provision for a system of public primary education.[2]

Meanwhile, a more general culture of letters—abetted, in the case of propertied elites, by prerequisite plenties of money and leisure, but also among merchant and professional classes by corresponding educational background and intellectual appetite—hitched itself to both the spoken and the written word with alacrity. Political oratory became a virtuoso form, as did the literary declamation and the lyceum and/or philosophical society lecture. Newspapers, pamphlets, literary journals, and popular magazines, both local and regional, found wide circulation. Newspapers, particularly, served as a venue for poetry. Also, in the case of the frontier humorists, newspaper pages became the first locations for most of their works to see print. Further, as to overall print interests, they served as a register of trends in popular book production and consumption, a forum of public opinion, so to speak, on literary tastes and reading habits, and, among the more affluent, buying habits as well.

Book culture itself flourished with the purchasing and reading in large numbers of works by figures of regional, national, and transatlantic reputation. Favored poets included Hemans, Byron, Campbell, Moore, Burns, and the graveyard school. American counterparts were Longfellow, Bryant, and—strictly in his non-abolitionist mode—Whittier (Ellison, *Early Alabama Publications* 43–55). Novelists were led by Scott; but, like many Southerners, Alabamians also liked Cooper and Simms. Irving was cherished too, as was the ubiquitous Shakespeare (63–67). In writing, an early professionalism among male figures often came about as a result of newspaper editorship, legal practice, or experience in politics or the judiciary. And even among figures eventually achieving something of a properly literary reputation—authors of mainly local and/or regional importance, for instance, such as William Russell Smith, Albert J. Pickett, or A. B. Meek, or writers eventually coming to national eminence, such as the humorists Johnson J. Hooper and Joseph Glover Baldwin—much would continue to be made of gentleman-amateur status. Among women, as with the travel diarist Anne Newport Royall or the estimable literary Mobilian Octavia Walton Le Vert, feminine literary production likewise remained largely the province of the gifted amateur. On the other hand, and with no small gender irony, in the case of such widely read domestic realists of midcentury as

Caroline Lee Hentz and Augusta Jane Evans, Alabama women's writing, imaging national trends, could also be seen quickly giving way to the rise, in essentially modern definition, of the mass-market literary professional.[3]

The key ingredient in all cases of the flourishing of a culture sufficiently thick and complex to support something that might properly be called literature was plenty of money—albeit, in a given locale, a given time span, or a given set of circumstances, money that could turn out to be as easily imaginary as real: first, land money, especially in the case of rich agricultural land, largely gained at the expense of original inhabitants, and then doubled, tripled, quadrupled in value through speculative enterprise; slave money, basing itself first upon the value of imported Africans for the labor of their muscles but then likewise rapidly increasing itself through profitable market speculation on the sale of their bodies; crop and commodity money, funding a flourishing mercantile and shipping community; and last, but certainly not least, enormous amounts of money existing in various forms of paper instruments, ranging from banknotes and other wildcat currencies to investment certificates and formal documents of indebtedness, and funding whole classes of professionals in law, banking, factoring, account keeping, and attendant areas of finance and investment.

This is to say that from the late 1820s onward, especially, following the first great influx of citizenry into the new state and the rapid development of its vast resources into a conventional socioeconomic base, there was already enough money in Alabama to support, in a rather traditional Anglo-European sense, a high culture. To be sure, it was not a court culture or even anything resembling the culture of a traditional nobility. Nor, on the other hand, could its values and assumptions be said to have replicated even those associated with the aristocratic pastoralism of the older regions of the middle and lower South. If anything, here, rather, was something like a feudal nobility of planter elites, albeit with the fruits of their wealth and the projections of their values disseminated among mercantile and professional classes often of commensurate standing and influence. In sum, it was a society of the gentry.

The result, to be sure, was a kind of living anachronism. A whole society founded on that great, ephemeral American quintessence, money, oddly found itself more like a nineteenth-century England, France, Germany, or—perhaps in the closest parallel of the time—Russia. Certainly it was far from the bustling egalitarianism of the Midwest and North; but even as a Southern precinct, just as little did it resemble Jefferson's dream of an agrarian landscape populated by its own natural nobility of planter and yeoman. Rather, as in analogous cultures of the gentry, a proprietary aristocracy quickly found itself pitted against insurgent middle- and lower-class aspirants to wealth, power, and status.

On the other hand, in comparison even to other Deep South counterparts,

Alabama also remained distinct in the relative uniformity of the ideological foundations of culture. Despite the radical carvings out and configurings, that is, according to the desires of various interest groups, of what Mills Thornton has described as power and politics in early Alabama—Whigs versus Jacksonians; fire-eaters versus Unionists; planter elites of the Black Belt versus yeoman farmers of the north; business and commercial interests versus assorted banking and currency factions—even here one would have remarked on a pronounced cultural homogeneity.

In terms of political demographics, the most active and/or influential figures were nearly all Anglo-American, with a preponderance of English stock from the traditional upper South in the planter classes and Scotch-Irish in the yeomanry[4]—albeit with the latter, if descended from earliest traders and settlers, frequently admitting to native admixture and proud of it. The single exception to the Anglo-American rule would have been Mobile, with its representation of the descendants of the colonial French and Spanish; and so, for most of the antebellum period, the basic early pattern would continue, save for a few pockets of new admixture as a result of early-nineteenth-century European immigration.[5] As to other external connections, there was but a minimal historical legacy, except among Creek chiefs of mixed descent, of the often bitter struggle that had taken place across the frontier South between revolutionary and loyalist; and as the national party scene evolved into the new century, the state nonetheless remained largely mainly Whig and Democrat, with virtually no incursions of republicanism.

In economics, the dominant order remained largely agrarian, with deep connections to the mercantile and professional classes, but as yet largely untroubled by the new complications of a rising industrialism;[6] and in jurisprudence, the system remained resolutely Anglo-American, with English common law engrafted upon only as far as necessary by the American Bill of Rights. In religion, the state was Protestant, with the Episcopalianism of the traditional elites beginning to jostle with other newly emerging evangelical Protestant denominations—Baptist, Methodist, Presbyterian.[7]

In sum, then, among the new political jurisdictions emerging on the antebellum Southwestern frontier, Alabama here distinguished itself even from such near neighbors and analogues as Mississippi and Louisiana, with their deep admixtures of other cultural influences—French, Spanish, African, Creole—to pursue an experiment in statehood remarkable in its Anglo-American demographic purity. In this degree, in fact, if there was a model, it was the more "traditional" pre-Revolutionary Anglo-American Southern cultures such as Virginia, North Carolina, South Carolina, and Georgia—not surprisingly, the regions from which most of the settlers emanated.[8] And so, almost uncannily, would follow a replication even of the geographical politics of the earlier land-scapes, with the residents of the Appalachian ridge seeing themselves in contra-distinction to those of the Tidewater, or those of the Piedmont to those of the Carolina low country. In Alabama likewise the index of cultural aspiration, landed status, would follow the movement into the broad, rich, agricultural landscapes of the Tennessee Valley and, to the South, of the Black Belt, with the plantation and its Greek Revival great house, the Episcopal parish, the court-house and commercial center. The cosmopolitan precinct of Mobile would con-tinue to mark the interfluence of cultures as in a port city like Charleston, Savannah, New Orleans, or an old trading center like Natchez. Meanwhile, the placement of the capital, following a zigzag course of political necessity from St. Stephens, to Huntsville, next Cahaba, then Tuscaloosa, would stabilize itself in deference to the rich Black Belt planters at Montgomery. Accordingly, as a not unmarked signature of affiliation with the mainly British postcolonial South, with its early centers of learning such as Chapel Hill, Athens, and Charlottes-ville, one of the first acts of the legislature in 1819—although not fulfilled until 1831—would be a provision for the establishment of a state university—a "semi-nary of learning" it was grandly called—in Tuscaloosa.

To be sure, the Anglo-American cultural elites actually presiding over most of the developments described above constituted a relatively small segment of the population.[9] Yet precisely in the degree to which they quickly came to dominate political, economic, legal, educational, and even religious life in early Alabama, they also supplied a corresponding center of cultural mass frequently missing in more egalitarian precincts, and often with distinctive literary results. The result, as will be seen, was the surprisingly early emergence in at least one outpost of culture on the putative Deep South frontier of virtually all the major literary forms of the era: satire; the novel, the romantic sketch, the philosophical essay, the legal-juridical treatise; autobiography, biography, history, epic poetry; and, shortly, even the more refined emanations of belles lettres—the poetry col-lection, literary magazine, travel book, and cultural memoir.

To enumerate by title and simple description the first books so produced is even now to sense the ebullience and vigor of cultural energy translating it-self virtually overnight into a startling richness of literary production. The first known literary text to find itself into print, for instance—a rollicking verse sat-ire about a would-be backwoods *miles gloriosus* entitled *The Last Campaign of Sir John Falstaff The II; or, The Hero of the Burnt-Corn Battle. A Serio-Comic Poem by* ***** *******—actually comes of the pre-statehood era; but even by now, perhaps appropriately in a new territory distinguished by Indian wars, land acquisitions, and the raffish tussle of seekers after fame and fortune and their parties, we see a literature already down to its grandiloquent title styling itself in the vein of major cultural chronicle. Here, an early Alabama author, Lewis Sewall by name, had already found world enough to write satire in the territories.

Accordingly, equally appropriate to a new country as soon as it acquired statehood status proved to be a properly political and ideological first book in the most utilitarian senses of those terms. The actual first production written and printed in the state by an Alabama author, Henry Hitchcock of Mobile, this was a law-and-order manual for courts administration, a combination digest of the laws and comprehensive guide to legal and judicial procedure, concealing its status as landmark legal and juridical treatise under the simple title *Alabama Justice of the Peace.*

Next came a new attempt to address the great Creek war of the early century, this time as a subject of romantic fiction—and accordingly, this time as well with the high seriousness that would mark its ongoing treatment as the focal, even obsessive topic of much of the state's early literature. Not surprisingly, the result here was a huge, garish, teeming Fenimore Cooper and/or Walter Scott–like epic of the forest, complete with fair heroine, genteel hero, noble savages, shadowed miscreants, and other mysterious presences abounding; and also including guest appearances by Andrew Jackson himself and his noble adversary, the Creek chieftain William Weatherford, known to history as the Red Eagle. Variously credited to "Don Pedro Casender," "Wiley Conner," or "the Rev. M. Smith," and grandly entitled *The Lost Virgin of the South: An Historical Novel, Founded on Facts, Connected with the Indian War in the South, in 1812 to '15,* it truly set itself forth as nothing less than a backwoods literary *incognito's* attempt to write the great nineteenth-century American romantic novel.

Evidence shortly followed of what seemed the possibility of genuine belles lettres in a new country. At the nascent university in Tuscaloosa, William Russell Smith, a young matriculant of poetic inclinations, published a first collection of romantic lyrics, demurely entitled *College Musings; or, Twigs from Parnassus;* there too, shortly, Smith's friend, the budding politician and man of letters Alexander Beaufort Meek, would found a literary journal called *The Southron;* and by the end of the antebellum era, Mobile's Octavia Walton Le Vert would gain international literary celebrity for her famed belletristic account of the grand tour entitled *Souvenirs of Travel.*

On a grander literary scale, it would also be A. B. Meek in 1855—the year, it turns out, of the publication of both Longfellow's *Song of Hiawatha* and the first edition of Walt Whitman's *Leaves of Grass*—who would make Alabama's contribution to the great American nineteenth-century epic poem with *The Red Eagle.* Again, the great subject would be the great Creek war; and again, against the backdrop of forest war would be set a tale of heroism and romance. And shortly would follow a weighty contribution to prose historical chronicle in the epic vein as well, with Albert J. Pickett's *History of Alabama, and Incidentally of Georgia and Mississippi, from the Earliest Period,* the quintessential achievement of history in the planter style.

Finally, a number of Alabama authors from the 1840s onward were making national literary reputations as well. The rumbustious humor of the frontier would find itself served in such popular productions as Johnson Jones Hooper's *Adventures of Simon Suggs* and Joseph Glover Baldwin's *The Flush Times of Alabama and Mississippi;* and the vigorous genre of the nineteenth-century women's novel would find Alabama practitioners even more well known on the national scene, with works such as Caroline Lee Hentz's *The Planter's Northern Bride*—itself a direct Southern riposte to Harriet Beecher Stowe's *Uncle Tom's Cabin*—and Augusta Jane Evans's *Beulah,* the attempt to transmute the novel of female education into the novel of ideas that would launch her on the most successful career of any domestic realist of the century.

In this connection, from the perspective of the historical observer, at least, the single most distinctive feature of Alabama literature of the territorial and early statehood period must surely remain its complex response to the tragedy of race. On one hand, as throughout much of the literary South, there remained the large and obdurate refusal of the culture—save, that is, for the utility of the political, legal, or scientific discourse,[10] or, as in the case of Hentz, the direct anti-abolitionist riposte—to write about the single fact of political and economic life that largely made it possible: the fact of chattel slavery. And, complicating the matter, there remained equally the habit of compounding the denial by a recurrent gesture of literary-historical substitution and sublimation. In work after work, the intense, even obsessive contemplation of the subjection and eventual extirpation of native peoples became a way of not contemplating the other tragedy comprised in the newer racial curse. Especially among male figures, the Southern tendency toward epic and romance, along with their debased forms of picaresque and adventure chronicle, fostered a complex pastoral nostalgia comparable to the romantic primitivism of Gray or Scott, or, in the closer American connection, Cooper and Simms. Accordingly, as in both of the latter, with Simms in the most pronounced literary proximity, the world of the forest wars in America, in keeping with the Whig explanation of history, could remain the world before the fall into history, politics, the law, the need of governments; and in Alabama, that prelapsarian vision was also frequently made to encompass a world before the fall into slavery. When slaves appear at all, as in Smith's *The Lost Virgin* or Hooper's *Simon Suggs,* they appear not as persons or as subjects susceptible to literary depiction, but rather as a class, a type, a caricature—a figure of humor, occasionally of villainy. Indeed, ironically the closest we get to slaves in writing of the era is again in domestic fiction—in Hentz's novels and short stories, for instance, or period sketches by male sentimentalists such as William Russell Smith and others, with the essentially benign depiction of slaveholding and plantation life at the household focus.

And it is precisely here, in a concluding examination of the relationship between subject and authorship, that we must return to consider literature and ideology at one final intersection, one last ironic tie-in of issues of race, class, gender, and social power with both the question on one hand of what might be called the political content of these first books and on the other of what might be called the cultural politics of writing and of reading that made them possible. For there can be no question that the literature so produced was in a distinctive sense a literature of social, political, and economic elites, produced by members of a ruling class and designed to be read, within the region and without, by an audience of corresponding cultural status, interest, and outlook. This is certainly true as it relates to the issues described above of suppressed, sublimated, substituted political content—ironically, almost invariably a function of male writers, working nearly to a man in a scene or arena of male writing of elite political authority; and it is equally true in the general subscription of the body of writing so produced, male and female, to the conventional protocols of a generalized antebellum American gentility. As the sites of authority for the production of literary discourse were remarkably uniform—the writing desk, the lecture podium, the pulpit,[11] the election platform, the courthouse, the legislative chamber, the law or newspaper office—so were the basic locales of literary consumption—the library, the parlor, the reading circle, the study club, the philosophical and/or literary society. Further, this remained the case even, as has been famously demonstrated by scholars of American humor, when the literature itself seemed to take to the street or the backwoods clearing to find a subject visibly earthy, proletarian, vernacular. In the low-life jollity of the frontier picaresque, the issue remained, at least on the surface, political control, with meaning dictated by the status of the gentleman narrator who most frequently presides over the rowdy tales spun out for the audience's amused and horrified delectation. And control there was. The male writers were, nearly to a figure, planters, politicians, lawyers, judges, journalists, educators, men of letters, the occasional minister, maintaining their identity as literary personages as a dimension of a larger public personality, in an astonishing number of cases intertwined with active political careers, either as elected or appointed officials, or with deep involvement in party matters. Sewall was a territorial government functionary, Hitchcock a frontier jurist and member of constitutional convention. ("M. Smith," the odd man out among early figures, seems to have been an itinerant preacher, albeit an exceedingly well read one when it came to popular history and political biography; on the other hand, one is hardly surprised to find that the alternate claimant to authorship of the work in question, Wiley Conner, who at the very least served as the printer of a revised version, was a newspaper editor.) Both William Russell Smith and A. B. Meek, who might have vied equally for the title of the state's most eminent man of letters during the early period, also pursued extensive public careers in law, politics, journalism, and education, with the former elected to the U.S. and Confederate Congresses and the latter serving as speaker of the house in the Alabama legislature. The historian Pickett was a planter, active in Democratic Party matters; and the humorist Baldwin was a lawyer and jurist, a member of the state legislature, and eventually justice of the California Supreme Court. Even Hooper, perhaps the closest to a professional writer in the lot, was a lawyer and a journalist, eventually becoming secretary to the Confederate War Department. The cases of the women were somewhat more complicated, but not much. Again, they were products of their class, with Hentz, once more the exception, in this case proving the rule: the educator and woman author—of a breed rather more familiar in the North, forced, after her husband's death, to live by the pen. Evans and Le Vert, on the other hand, were both literary women impelled toward literature by their genteel origins and sustained by their cosmopolitan cultural milieu.

Male or female, what these writers all had in common was that mainly they wrote about their kind and subjects of interest to their kind. Even when they went outside class limits, they wrote within the essentially homogeneous political and demographic assumptions of their race and region. Accordingly, in this connection, it should thus not surprise us excessively that the vast preponderance of the literature produced was not great, or perhaps not even accomplished, but probably more like merely competent—although the closer it approached the properly professional sphere, certainly the more visible it frequently found itself in the national venue. Hooper's work, first appearing locally, found its larger audience in Porter's *Spirit of the Times* and through the Philadelphia publisher T. B. Peterson; Baldwin's, published initially in the august *Southern Literary Messenger,* came out in book form with the New York publisher D. Appleton. Hentz went into standard edition with the Philadelphia firm of Carey and Hart, later A. Hart/T. B. Peterson. Evans's New York publishers included Harper and Brothers, Derby and Jackson, G. W. Carleton, G. W. Dillingham, A. L. Burt, and Grosset and Dunlap. In London her publisher was W. Nicholson and Sons. And Le Vert's 1857 travel memoir, first published by S. H. Goetzel of Mobile, was reissued in 1866 by G. W. Carleton of New York.

Further, if most of the writers considered here thought of themselves as representatives, if not active proponents, of regional letters, they also certainly saw themselves as part of national and even transatlantic conversations. Whoever he was, "M. Smith," for instance, surely saw himself as talking with Scott, Simms, and Cooper, as well as popular chroniclers such as John Eaton, Timothy Flint, and Joseph Holt Ingraham. Smith began his poetry volume with an homage to Shakespeare and ended with a eulogy for Scott, making time along the way for echoes of Byron, Wordsworth, and William Cullen Bryant, not to mention such fellow Southerners as Edgar Poe, Edward Coote Pinkney, and Thomas Holley Chivers. As a man of letters and apostle of Southern literary culture, Meek worked in conscious emulation of his idol, William Gilmore Simms; as a poet working in the vein of the popular epic, his example was clearly Longfellow. In his *History*, Pickett reeled off his debts to fellow Southern historians, but also invoked the names of eminences outside the region, including Jared Sparks of Massachusetts and Theodore Irving of New York.

Hentz, of course, became the most celebrated of all the Southern literary controversialists on the slavery issue with her direct riposte to Harriet Beecher Stowe. But she also wrote the larger body of her fiction in direct awareness of other such national counterparts as Catherine Maria Sedgwick, E.D.E.N. Southworth, Susan Warner, Maria Cummins, and others. Evans similarly revealed her awareness of female contemporaries—Southworth, Hentz, Warner, Cummins, and the like—but her texts were also filled with philosophical debate involving virtually every major writer in the nineteenth-century canon—Ruskin and Mill, Coleridge and Carlyle, Emerson and Poe. And as a travel writer, Le Vert cast herself in the distinct role of the literary cosmopolite as well, invoking along the way all the requisite departed worthies and meeting as many of the prominent living ones as possible.

Indeed, in the larger literary dimension, one's final response to the general body of the work in question can only be the profoundest sense of admiration—as with much antebellum American writing at the local and regional level—for how supremely competent so much of it actually turns out to be: that in a world where the urge toward literary expression itself once stood out as a kind of educational competency, so many people actually could write a passable poem, a playlet, a sketch, a story; and that so many not only tried their hands but found some measure of accomplishment, writing an ode, a sonnet, a satire, a literary essay, a personal or political memoir. A professional corollary of this, in fact, would be that established writers—people visibly esteemed as men and women of letters—themselves invariably worked in multiple genres and subgenres and/or modes. Hentz, for instance, is remembered as a novelist, but she was also an extremely popular and successful early practitioner of the literary short story; in her earliest literary efforts she was a dramatist; and as demonstrated by an 1839 appearance in A. B. Meek's literary magazine, *The Southron*, she proved a more than passable poet. Likewise Meek himself, in terms of variety of production, proved a man of multiple literary talents: an editor, critic, and literary essayist, he was also a poet, writing both distinguished lyric and epic, and a romantic historian. His cohort Smith was even more diverse: a poet, novelist, and dramatist, he also produced a number of well-known legal treatises.

But equally important to the culture at large was how the pattern also recapitulated itself endlessly across what might be called the vast substratum of everyday literary activity. In all the major antebellum urban centers—Mobile, Huntsville, Tuscaloosa, Montgomery—and in countless lesser places with names like La Fayette, Wetumpka, Gainesville, Marion, and Greensboro—local aspirants answered the call to literature. In newspapers like Tuscaloosa's *Flag of the Union*, Huntsville's *Alabama Republican*, Greensboro's *Alabama Beacon*, and Cahaba's *Southern Democrat*, they published poems entitled "Florida Volunteer's Farewell," "Chonelar—the Creek Maiden," "The Maid on the Banks of the Tar," "To Caroline," and "The Steamboat Explosion" (Ellison, *Early Alabama Publications* 57–58). They wrote plays with names like *Alfred and Inez; or, the Siege of St. Augustine,* and *Volentia* (189). They published novels with triple-barreled titles like *Onslow, or the Protege of an Enthusiast: A Historical-Traditionary Tale of the South,* by a Gentleman of Alabama, and tearful memorials like *The Admirable Young Man: A Discourse Occasioned by the Death of George Richard Wright, Editor of the "Alabamian"* (202). At once a record of social celebration and a testament of the society's deepest denials and avoidances, the early literature of a Deep South state carried out the groundbreaking work of cultural formation.

1

Satire in the Territories

~

Literature and the Art of Political Payback
in an Early Alabama Classic

It is a commonplace of American literary study that the culture has always somehow eluded traditional satire in its broad-scale social dimension. Such impoverishment was once understood to have cast its shadow across the colonial era and the early Republic through at least the whole pre–Civil War period, with the explanation that only in the decades after 1865 could one even begin to speak in a institutional sense about American manners. And even so, apologists for something like satire in the works of the great American realists—Henry James, William Dean Howells, Mark Twain, for instance—continue arguing among themselves to this day if things ever stabilized enough or acquired sufficient texture for a social satirist to write classically in the form. Even Twain, whose debunking frequently married social comedy to the explosive possibilities of frontier humor, at most wrote incidental satires of folly.

Likewise, whatever their socially corrective inclinations, American naturalists—Crane, Norris, Dreiser, and the like—found satiric impulses mired in visions of biosocial necessity. And their ironist successors in our own century, confronted with the endless new dehumanizations of technology, bureaucracy, and mass psychology, have in turn found themselves looking out on a landscape of sociocultural waste so garish and vast as to outrun the imagination of even the most resourceful humorist. Against the best efforts of figures as diverse as

Edith Wharton and Kurt Vonnegut, America's peculiar gift to social comedy has been somehow to make the world safe for Michael Jackson.

As to early developments in what might now be called a native tradition of satire, some progress has been made in revisionary understanding. If nothing else, it is admitted that from the earliest days onward, colonial and pre-Revolutionary Americans were not only trying to write satire more often than was thought, but were often actually writing it rather successfully within a given cultural context. Such works such as Nathaniel Ward's *Simple Cobler of Aggawam* and Ebenezer Cooke's *The Sot-Weed Factor,* the first from late-seventeenth-century Massachusetts and the second from early-eighteenth-century Maryland, we now know to have carried humorous meaning and appeal for a transatlantic audience. Diarists such as Sarah Kemble Knight and William Byrd likewise reveal themselves to have been skilled satirists of provincial manners. Franklin's career, from the *Dogood* papers onward, was marked by frequent successful ventures into topical satire. And the sociopolitical ferment of the Revolutionary and early national periods was often kept humorously aboil by poetic efforts such as *The Anarchiad* and *The Battle of the Kegs,* plays such as Royall Tyler's *The Contrast* and Mercy Otis Warren's *The Group,* and prose works such as Brackenridge's *Modern Chivalry* and Irving's *History of New York.* Indeed, it could be argued that through extensions of the Knickerbocker hoax in "Rip Van Winkle" and "The Legend of Sleepy Hollow," Irving's *Sketch-Book* became the new nation's first transatlantic best-seller largely by proving that American social humor could lend itself successfully to satire.

My purpose here, in bringing to light the work of an early verse-satirist of pre-statehood Alabama, is to show that it also could be done and in fact was being done in other portions of the new country even before nationhood officially reached the landscape of an ever-extending frontier. That is, in at least one instance, it truly does seem to have been possible, with considerable skill and literary success, to write classic satire in the territories. At the same time, I also propose to show how one of the first productions of humorous literature in the Old Southwest, like much material to come in a celebrated regional genre, can also provide an early opening on a familiar political archaeology—in this case with a freewheeling literary lampoon arising out of a clash of partisan interests in a complex of unsavory political and economic relationships all too typical of territorial administration in the early decades of the Republic; and with the result cementing the eventual reputations of the two figures involved— neither of them strangers to local corruption—largely as a consequence of one's exercise of a minor gift for literary improvisation and the other's inability to dodge a judgment for military foolishness already administered by local memory. To put it more directly, anticipating the popular prose classics of South-western successors such as George Washington Harris, Augustus Baldwin Long-street, and—most notably in Alabama itself—Johnson Jones Hooper, here a gifted literary amateur found it possible to successfully cast a political enemy as an early original of the homegrown *miles gloriosus* who would become the butt of anti-Jacksonian humor—the grotesque frontier hybrid born often and in equal measure of the backwoods buffoon and the natural-born killer, the Lion of the West, the ring-tailed roarer as canebrake Napoleon.[1]

The example chosen to illustrate both points, my subject here, turns out to be the earliest known work of literature produced in the Mississippi Territory—and more specifically, in the portion that was about to become the Deep South state of Alabama. Its title: *The Last Campaign of Sir John Falstaff The II; or, The Hero of the Burnt-Corn Battle. A Serio-Comic Poem by* ***** *******. Its subject: the true misadventures of one Colonel James Caller and his equally feckless, over-officered band of local militia in an 1813 engagement with the Creeks glori-fied under the title of the Battle of Burnt Corn Creek—but in fact a failed am-bush upon an Indian caravan followed by an ignominious rout, the Americans having stopped to plunder the pack animals, by a force one-fourth their size.[2] Its date: 1815. Its place of publication: St. Stephens, a center of territorial adminis-tration upriver from Mobile, claiming the honor of an early printing press, and soon to serve as the new capital of Alabama.[3]

The identity of its author, as will be shown, would have been made obvi-ous to a local audience by means of an attached preface—although nearly two decades would pass for him to acknowledge it on a title page.[4] He was Lewis Sewall, himself an territorial functionary having served as "Register of the Land Office" and later as official "Receiver of Funds" under the territorial administra-tion of Judge Harry Toulmin. Further, in these connections, he had also been a frequent associate of James Caller and his brother John, both of whom had achieved quick notoriety for constant meddlings in matters political, financial, and military.[5] In fact, to such a degree had Sewall been linked with various influ-ence-peddling and land-acquisition schemes set afoot by the brothers Caller and their associates that Toulmin—himself a figure of such rare probity as to have gained the epithet of "the Frontier Justinian"—seems to have harbored few doubts about where his subordinate's bread was buttered. On 26 February 1812, for instance, he wrote to the secretary of the treasury warning of an attempt by James and John Caller and others to replace "the Receiver of Public Monies for the District East of the Pearl River." And further facilitating the scheme, he went on, appeared to be the lamentable fact that "the present Register of the Land Office is too much the mere creature of these men" (Carter 6: 275). The functionary in question was, of course, Lewis Sewall.

As for the brothers Caller, there simply seems to have been no end to their energies for participation in corrupt schemes. John, an early colonel of militia briefly appointed county judge (Carter 6: 367), seems to have specialized in general influence peddling, while James, besides serving as a territorial commissioner (6: 345) and general accessory to his older brother's machinations, seems also to have become increasingly obsessed with developing his own high-profile military reputation. In any event, the spurious acquisition of large amounts of land was invariably at the bottom of things. And in most instances of the sharp dealing, the names of the brothers appear in tandem. As early as 25 November 1803, for instance, both appear as petitioners for a separate territorial government for "the District of Washington situate on the Mobile Tombechbee and Alabama Rivers" (5: 290). And, not surprisingly, both become signatories to a nearly concurrent petition (28 November 1803) for the finalizing of preemptive sales transactions hazarded earlier by themselves and others on lands under native claim in the forks of the Tombigbee and Alabama Rivers (5: 292–95). On 27 November 1804, both were again on record as conspiring to install as territorial judge a cat's-paw named Rodominick H. Gilmer. (As things turned out, Toulmin got the job.) And by 1810, according to James F. Doster, turning to more warlike activities as militia recruiters, the two had raised "what amounted to a private army" with the purposes of provoking a border conflict over trading concessions with neighboring Spaniards (92).

Most fatally, by the spring of 1812, with local tensions already on the rise through visits to native tribes by the Shawnee chief Tecumseh, James had also taken the lead in trying to incite the Creeks. Or, as Judge Toulmin recorded in official correspondence, "A party of rangers have been sent out by Col. Callier [*sic*], without any occasion,—and whose avowed design is to murder indians:— two companies of militia were ordered out by him on a groundless, idle rumour;—a party of indians were wantonly & without provocation fired upon by others,—and some peaceable Choctaws were almost beaten to death" (Carter 6: 307).

That provocation may have failed. But the ensuing one, again led by Caller, this time at Burnt Corn Creek, succeeded in making territorial history beyond anyone's most horrific imaginings. To be sure, the proximate issue of events was an ignominious American rout—with Caller's command scattering to their homes, and with their bold commander and one hapless aide eventually found without their horses and wandering dazed and half-dressed in a nearby swamp. Unfortunately, the Creek Nation at large was outraged by the ambush; they quickly retaliated with an attack on the incompetently defended Fort Mims in which the entire population of the settlement, in excess of five hundred men, women, and children, were slaughtered; and from this atrocity against the white settlers, two more years of exterminatory war would follow. This time, however, more skilled and ruthless commanders, headed by Andrew Jackson, would be at the helm of the militia; and it was, of course, this time inevitably the Creeks who would be reduced and driven from the land. On 27 March 1814, Indian forces under the command of William Weatherford, the Red Eagle, were summarily defeated in battle at a place called by them Tohopeka and by the whites Horseshoe Bend; and on 9 August of the same year, by the Treaty of Fort Jackson, cession was made of all Creek land west of the Coosa River.

Treaties followed with the Choctaws, voiding similar claims to original possession. And by 1815, with the vanquishing of native peoples accompanied by a favorable peace treaty with the English, would-be nabobs in the Mississippi Territory found themselves operating quite literally on a new geography. Basically, the whole Southwest frontier was up for grabs, with vast new land dealings afoot. And, hardly to anyone's surprise, among those involved in the latest unseemly scramble was the disgraced commander of Burnt Corn. With new ambitions for the legislature, he was seeking political rehabilitation; and with an eye to new economic chicaneries, he had also filed an official petition against Sewall, accusing him of financial misfeasance. Sewall, he alleged, had taken his money on a land option, and then failed to record it. The option had lapsed. Sewall, presumably, had pocketed the funds, leaving Caller with an empty claim on a notice of nonpayment. So Caller had complained to local officials, basically accusing Sewall of embezzlement; and so Sewall likewise described the action as he sought to defend himself in various letters to political superiors.[6]

At the same time, however, Caller also seems to have circulated in print one or more expressions of public insult to Sewall, perhaps in the form of broadside or pamphlet. Whatever the texts, they have been lost to us; we can only rely on Sewall's description of Caller's pronouncements in some fairly impenetrable references appearing as part of his literary efforts.[7] In any event, this, as much as the accusation itself, seems to have been the proximate cause of Sewall's literary exertions.

On the other side, of course, Caller's misfortune was that, whatever his ad hoc skills for political troublemaking and trail-covering, his ignominious role in recent history was largely settled as a matter of public record. While there had been some argument over his complete responsibility for the course of events at Burnt Corn, and while he had also found defenders on the issue of personal courage, as with virtually all the participants, the disaster itself was something he could not get off his back.[8] Moreover, the recently triumphant conclusion of the Creek war had made matters even worse. To put it baldly, Caller now presumed to stand amidst a cast of heroes having emerged from the conflict streaming with real martial renown—Jackson, Coffee, Flournoy, and others—

and to do so not only as an egregiously failed glory-seeker but also as one with his name inextricably linked to one of the most inglorious episodes in all of frontier warfare. Accordingly, whatever the debates that had continued over his responsibilities for the disaster, and whatever his ensuing attempts to paper this over along with his various other intrigues and venalities, he presented, as Sewall seems astutely to have reckoned, a historical target too large to miss. Were the right kind of humorous literary weaponry to be focused on Caller's role in the most shameful military debacle in territorial history, laughter would do the needed work of political demolition.

As it turns out, Sewall the satirist was also up to the task. Partly, as will be seen, this is because he truly did discover himself to possess a certain gift for humorous invective *and* a capacity for spirited mock-epic narration and exposition, in the latter case sustained by something of a natural bent for the well-used heroic couplet. Most important, however, was a prize of inspired insight born of the author's obvious familiarity with Shakespeare. This was his recognition of how thoroughly the victim at hand had been cast as a backwoods likeness of the bard's fat, conniving, venal Falstaff: a self-important braggart, coward, liar, and thief; a low political intriguer with astonishing public effrontery yoked to enormous martial presumption. Indeed, given his precise aims, Sewall must simply have rubbed his eyes at the realization of how completely the subject at hand—the Burnt Corn debacle and Caller's feckless leadership of the band of routed brigands—seemed a wondrous conflation of virtually all the great rogue's misadventures in *Henry IV*, Part I: his poltroon's part as ringleader in the botched Gadshill robbery; his lying cover-up before the amused Hal and Poins; and his culminating ineptitude upon the field at Shrewsbury at the head of a personal army he has managed to recruit from cowardly scum like himself. In short, an entire satirical architecture of plot and character seemed to have played itself out of literature into Sewall's historical hand. His title, he could aver, simply did not lie. The Hero of the Burnt-Corn Battle had to be seen truly as nothing less than the incarnation of "Sir John Falstaff The II."[9]

So the title announced. And so the poem delivered, in rollicking Shakespearean reverberation, but also with admixtures of help from other noted literary forebears. The concisely damning epigraph, for instance—"He who fights, and runs away, / May live to fight another day; / But he who is in battle SLAIN, / Can never rise to fight again"—came from Butler's *Hudibras,* perhaps by way of Goldsmith. A bare two lines beyond the title, we find the poet congratulating himself on parodic improvement of Homer's *Iliad* as well. And once the fated encounter has plunged Caller and his aide into their hallucinatory wilderness adventures, Cervantes clearly enters the poem as a major guide.

In the meantime, however, as Sewall's couplets quickly begin to move the narrative along in energetic six- and eight-line stanzas, it is clearly Shakespeare's robust original who fuels the main engines of satire. For the would-be hero, venality coupled with martial ambition is the burning motive:

> Roused by a *zeal* which *fertile lands* inflame,
> And *vainly* hoping for a *warlike* name,
> JOHN calls his troops around, declares a foe
> *Was* gone, or *would* to Pensacola go;
> Where powder he'd procure, and arms and lead,
> And swift destruction on our frontier spread. (5)

And for the assembled mob, military bombast is the ignition:

> "Is any here," he cries, "afraid to go;
> "A *pale-faced* wretch, who'd shun a savage foe:
> "Let him remain behind, while we, the *brave*,
> "Will instant march, and our lov'd country save." (5)

Quickly, with "our *Hero*" at the head, the troops advance "in warlike honor" and "proud array" (6). Quickly the desired attack is made. And as quickly, when attacking yields to looting, the hero finds himself out ahead leading the same force rapidly in the opposite direction as part of a humiliating rout. Ignoring the cries of a wounded comrade, he abandons the latter to execution, meanwhile continuing to bellow "retreat! retreat!" at the top of his lungs. And shortly, having abandoned the whole command to their own designs, only John and a single aide are left in the trackless swamp, imagining every tree a warrior and every owl's call the sound of Indian bloodhounds. Vainly, Sir John confesses his sins to heaven. Vainly he implores his imagined captors to spare him. Vainly he seeks God's mercy. Mistaking a papaw tree for a Muskogee, he hews the offender to the ground. Attempting to exercise of the skills of the woodsman, he idiotically puts his boots on backwards to reverse his tracks; later he tries to simulate the footprints of a monster. When, at long last, he is found, he is shirtless, trouserless, and hatless, albeit still attempting to brag of late feats of arms; but once ahorse and headed home, he finds only new woes in his wake. To wit: "*sad calamity, effect of fear,* / In form of *Dysentery* gained his rear! / Kept up a firing which his foes would shun / With greater care, than pistol, sword or gun" (20).

To put it mildly, this is mock-heroics with a wonderfully scurrilous vengeance. And really, in the midst of the reporting of such misadventures, it seems little to matter when actual Creek vengeance is exacted on the helpless garrison at Fort Mims and war eventually takes its course. For his part, Sir John remains obdurate in his martial pretensions, convinced his cowardice remains a secret. Still, the poet avers, one stigma proves impossible to shake, at least as long as the conflict continues. Only with the coming of peace do "John's *fears* and *dysentery*" jointly abate; and only then, newly fattening[10] "like a Bullock in a stall" (22), does he muster courage for new corruptions and slanders. Yet even now, according to the poet, he will not get away from new broadsides echoing in the streets. As he has once made his exit, pursued first by Creeks and then by diarrhea, the hero now departs again, this time pursued, for good measure, by a final strain of mockery. Conveniently provided by the author at the formal poem's conclusion, presumably for everyday use, it is a scurrilous ditty easily sung on the street to the tune of "Yankee Doodle."

We do not know how much misery the long-abused Caller endured from either Sewall's formal lampoon or the street version before going to his grave in 1819. We do know, on the other hand, that Sewall's literary efforts, presumably encouraged by some measure of success, not only continued but also became eventually the basis of something of a reputation. One reason we know this is because of the publication in 1833 of *Miscellaneous Poems,* headlined by the old Caller saga, this time in a lavishly revised and expanded version, but also containing much ambitious new work in a similar mock-epic historical vein. But we also have the record of later cultural commentary, including recollections of Sewall by Mary Welsh, published in *Transactions of the Alabama Historical Society, 1898–99.* Amidst other personages of old St. Stephens, she recalled, "there once wandered around an erratic individual, something of a poet." Of Sewall's work, she went on, "I have often heard my father repeat with great gusto a comic poem written by him on a very common subject. I remember the lines jingled harmoniously, and the rhythm was smooth and flowing, but it was not at all refined. Still it was enough to credit the old town with a poet—Captain Sewall" (222).[11]

Colonel Caller. Captain Sewall. "Some may think that there was quite an array of titles among the old inhabitants," Welsh went on. "Well, so there was," she was forced to admit; "and," she concludes, "let us bear in mind that those were days when a title, either civil or military or professional, stood for something" (222–23).

One could not have put it any better, then or now. In the early decades of the nineteenth century, the territories soon to become the newest states in the Jacksonian free-for-all called America were a cultural wilderness in every sense of the term. In the scramble for political ascendancy; in the vast grab after lands newly vacated by native peoples; in the relentless quest after glory and honor, fame and fortune, property and position: for a figure in the territories acting in any public capacity, the gaining of a name was everything. Never mind that vainglory and venality were a way of life and virtually no one got away untouched. The distance between immortality and ignominy had to be measured in terms just that grubby.

Here, the record shows beyond a doubt that the feckless *miles gloriosus* and his literary tormentor had both been in all of it up to their ears and in equal measure. Still, in the unequal distribution of literary talent, the political battle finally also came out most unevenly. Sewall, with an eye for the brilliant source and a gift for verse satire, would parlay his literary skills, such as they were, into a modest but enduring historical eminence. Caller, through his opponent's exercise of those skills, would suffer further literary consignment to an already considerable historical ignominy.

It all turned out, then, as Sewall—himself something of a braggart—had boasted in his early preface in the war of dueling broadsides. "Crude and predictable as the piece is," he boasted, "the author ventures to predict that it will stick." Or, as he might have put it more directly, he was laying odds on the idea that humorous literature really could make history.[12] The difference to posterity between the author of a satire and his victim, he seemed to suggest, really could turn largely on a contest of backwoods effronteries. On one hand was Caller's political effrontery to believe that, given a new field of postwar opportunity, he truly could pursue new political and economic advantages in spite of the historical stigma of command at the war's opening disaster; on the other was Sewall's literary effrontery to believe that such stratagems could be countered by writing a humorous poem about the disaster and making it stick. To be sure, with or without Sewall's efforts, it is certain that Caller would have come down to us carrying the shame of Burnt Corn.[13] On the other hand, as for Sewall's small literary celebrity, if a minor eminence, surely it was better than nothing. For therewith he had, after all, escaped not only the fate of a James Caller but also that of a John Caller or a pre-literary Lewis Sewall or a hundred others just like them—the fate of being remembered as just another frontier rapscallion.

2

First Book

∽

Henry Hitchcock's *Alabama Justice of the Peace*

Regularly affirming a new alliance between culture and mass-print literacy, the first books of early American places nearly always speak volumes about the groundbreaking work of social organization. We find it appropriate, for example, that the first book written and printed in Puritan New England should have been the *Bay Psalm Book,* a 1640 torturing of the English psalter into hymn-book rhyme and meter for use in common worship. Nor are we less gratified to find decidedly more earthbound Virginians of the era laying claim to their version of the honor with a 1626 translation of Ovid's *Metamorphoses* by a well-connected literary traveler—son of an archbishop, to be exact, and brother to the royal treasurer—George Sandys.

Least of all should we probably be surprised, as the new nation extended itself westward into the territories, to find that the first such production in the Deep South state of Alabama turns out to have been a volume on law and order. Its title: *The Alabama Justice of the Peace: Containing all the Duties, Powers, and Authorities of that Office and a great variety of warrants, recognizances, bonds, deeds of bargain and sale, together with the Constitution of the State of Alabama.* Its date of publication: 1822. Its place of publication: the newly established state capital of Cahaba. The author's identification would have been greeted with respectful familiarity by any Alabamian conversant in statehood matters. He was Judge Henry Hitchcock of Washington County, who at the Huntsville convention of 1819 had helped prepare the final draft of the state constitution and shortly had also been selected Alabama's first attorney general.

Indeed, throughout the first two decades of Alabama statehood, few public figures would have exceeded Henry Hitchcock in reputation for judicious public service. Nor, as it turns out, would many public biographies have provided a closer mirror of culture. A native of Vermont and grandson of Ethan Allen, the hero of Ticonderoga, Hitchcock set out after completion of his legal studies with the express intention of making a life for himself and his family in the territories then known as the Great American Southwest and now comprising the states of Louisiana, Mississippi, and Alabama. His first destination was Natchez, but, unenthusiastic about his prospects there, he pushed on to Mobile and then St. Stephens, at the time the territorial capital. His legal business flourished along with his local renown, and within two years, at age twenty-six, Hitchcock found himself appointed by Governor William Wyatt Bibb as first secretary of the Alabama Territory—a post essentially requiring him to manage affairs in the governor's absence. Appointment quickly followed to the Huntsville constitutional convention of 1819. There Hitchcock was among the fifteen out of forty-four attendees delegated to prepare a first draft. In turn, he and two others reduced the document to the final form in which it was adopted essentially without revision.

Upon admission of Alabama to the Union, the new legislature elected Hitchcock the state's first attorney general. And it was in consequence of these responsibilities that Hitchcock turned to the composition and publication of *Alabama Justice of the Peace,* the state's first book. The attorney generalship and subsequent appointment to the supreme court were attended by a burgeoning private practice, first in Cahaba, and afterward, when the capital was moved to Tuscaloosa, in Mobile.

Unfortunately, it was here on the other hand that in the realm of private affairs, Hitchcock's biography also turned out to be a less happy parable of early life in the state, where sudden wealth *and* overnight ruination came frequently to individuals and families through recurrent cycles of boom or bust economics. Here the house of Hitchcock was no exception. Once in Mobile, the jurist devoted himself increasingly to real estate transactions and development of various commercial properties; and by 1836—also the year, it turns out, of his much-publicized religious conversion—he was reputed to be the richest citizen in the state, with assets in excess of two million dollars. The Panic of 1837, fomented by Andrew Jackson's feud with Nicholas Biddle's Bank of the United States, claimed nearly everything; and despite a series of desperate attempts at refinancing, Hitchcock failed to shore up his overextended empire. When he died two years later, in the Mobile yellow fever epidemic of 1839, his affairs were in receivership. From the estate, Hitchcock's widow and children received a cash payment of $150,000, much of which was used to pay unsecured creditors. The mortgaged property became the possession of the banks. One of the most distinguished jurists of the early national era thus became simultaneously another victim among many of the flush times of Alabama and Mississippi.

At least at the height of his reputation, however, as a pioneering jurist, Hitchcock was perhaps second in territorial renown only to Harry Toulmin, a figure so prominent as to have been accorded the title of "the Frontier Justinian." The latter had published an 1807 digest of the laws of the Mississippi Territory and a companion volume entitled *The Magistrate's Assistant*. His new *Digest of the Laws of Alabama* was also to come forth from the Cahaba printers within the year. Not surprisingly, when it did appear, it would carry an index supplied as a public service by Hitchcock when Toulmin proved too ill to complete it and supervise final printing.[1]

What was the distinguishing feature of Hitchcock's Alabama volume as a first book? The difference is most readily explained by the decidedly functional emphasis of his title—not to mention the reason, one might add, why it had been heralded as a subscription project nearly since the day the Huntsville deliberations had adjourned. To put things simply, in its desperate need to implement the rule of law and order in arguably some of the most lawless precincts of the English-speaking world, Alabama had a justice system that needed a jump start as far as some guide to basic operations was concerned. To be sure, at the top tiers, experienced jurists were at hand to staff a fairly traditional structure. A supreme court would preside; and six circuit courts would provide original trial jurisdiction, with one judge handling three to six counties, and each county court meeting at least twice annually. (Until 1825, it was further mandated that the latter would actually perform the duties of the supreme court.) In addition, however, there would also be numerous other judicial venues. Chancery court, for instance, would handle "original and appellate equity jurisdiction"; and in each county, a court of probate would be established "for the granting of letters testamentary and of administration and for orphans' business." Most importantly, it would also fall to the assembly to secure continuing appointment of "a competent number of justices of the peace in each county to try petty civil cases" (Moore 141). And it was at this ground level of the judicial edifice, so to speak—with the "petty civil cases" so described in fact encompassing everything from horse-stealing to homicide, *and* with the authority of the courts quite likely vested in countless persons with incomplete legal training—that basic operational wisdom would be sorely wanted.[2]

Accordingly, taking its lead from Toulmin's earlier development of companion territorial volumes, Hitchcock's text attempted to answer the same need of local functionaries in the new state for such material in an all-in-one compendium, best described as a combination statutory reference and manual for law enforcement and courts administration, with a running glossary of legal terms and a copy of the state constitution thrown in for helpful measure. To put it more directly: here, in a single, free-standing volume, could be discerned both the lofty instruction of the law itself *and* practical guidance on the various more workaday matters of administering justice the frontier magistrate might expect to encounter. With such a book in hand, then, even a backcountry electee, presiding over a newly created jurisdiction, could presumably read himself into a position of at least rudimentary expertise on a given case, thereby finding enough information and professional guidance to turn the site of his deliberations into something resembling a courtroom and himself into something resembling a judge with his *bona fides* and *habeas corpuses* roughly in place.[3] The matter might be something as abstruse as the limits of constitutional authority; or, it might be as pedestrian as the wording of a specific statute or the standard form for a particular kind of brief or pleading. Rules of procedure jostled with poor laws and guidelines for jury qualification. Legal exemption of educators and ministers from work on road maintenance got equal treatment with justifiable homicide.

Given the array of information to be presented, a second question naturally arises. Granted, Hitchcock may have been as much a compiler or anthologizer as an author in the traditional sense, with most of the legal references, by his own admission, copied from Burn's English *Justice* and adapted where appropriate to the constitution and particular laws in force in Alabama. Still, how did he manage to wrestle all this cumbersome and unwieldy material into one ordered collection available for ready reference? The answer is that he exercised the simple genius of alphabetizing it. Thus, under A, the definition of "*Actions Qui Tam*" was followed by an equally businesslike entry on "Adultery and Fornication." "Barratry" and "Bastards" led on to "Bigamy," "Bribery," "Burglary," and "Burning." "Ferries and Toll Bridges" shared a page with "Forcible Entry and Detainer," "Lotteries" with "Lunatics," "*Ne Exeat*" with "Nuisance," "Taverns" with "Treason."

For the country justice confronted with a bewildering body of juridical lore and terminology—and in those days of rough-and-tumble frontier politics, a country justice quite frequently was not a lawyer by training—such an arrangement, albeit striking us perhaps as somewhat strange and arbitrary, must surely have seemed a commonsense convenience and a comfort. At the same time, for the student of its mysteries, it must have seemed a beckoning window into a whole world of magisterial lore and glittering generalities, the very stuff of civilization itself. Accordingly, for the modern reader, precisely through the same compounding of arrangement and serendipity, the volume now offers the parallel opportunity of re-creating social history in uniquely vivid and spontaneous ways. Sometimes—as many of us are wont to do, for instance, when we turn to a reference text for one purpose and wind up reading a page or so more out of curiosity—we can find ourselves plunging ahead serially, as above, in a kind of garish, careening, alphabetized free ride; or sometimes—perhaps trying more methodically to reimagine the actual work of a frontier jurist—we may attempt to navigate between and among related topics in an intricate system of cross-reference. Whatever our initial interest or method, here an antiquarian browse quickly transforms itself into a genuine cultural odyssey, a complex journey of political and historical return. We reconstruct, working in precise scale and contour along its intricate patterns of legal relationship, the full configurings of a world.

Part of the interest of the effort of cultural reconstruction, as one may have noticed from even the preliminary sketch of headings rendered above, is a curiosity born of recognition, even in such rudimentary social and legal circumstances, of much that already strikes us as familiar. As shown elsewhere, we may rightly conceive of the backdrop of the text as a teeming, rumbustious frontier, a hodgepodge of jurisdictions and petty fiefdoms, short on law and lawyers alike, with "disputes over land, women, horses, cards, and slaves," in Leah Rawls Atkins's memorable phrasing, still seeking primary resolution in "fistfights aided by knives, sticks, and teeth" (Rogers et al. 122). At the same time, here, against that same backdrop, we witness long-accredited terms and concepts of legal tradition elaborating themselves in steady alphabetical progression into the overarching structure of a government of law and a mechanism of authority for its enforcement. "Accessory"; "Arrest"; "Bail"; "*Certiorari*"; "Confession"; "Contracts"; "Conveyances"; "Evidence"; "Felony"; "Indictment"; "Information"; "Limitation of Actions"; "*Mandamus*"; "Partnership"; "Recognizance"; "Summons"; "Warrant": under all these heads, we recognize ourselves already to be in a realm of legal doctrine and usage having much in common with our own.

On the other hand, of course, there is also the frequent recognition of difference. We revisit often a distant world of quaint terminology applied to matters of legal definition and/or conduct both rendered similarly remote by the passage of years. "Affray" we discover to be "the fighting of two or more persons in some public place to the terror of the people" (15); "Barratry" the fomenting of a quarrel or contention (64); "Forestalling" the propagation of rumors inflating common prices of merchandise (236); "Maintenance" the "unlawful taking in hand or upholding of quarrels or sides, to the disturbance or hindrance of common right" (340). The latter we also find to include "champetry"—assisting another's suit in hope of sharing an award; or "embracery"—trying to influence a jury deliberation toward similar ends.

In some cases, terms may be familiar; but most of the behaviors they describe we now take pleasure in contemplating as lurid relics. While brawling may always be with us, for example, a special section of the statutes would no longer seem to be required for "Maim"—defined matter-of-factly as the attempt to "cut or bite off the ear, or ears, or cut out, or disable the tongue, put out an eye while fighting or otherwise, slit the nose or a lip, cut or bite off the nose or lip, or cut off or disable any limb or member"—so as to gain unfair advantage over a fellow combatant (339). Likewise, "Duelling," "Cockfighting," and "Horseracing," while still on the books as legally proscribed, have ceased to crowd local dockets. "Pillory" has fallen out of favor as the recommended punishment for "persons guilty of forgery, perjury," or "cheating by means of some artful device" (376); and such colorful gaming pursuits such as "ABC," "EO," "Rowley Powley," "Rouge and Noir," and the "Faro Bank" no longer seem to warrant itemization as matters commanding detailed legal scrutiny (237).

Other topics once of important everyday concern—"Marks and Brands," "Mills and Millers," "Strays"—have vanished from the legal horizon. And in still others, entries refer to matters of private conduct having come over the years to be deemed outside the domain of legal jurisdiction—albeit with some of them only leaving the statutory lineup in recent decades of our own century. There is the aforementioned "Adultery and Fornication," for instance. And likewise "Immorality" is seen as once casting its wide net to include nakedness, cohabitation, and cursing, as well as profanation of the Sabbath and disturbing religious meetings.

In the domain of social administration, some inclusions may evoke in us, at least at this remove, a certain antiquarian bemusement. Coroners, for instance, as befits a world of astonishing physical violence, get a detailed amount of guidance on their likely work, with pre-headed inquest forms provided to cover a host of fatal eventualities: "murder"; "where one drowns himself"; "where one dies a natural death"; "where the murderer is unknown"; "where one hangs himself"; "for cutting his throat"; "for killing another in his own defense"; "where the death was occasioned by chance-medley" (166). And in a similar vein, the education profession also rates a special entry on the limits of physical discipline, being warned that "where a schoolmaster, in correcting his scholar, happens to occasion his death; if on such correction he is so barbarous as to exceed all bounds of moderation, he is at least guilty of *manslaughter;* and if he make use of an instrument improper for correction and apparently endangering the scholar's life, as an iron bar, a sword, or kick him to the ground, and then stamp on his belly and kill him, he is guilty of murder" (406).

Others, of course, at whatever remove we imagine ourselves, provide no such occasion for humor. Rather, they painfully remind us that for various classes of individuals within the new state, institutional standards of political freedom and legal protections were decidedly a relative thing. A detailed section on "Patrols," for instance, reminds us that in the pre–Civil War South, the slave-holding citizenry of any given state had to consider itself as basically existing within a permanent condition of martial law, with the threat of uprising never far from waking thought, and with local alert and mobilization the matter of a moment's notice. And in the section of the code itself pertaining to slavery—not surprisingly one of the longest in the text—we find laid out an intricately evolved set of strictures, covering everything from manumission (not surprisingly, hedged with forests of legal obstacles) to specifications on the precise numbers of lashes to be administered for given infractions. Further provided, one might add, are handy forms to cover a host of possible code violations by individual slaves, ranging from fomenting a riot to illegal possession of a gun or spending more than four hours unsupervised in a house or kitchen.

At the same time, as to political and economic association even among technically free individuals, we are similarly reminded that this was still a world of masters and servants, of indentures and other forms of legal and financial binding in a host of carefully defined gradations of relationship: menials, domestics, apprentices, laborers, stewards, factors, and bailiffs (350). Likewise, a detailed calculus was presented to delineate the differing property rights of husbands and wives in relation to marital assets. As Leah Rawls Atkins points out, up to the eve of the Civil War, it was clear that the old common law ruled. "A married woman's possessions," she writes, even "including her personal clothes, were owned by her husband." In addition, and much more importantly, "any real estate a married woman might inherit" also "could be controlled by her husband." Further, "he could sell it without her consent and appropriate the money for his own purposes" (Rogers et al. 113).

With equally brusque dispensation through legal category into arbitrary power, this was also a world in which the insane found themselves summarily sorted out into four basic orders of misery: "*Ideots,* who are of *non sane memory* from their nativity, by a perpetual infirmity. Secondly, those that lose their memory and understanding by the visitation of God, as by sickness, or other accident. Thirdly, Lunatics who have sometimes their understanding and sometimes not. Fourthly, Drunkards, who, by their own vicious act, for a time deprive themselves of their memory and understanding" (336). And the same was basically the case with insolvents, minors, the poor, and various other categories of the disadvantaged. All received sternly cursory notation in the canons of justice.

In sum, even where one does not find patent injustice, one may look in any number of other places to see uncomfortably short shrift and summary disposition being given to problems now more fully addressed by law and the courts with heightened compassion and understanding of their human complexities. On the other hand, for all the injustice of its frequently short-circuited and summary justice, one still honors at least the attempt at a comprehensive manual for judicial administration that tried not to waste words on making matters any more complicated than they seemed to have need of being. For it all truly had to be gotten up in short order with the full knowledge that magistrates would frequently lack legal training, and their courts nearly anything else in the way of judicial trappings, let alone any of the more standard texts of legal reference. Courtroom justice of the time, after all, as Albert Moore records, literally *was* being played out in people's dwellings "or on logs under the boughs of trees" (141), with "cases galore" moving through the sprawling, informal network more quickly than a newly formed supreme court could hope to subject them to judicial review. New lawyers vied with more experienced counterparts from other jurisdictions, with the former compensating for any lack of "learning" with "florid and impassioned oratory" (141). Meanwhile, with each legislative session, statutes poured forth. In the first year alone, for instance, new laws provided for everything from the creation of additional counties to the prohibition of usury and the setting of quality standards for "cooperage stock, tar, pitch, turpentine, and rosin." Policies were devised for the leasing of salt springs and for the legal holding of lands by religious societies, albeit "not to exceed fifteen acres" (112).

However fast the pace of change, anything surely had to be an improvement over that meeting of the Washington County judiciary of two decades earlier, recalled with bemusement by the early historian Albert S. Pickett. "These justices," he wrote, meeting in the first court to be held in the new territory, "had no code before them, and coming from different States, decided cases according to the laws of their native land, so that the most amusing differences of opinion often prevailed." Indeed, for the moment, he went on, this seemed to be "the case all over the territory," with the only consistent result at the time seeming to be the success of jurists hailing from Georgia in "holding the laws of South Carolina, North Carolina, Virginia, and the whole of New England in great contempt." "With their usual success," he concludes, the local mafia thus "generally managed to carry their points" (475).

For most people today, the idea of the absence of a uniform code of law and system of courts administration must surely seem as dated as that conclave of squabbling territorial appointees. Indeed, for many persons today, the concept of the justice of the peace itself is similarly a legal archaism—albeit a development of recent memory surely unlamented by an older generation living in dread of a run-in with some local Judge Roy Bean. City and county magistrates presiding in regular session now do most of the workaday business of the office, with weightier matters of state law being reserved for sittings of the circuit and district courts, each with separate civil and criminal divisions, over which in turn a supreme court exercises final jurisdiction. Likewise, the day is long gone when anyone might even think of trying to put even the administrative or procedural basics of judicial operation into a single volume. The Alabama *Rules* alone now require two, with the statutes filling an additional twenty-four. As to case law and precedent, reported decisions still appear in annual published volumes; as to basic information gathering by lawyers and jurists, on the other hand, books themselves have largely gone by the board, with most legal research conducted through various electronic data recording and retrieval systems. In sum, here, as in virtually every other area of human endeavor, it has become downright poignant to contemplate the idea of a single book like Hitchcock's devised for an astonishingly heterogeneous constituency to supply the basic elements of professional legal and judicial knowledge. And never mind, of course, that while the estimable jurist may have understood a host of immediate problems of the administration of justice to be his practical subject, the larger goal he clearly envisioned was the legal foundation of a cultural polity.

Accordingly, our admiration goes out across the years to that pioneering legal soul who tried to get a start on the problem of uniform, equal justice under the law in a place called Alabama by trying to put into a single, usable volume enough information to supply at least a first, provisional mode of solution. As with so much else in the early Republic, the whole business was a quintessentially American blend of practicality and idealism. In Judge Henry Hitchcock's making of a first book that would attempt to engineer from the ground up the making of that greater thing called justice, the state could claim a bold effort and a worthy beginning.

"The First Production of the Kind, in the South"

~

A Backwoods Literary *Incognito* and His Attempt at the Great American Novel

One of the most remarkable stories in American literary and publishing culture of the Old Southwest can be found in a small, workmanlike volume entitled *The Lost Virgin of the South: An Historical Novel, Founded on Facts, Connected with the Indian War in the South, in 1812 to '15*. Billing itself as a "SECOND EDITION, ENLARGED," it lists its printing origins as "COURTLAND, AL," "PUBLISHED BY, AND FOR, M. SMITH," and its date as 1832. And, surely enough, a Florida copyright notice printed among textual preliminaries leads us to a prior version, somewhat condensed, and set in different typeface, but otherwise corresponding, published "By, and for" the same figure, a year earlier at Tallahassee.[1]

Although the work's author is named on the title page of both editions as "Don Pedro Casender," actual authorship has been variously attributed, and is probably, at this remove, impossible to authenticate. Within a preface to the text, identical in both versions, an "editor" identifies Casender as "the Spanish author . . . of the original outline of the facts of the work." The matter is further complicated by correspondences between this name and those of certain figures within the text of the novel itself. One minor character, a brother of the titular heroine, Calista Ward, the daughter of an English colonel and a Spanish lady, is named Pedro Ward. A more important personage, a second brother who figures heavily in the action throughout, is named Casender Ward. As to "official" attribution, Library of Congress bibliographers, tracing the novel from the Florida text through the Alabama version by the phrase "Published by, and for, M. Smith," credit it to one Rev. Michael Smith, likely an itinerant Baptist clergyman. Alabama literary historians identify the author as Wiley Conner, known to have been the publisher and printer of the *Courtland Herald* from 1826 to 1841, and alleged by some accounts also to have become a traveling preacher.[2]

Thus reads the story *of* the text, beginning in the mystery of authorship, and extending forward to what the artifacts themselves tell us about the quaint, almost poignant details of producing a lavish historical-gothic-sentimental-picaresque novel-romance in a territorial capital; and then, at a outpost of culture to the north on the Alabama frontier, of trying to reset and market anew a breathlessly enlarged version, composed in blocks of two alternating typefaces, on a press no doubt some few years earlier trundled in over the mountains or down the rivers from Tennessee; of trying, in sum, to write a new literature apace with the rise of a new culture. Then, as if all this were not sufficiently complicated, there is the story *in* the text: a lurid, teeming mishmash of sentiment and adventure, of actual history and outrageous fictive invention. Arising from its generic shipwreck-kidnap plot, it evolves eventually into a spectacle of early settlement in the Old Southwest—English, French, Spanish—in its tragic collision with the great native cultures—Seminole, Cherokee, Chickasaw, Choctaw, Creek. And further, as noted above, it does this through a "literary" design so concocted as to beggar the possibilities of early American genre.

Indeed, to attempt a literary overview of this work is to challenge both our taxonomies and our histories of reading across a range of Anglo-European and American texts. In the vein of Cooper, whom the author explicitly inscribes, this saga of a virginal heroine, shipwrecked, captured by Indians, cast into the tumults of the great wars of the Southwest, eventually united with a faithful lover and, after a sojourn in Europe, returned to happy domesticity in the city of New York, is above all a vast historical romance.[3] With a dark energy of execution that reminds one of the labyrinthine narratives of Brockden Brown—but in the present case, with its mysterious Europeans, fallen nobles, defrocked clergy, murderous pirates, lascivious seducers, and unprincipled robbers, probably derived from a variety of Anglo-European and American popular sources—it is also a complex, involuted gothic mystery and tale of terror.[4] Centering on the physical and spiritual—and thereby emphatically sexual—perils of its titular heroine, and in that connection further inscribing the popular genre of the captivity narrative, it is a sentimental novel of threatened virtue, wise perseverance, and rewarded love. With its brigands, half-breeds, rustics, and *incognitos,* and their sundry roughhouse adventures and peregrinations, it is an American frontier picaresque. Focusing on contemporary events of national expansion and conquest amidst vivid adventure and romantic complication, it is also clearly a work of uncommon political realism, a "non-fiction" novel of precocious wisdom and insight. With its sundry levels of attribution and narration, its intertwining narrative lines, its inscriptions of shadowed, even paranoiac agencies, causalities, congruencies, it is also a metafiction of compelling challenge, a book, as in the vein of many early American gothic and historical texts, where the form of fiction also becomes in many ways the great theme of fiction. And finally, then, like many teeming, rumbustious works of the early Republic, it comprises a whole mysteriously larger than any sum of its parts, a profound statement about the aesthetic and the cultural politics of something called "literature" in a new nation, about the beginnings of a critical realism that must itself begin by investigating its own literary, political, epistemological, and even ontological status.

All this barely manages to get itself contained within two teeming volumes of small print, bound between a single set of green boards; and, even in outline, it can still give some sense of the complex ambition of what is being attempted. The text proper of the expanded Alabama edition begins, as noted earlier, with various matters prefatory. A chief addition, reflecting the hubbub and bustle of a Southwest frontier quickly becoming the nation's most important new political precinct, is a three-page dedication to Andrew Jackson. This, however, is also prefaced by a quite official and stern notice of the work's prior copyright, issued and signed by the clerk of the Middle District of Florida. The long, odd salute to Jackson begins by explaining several motivations which should *not* be inferred. The work is Jackson's, the writer avers, "not because Andrew Jackson bears the title of L. L. D."; "Not because the author and publisher is a sycophant"; and "Not because Andrew Jackson has millions of admirers and many defamers." Rather, it is to mark Jackson's role in many events described, his twenty years of service to the American people, and his qualities of perseverance, patriotic duty, and self-sacrifice, "notwithstanding the occasional moral and political errors."

Finally, there follow two more closely "authorial" prefaces. The first, taken verbatim from the first edition, notes the "design" of the work "to instruct in some matters, both new and interesting, relative to the Indian war in the South," as well as "to amuse and delight the fancy, and to console the heart under circumstances forlorn and distressing." As to origin, the narrator dismisses questions regarding "How or when, the editor became possessed of the original outline of the facts of this work, from the Spanish author." Suffice it to say that "the editor was instructed to copy the original MS. and to dress it in such as garb as his genius and fancy may dictate." At great personal "expense and responsibility," this he has done, but under very unfavorable circumstances of much hurry and sickness. Hence, "he must bespeak the indulgence of the readers and critics, and will solicit them to recollect, that it is the first production of the kind, in the South."

The second preface, two short paragraphs supplied for the new edition, spins off excitedly from the first. "Such has been the demand for, and general approval of this work," it asserts, "that the proprietor has been induced to print a second edition enlarged and revised, and in two volumes; and in such a state of perfection, that no fault can be found with the work." He then concludes, "Although many typographical and literary errors existed in the first edition, yet the work seemed to be universally acceptable; but in this edition, all these faults are corrected, and one hundred pages of new and interesting matter added, which renders the present edition more valuable than the first."

Thus born of a characteristic American marriage of apology and advertising, the text proper opens in 1810 aboard a foundering ship just off the tip of Florida at Key Biscayne. Passengers include an English colonel named Ward, his wife, their two sons, Casender and Pedro, and their two daughters, Calista and Cirephia. In the ensuing wreck, parties are separated and fall among various bands of Indians, with Calista, the book's child-heroine, rescued by a youthful Spaniard, Perendio Civello, who, before she is taken off by a band of Seminoles, places a gold chain around her neck with a locket containing his portrait. Calista is made to join the family of Ropaugh, which includes a beautiful daughter, approximately her own age, named Jula. With the Seminoles, who have proven kindly, they travel up the peninsula and eventually make their way into southern Alabama.

In the new territory, where relations between whites and Indians have been inflamed by agitators sent by Tecumseh, the family will shortly be involved in Jackson's battle with the Creeks at Tallushetchee, and, we are peremptorily told, Calista will be wounded by her own brother Casender. But first we pause for the interlude of Calista's conversion in the wilderness. Then we proceed back to historical action, with the appearance of the Creek chieftain Weatherford, a first heroic figure from actual history, and the battle itself.

As predicted, Casender appears among Jackson's forces and, in shooting Ropaugh, also wounds Calista. As he is about to kill her with a sword, he is disarmed, however, by Cevillo, who has also just appeared, and who wounds him in the thigh. Ministering to the supposed Indian maid, Cevillo notices the chain and the locket and its resemblance to that given Calista, but the recognition proceeds no further than his wondering about how it came to be in her possession.

With Perendio in attendance, Ropaugh dies of his wounds. Calista and Jula also minister to a captured white soldier, an Irishman named Jones. The family attempts to move to safety in the East, with Calista and Jula now disguised as boys, to prevent their abduction and rape by white soldiers, but they are captured as bearers by a war party of hostile Creeks. They become involved in new combat, in which Perendio is now wounded by Casender, and in fact is prevented from killing him only by Calista's shooting of her brother's horse.

Chapter 5 introduces a major new figure in the tale, the mysterious ex-priest Don Ricardo Duville, who makes his appearance as a shadowy, half-breed "*incognito*." His function is multifold. In a scene directly out of *The Spy*, he plays Harvey Birch, as noted by the narrator, to Jackson's Washington, providing an inside narrative of political-military events to date. He also then, Natty Bumppo–like, engages in a lengthy debate with the Rev. Mr. Blackburn (another actual "historical" figure), whose inspirational abilities have caused the pragmatic Jackson to attach him to the military staff, but whose doctrinaire Calvinism, like that of David Gamut in *The Last of the Mohicans*, is now vanquished by Duville's clear, commonsense deism. Then, at length, Duville reveals his own story, which includes his early service in the French priesthood, his marriage to a Spanish noblewoman who bears him a daughter, their capture as part of Napoleon's expedition to Santo Domingo by Caribbean pirates, the presumed death of the wife and child in a shipwreck, after an escape in Cuba, and Duville's eventual joining forces with the Indians, to whom he has decided to devote his life in ministering.

Meanwhile, Calista and the rest of Ropaugh's band have been swept up in the enormous, decisive battle of Tohopeka, known to the whites as Horseshoe Bend. During Jackson's rout of Indian forces, Calista is nearly raped by a white straggler, one of Coffee's volunteers. Cevillo appears, saves her momentarily, and is then himself nearly killed by the assailant. At the last minute, Calista shoots and ostensibly kills him, rescuing Cevillo. She and Jula then vanish back into the confusion of war.

At the same time, in a post-battle encounter, Perendio Cevillo and Duville meet and decide to become comrades. They witness Weatherford's magnificent speech of concession to Jackson. Duville reveals himself to be Calista's uncle. The two begin the search for the "Lost Virgin!"

They return to Tohopeka and, in a scene recalling the deserted field of death at Cooper's Fort Henry in *The Last of the Mohicans*, the two muse on the origins of the Southwest wars, the repeated misapprehensions of Indians by whites and vice versa, the provocations on both sides, the growing outcries for vengeance, the mistakes, the cruelties, the British agitations. Jackson is discussed as neither a saint nor a pitiless warrior, but a man of duty first and of commonsense *realpolitik*.

It is now the fall of 1813, and Calista, Jula, their old Indian "mother," and the remnants of Ropaugh's band have established themselves in a bower somewhere between the Coosa and the Tallapoosa. A mysterious English-speaking

Indian, who turns out to be Duville, appears at Calista's forest cottage and inquires if she may be Calista Ward. Duville bargains for the return of Calista, offering money to the old mother and also writing Calista a letter. Meanwhile, Jula laments, with much weeping on her part and Calista's, that she may be left alone. Calista verifies her uncle's identity from her remembrance of an ancestral portrait, and writes back "I am Calista Ward—Come!" At the recognition scene itself, Duville for the first time perceives the likeness of Jula to his lost wife. Duville also relates his adventures and those of his comrade Cevillo, whom Calista and Jula now remember from earlier appearances. In addition, Duville has a key to the locket, which he opens, revealing Cevillo's portrait, and causing Calista's memory of her rescuer to blossom into love.

In the fall of 1814, led by Duville, the party sets out for New Orleans. On the way they are beset by three brigands, two white and one black, whom Duville vanquishes. He also rescues from their clutches, nearly dead, the same Jones whom Calista and Jula have aided at Tallushetchee. Duville, as a priest, shrives the two dying white pirates, a Spaniard named Es Joebe and a German named Hosmer Sprouse. They both turn out to be part of the band from which he and his wife escaped in Cuba in 1804. Both have left behind manuscripts. After their burial along the Jackson trail at "Pirate's Grave," and the party's arrival at New Orleans, we are given the manuscript relation of Es Joebe.

A profligate son of indulgent parents, Es Joebe has squandered his prospects, turned to piracy at an early age, and shortly found himself in command of a party herding a large group of Santo Domingo captives, mostly noble young men and their fair brides, to a place of execution. He has culled out Duville and his wife on the promise that the latter will serve the pirates as a resident intercessor. Es Joebe also selects one young woman for his personal purposes. At a cliff, after the men are massacred by a firing squad, he invites his comrades to select women for themselves. The bound women throw themselves over the cliff and into the sea. In the confusion, Es Joebe's personal selectee plunges a knife into his breast and jumps as well. He survives, however, and by 1807 he is again a pirate, now en route to Monserrat in France, where his party has taken a vessel whose captives include his own father and mother. Here the narrative of the first volume ends.

As the second volume begins, Es Joebe's tale continues. His mother reveals to him that he is not his alleged father's child, but rather the bastard son of a nobleman who has seduced her. Es Joebe stabs her in the breast, and she falls overboard. Onshore, he confesses to a priest. Shortly, events carry him back to the New World, and to adventures leading up to his just-recorded demise.

Now, in New Orleans, under the patronage of Bishop Dubourg (once more, an "actual" figure), both Calista and Jula, adopted by Duville, are educated as young gentlewomen at the convent of the Ursulines. Although Duville still does not recognize Jula, her appearance continues to remind him of his lost wife. Shortly ensues the Battle of New Orleans. Calista and Jula are enlisted as nurses, whereby they become involved with "two very interesting young men" who appear among the wounded. One looks like Calista's brother Casender. Under the two women's care, the young men, near death, miraculously recover. The second, the reader quickly realizes, is Cevillo. Casender—who, it turns out, has been serving with the British—is now recognized. Then, shortly, Perendio is recognized by Duville, but not by Calista or Jula. Perendio confesses his love for Calista. Duville hatches a complicated recognition plot, with Cevillo in his *incognito* status impersonating a new suitor, to test Calista's fidelity. Meanwhile, among the British wounded, Duville discovers Colonel Ward, Calista's father and his brother-in-law. He orchestrates a lavish Valentine's Day party in which Perendio's identity is revealed, father and daughter are reunited, and Casender is also brought forward. Cevillo sues for Calista's hand. Meanwhile, the whole complicated story is rehashed and brought up to date. Jones, having come along to New Orleans, is married to the girls' quadroon maid. With Calista now nearly sixteen years old and Jula nearly fourteen, the whole party sets out for Europe.

After another great storm and devotional interlude at sea, they arrive in Spain, where the Ward family is reunited and, in gratitude, sets out on a pilgrimage to Monserrat. There they come into contact with a female religious hermit, deposited at the place by the same shipwreck involving Es Joebe's murder of his mother. Her name is Jula. By a birthmark, she recognizes the child Jula to be her daughter. This family is now happily reunited.

Back in Spain, Perendio and Calista's romance is complicated by political-religious strife and the machinations of a blackmailing villain named Jorallo, who has Perendio imprisoned as a religious liberal and attempts to exchange his release for Calista's virtue. She defies him and receives a wound in her breast from his stiletto.[5] Perendio then stabs Jorallo, who survives and repents.

In France, Calista and Perendio are married. A guest at the wedding is a melancholy young woman with a handsome male child. She excites Duville's curiosity, and he elicits from her a manuscript. She turns out to be Cecilia, of the Santo Domingo massacre, who has survived her plunge after stabbing Es Joebe. She has also rescued her still-living husband from the pile of corpses. Although they have made it back to Europe, he has been lost in action at the recent battle of Waterloo, leaving her widowed and bereft. Duville, however, has by now noticed a wedding musician who resembles the husband as he appeared in Cuba. After further elaborate reunion plotting, this couple is reunited, with an attendant revelation that Cecilia is also Perendio's long-lost sister.

Now, amidst the disruptions of post-Napoleonic Europe, the principals return to the New World. They arrive at New Orleans and revisit the woodland bower, where the old squaw reveals the story of her adoption of Jula. At the last moment a mutilated white veteran of the wars also straggles out of the forest. It is the would-be rapist that Calista, miraculously, has not killed after all. He begs forgiveness and receives her blessing.

The party then proceeds up the East Coast. It is now 1818. Jula has been married, we are told, to a young New York man, and Casender to a young New York woman. Calista has become the mother of four children and Jula of three. They live happily in the city. Duville and Jula, it is revealed, have also produced a new child. She has been lately placed, according to her mother's vows, at "the Monastery at Montreal, in Canada, with a view to taking the veil." Once more, however, romance looks to intervene, and "we understand this young virgin is to be stolen away from old mother church, by her lover." That "romantic affair," however, the narrator concludes, "will cost the world the reading of a new book" (2: 152).

From its bizarre prefacings of origin and authority, through its stunning historical-novelistic complications, and down to the "soon-to-be-continued" titillations of its last line, then, for all its crudities of execution, *The Lost Virgin of the South* is somehow incredibly "literary." Indeed, one nearly staggers under the sheer amount of "material," factual and fictive, that the author somehow manages to combine in a single fabric of assimilations.

Most especially, in the American scenes of the first volume, the chief of such literary presences is Cooper, and to a degree suggesting that the author had read everything the latter had written virtually up to the instant of composition. As mentioned, both *The Spy* and *The Last of the Mohicans* inform Duville's first appearance as a mysterious *incognito* at Jackson's headquarters. Duville and Perendio's forest discussion, apropos of their remarks on Jackson and on larger national traits and issues, speaks of the kinds of dialogues recurrent in *Notions of the Americans*. As to pirate materials, while perhaps most likely indebted, as noted above, to popular legends of Jean Lafitte, the work also suggests *The Red Rover*. And while set upon the forest landscape of the Southwest, the scenes of Indian warfare and the captivity plot[6] resemble those of the Connecticut frontier in *The Wept of Wish-ton-Wish*.

While in some ways a kind of compendium of early Cooper, *The Lost Virgin* also remarks eloquently, however, as a Southwestern text, on the many kinds of Cooper it is not. Centering on the Southern Indians, for instance, of the Five Civilized Tribes, and involving an actual mixed-blood hero of romantic stature, the Creek chieftain Weatherford,[7] it contains little of Cooper's racial anxiety. No Leatherstocking declaims endlessly about being a man "without a cross" in his blood. The Indian hordes of the text provide not a single satanic villain. (The one bona fide attempted rapist is a white irregular.) One looks hard even for the covert racism of Cooper's "red" narratives at their most sympathetic. The adoptive parents of Calista and Jula, the Seminole father Ropaugh and the Creek mother Camera, are treated as complex and sympathetic in their motivations. They are Native Americans in a deeply political sense anticipating new historical understandings and clarifications.

Nor, in the same vein of ideological reinscription, does this Southern Cooper inscribe his mentor's party politics of religion. As the dialogue between Duville and Blackburn reveals, the work's hero is distinctly anti-Calvinist. Yet he lauds Jackson's pragmatic employment of Blackburn's spiritual charisma to motivate his backwoods religionists to battle. Comparably, Catholicism (and especially in a long conversational passage on papist abuses of money and power included in the first edition but excised in the second) is subjected to a good deal of Cooperesque caricature. Yet Duville, despite his fallen status, remains faithful to the Church, and it is at times explicitly credited for its advancements of New World civilization.

Such pluralism also manifests itself in other suggestions of regional difference in literary-cultural foregrounding. This Southwestern religious-historical epic, for instance, unlike Cooper's or those of the great New England romancers such as Hawthorne, Melville, and Stowe, is not remotely Miltonic. There is no tainted Eve, no Lucifer plotting his rebellion and revenge, no Adamic innocent. The titular "virgin," in fact, if anything, derives from the heavily Catholic flavor that overlays the bulk of the novel; and this non-Protestant orientation likewise probably helps to explain why, in contrast to Cooper, say, or Hawthorne, it seems so hard to isolate those customary Calvinist romance archetypes such as the fair heroine, dark heroine, genteel hero, and satanic villain. Nor, in contrast to virtually every other Protestant novelist-romancer of the era, from Hawthorne through Twain, does the author seem in any conventional way Bunyanesque. Rather, like much early Anglo-American writing of the South, it is really rather more directly Elizabethan and Jacobean. Biblical inscription is decidedly King James. From the initial shipwreck onward, Shakespeare appears in a number of turns from *The Tempest*. In this brave new world, Duville is a Southwest Prospero. Calista, evoking the memory of Sidney, recalls in her name Callisto, the mother of the Arcadians. Meanwhile, back in Shakespeare, she seems a Miranda who has borrowed part of her name from Caliban.

Then there is Spenser. From the allusive echoing of the titles, *The Lost Virgin* and *The Faerie Queene*, stunning intertextual parallels abound in these large dramas of historical destiny. Within both texts, virginal literary heroines become objects of perilous missions of noble rescue on a landscape at once charmed and sinister, wondrous and terrible. Casender's virgin Calista plays, as object of the quest, Una; as near-victim of several wilderness ravishers, not to mention as possessor of the golden locket signifying her true identity, Florimell; and, as part of the double rescue plottings with the noble Perendio Cevillo and Casender Ward, Britomart to her companion Jula's Amoret. The elder male hero of the quest, Duville, would seem a frontier Prince Arthur; the younger, Cevillo, provides a counterpart Red Cross Knight, even to Calista's nursing of him to recovery in the New Orleans convent hospital. "Feirce warres and faithful loves shall moralize my song," Spenser announces in his introduction, and this Southwestern romancer seems to have embraced his model with backwoods gusto.

Similarly, on the more immediate account of popular gothic inheritance, *The Lost Virgin*'s author presents a rich record of assimilations. In the strange intertextualizations of narrative authority; in the claims of high moral purpose and veracity commingled with sensationalism and promotional shill; in heroes and heroines forced to navigate a landscape of predation where, among savage and civilized alike, friend repeatedly passes for foe and vice versa: in all these things, one vainly waits to discover that the author had devoured Brockden Brown as obviously as he had Cooper. Perhaps, given the shadowed, clerical presence of Duville, one could also take the chance of inferring Matthew Lewis's *The Monk*. On the other hand, as suggested by the synopses of gothic potboilers supplied by Henri Petter, this author, with his outrageous concoctions of plot, the various origins of his characters, and the diverse and exotic settings ultimately traversed in the course of their adventures—England, Europe, the Southwest frontier, the Caribbean, the Americas—seems really, rather, just to have pulled out every gothic stop available in a popular literature of inexhaustible invention. Indians, pirates, defrocked priests, sainted heroines, noble *incognitos,* lost children, bereft parents—all navigate their imperiled ways upon a gothic landscape cluttered with the stage paraphernalia of mysterious manuscripts, letters, coinciding anecdotal relations; secrets of birth; charms, amulets, identifying information, and tokens.

The same may be said of related debts to the popular sentimental. In the travails of Calista, Jula, and various other female moral exemplars, not to mention their more unfortunate sisters—Jula the suffering wife and mother, the eventually sainted Cecilia, the murdered mother of Es Joebe—this proves relentlessly, with all the titillations and aggressions incumbent, a tale of virtue rewarded and vice punished. Further, one also finds new hybridizations of sentimental convention with the increasingly well developed American genre of the captivity narrative.[8] Here, amidst Indians, pirates, and sundry other clutches of Anglo-European irregulars, the plot is not nearly so often seduction as rape. During their Indian sojourn, Calista and Jula spend the better part of their time dressed as boys to avert just such a terror. Indeed, in one specific case, as mentioned, the crime is actually attempted on the former, with further perils also supplied by the skirmish with the Es Joebe pirate band, including a murderous black, and the perilous moonlight confrontation in Spain with the dagger-wielding Jorallo. Similarly, the scenes in the Es Joebe narrative involving his designs on Cecilia and the mass suicide of the women to avoid similar appropriation make no attempt to disguise the fate over which death becomes their necessary choice.

On the other hand, the more commonplace, domestic-sentimental strain is also fully exploited in the lachrymose scenes of parting, solitary musing on one's fate, new meeting, recognition, reunion, and final conjoinment in prospect of endless amatory and familial happiness. Mixed with all this, there evolves also a social minuet of marriage and manners, the orchestration of reunions, of courtship and betrothal, of confessions and recognitions. And finally, anticipating new variants of sentimental melodrama to come, the young heroine prefigures Harriet Beecher Stowe's Little Eva and others like her, somehow at once the Holy Virgin and the Virgin-Child, the example of a spotless life invoking the prospect of a world of adult relations transformed and even possibly redeemed.

Still, this is, after all, a text of the Old Southwest. Accordingly, amidst the romantic elevation—the sweeping historical drama; the hothouse gothic sensationalism; the genteel sentimentality and moral didacticism—the novel places itself locally as well in the tradition of the American picaresque. Brigands and rapscallions, rabble-rousers and sly miscreants, mix with noble half-breeds, gentleman-*voyageurs,* homegrown Napoleons arising with chaste heroism from amidst the ranks of their democratic brethren. And here further, in the Caribbean scenes and the Louisiana settings of much of the important action, the backwoods elements mingle with the piratical, the motley cast of cutthroats, half-breeds, and isolatos familiar from a host of gothic narratives and now tied in almost surely in the present case, as noted elsewhere, with popular accounts of the romantic renegade Lafitte. Along the way, the element of Southwestern narrative inscribes its peculiar, almost black-humor grotesquerie. Somehow out of Edgar Poe by way of Mark Twain, for instance, the ubiquitous Irishman Jones staggers in and out of the novel during the battle of Tallushetchee, reappears in the clutches of Es Joebe, and is finally united in marriage with a beautiful New Orleans quadroon. The nameless, would-be rapist of Calista, shot by her and presumed dead at Tohopeka, reappears at the last, halt and maimed, yet very much alive and the subject of a miraculous conversion. In good-natured raillery, the rumbustious chorus of staff officers at Jackson's headquarters celebrates Duville's rhetorical defeat of the pious, hypocritical Mr. Woodward. Likewise, the clever priest's securing of Calista's release from her wily Creek mother combines romance stratagem with sophistries that resemble those of many a horse or blanket trader to come.

In the related vein of what Philip Fisher has called *Hard Facts,* we also have something of a new composite order as well: and that is the attempt at an American political novel about extant, contemporary American political realities. To put this another way, by writing directly about the rise of Anglo-European and American frontier culture of the early 1800s and the resultant fate of the Native American civilizations in the process destroyed and displaced, the author is actually doing what Cooper could only do by historical indirection. Hence the frequent replacement of romance stereotypes, especially among male figures, by political characters who strike us as at least rudely problematic. Here we have, for instance, no formulaic confrontation of the genteel hero—upper class, Anglo-Saxon—with the satanic villain—dark-skinned, savage, violent. Here we have no greenhorn's progress, abetted by the legendary frontiersman. Similarly, apart from romance necessaries such as pious moralism and suitable attributes of face and figure, the women in this text, red and white, English, French, Spanish, nun and quadroon, seem uncommonly durable, brave, survivorly. Here indeed, across the ranges of gender, class, and race,[9] we have a politics of character, albeit literarily hasty in its hybridizations, shaped to the unfoldings of actual culture in the Old Southwest. The clashes of colonialisms eventuating in the rise of Anglo-Euro-American culture yield to the tragic removals of the Native American, which in turn prepare the way for the experiment of expansionist frontier democracy. In turn, such events are politically contextualized in the second volume by the convulsions of Napoleonic Europe. It is not for nothing that this book is presided over in the first volume by the American battles of Horseshoe Bend and New Orleans, and in the second, albeit much more circumstantially, by Waterloo.

All this literary-historical confabulation, one is tempted to say, must enroll *The Lost Virgin of the South* in a long tradition of precocious American metafictions: of literary art self-consciously attempting to justify its epistemological and ontological status as a way of investigating the forms of a culture still trying to reify itself into existential and political fact; or of prophetic postmodern conundrums spinning off into paranoiac congruencies or endless reflexive self-interrogation. But that would be to do injustice to the rare relevance of this fiction in the more fashionable interests of teasing out some academic allegory of art, a myth of cultural origin that is also a form of radical cultural critique. Here, one must insist, for all the historical-gothic claptrap, something emerges that often looks instead, if anything, like the material of the important contemporary "social" texts currently being rediscovered in nineteenth-century women's writing (and in the process once again calling into question frequent claims by male practitioners of romance about a lack of social material). Here, indeed, the cultural story of evolving American manners would seem exactly to the literary point. The mode of mythologizing here is meant to invoke the historically probable. The mode of critique is meant to be historically pragmatic. In a word, this novel is an attempt to be realistic in the vein of those two rather new and local realisms—the tradition of frontier humor and the tradition of domestic melodrama—that would in their confluence prove the special contributions of the Old Southwest to an emergent critical realism.

And that, of course, is the story behind the story as well, the story of M. Smith alias (perhaps) Wiley Conner alias Don Pedro Casender. That story is about the cultural and the aesthetic politics of something called "literature" in a new country. Further, it is "political" in certain "literary" ways that ought to make us keep rethinking our commonplaces about American literary and cultural attitudes in the antebellum Republic. As this is not a Northern romance of the forest, neither is it a Southern one of the plantation. For here the American frontier setting is, for the most part, yeoman farmer and backwoodsman South, as opposed to the aristocratic, landed South. It is the Gulf South, as opposed to the Atlantic South, and thereby an Anglo-Euro-American New World embracing not only England but also Spain, France, the Caribbean, and the postcolonial regions of Florida, Alabama, Louisiana. And similarly, the New Orleans and the sundry European capitals and watering spots of the second, more "cosmopolitan" volume, albeit in their hasty, sketched-out, gothic way, represent the great world of international culture whose vistas were to be opened by Hawthorne and James. The society represented is a multicultural society and, in certain limited ways, even a multiracial society, with not only the possibility but the fulfillment of various crossings: French-Spanish-English-American. And on this side of the Atlantic as well, new possibilities become equally diverse: as in the case of Ropaugh and Camera, intertribal; as with the noble Weatherford, white and Indian interracial; even, as in the case of Jones and the ladies' maid Urana, an Irishman and a quadroon. Here, indeed, the "marriage" theme that becomes the dramatic counterweight to the history-adventure theme forces no precipitate giving in either to Cooper's and Hawthorne's Manichaean necessity of antiphonal tragic and comic discourses, or to Melville's and Twain's alternative fantasies of a homosocial brotherhood. And that—the possibility of a multicultural society, albeit on Anglo-European and American terms—*is* the great social theme of this novel, and the one that distinguishes it from many of the romances of the nineteenth century which tried to articulate the prospects and promises of American history, and wound up so often recapitulating its bitter irony.

Neither, in the larger "political" domain, does it correspond to major versions of official narrative. As to the matter of Jackson, it contrasts itself both to the campaign-biography hogwash and to the aristocratic invective coming out of the South and assumed to be the dominant tones. The great Democrat stands astride the action, but as neither the proletarian demigod nor the Whig anti-Christ. Similarly, the Indians, if they incline to the Rousseauvian, are not prelapsarian. On the other hand, it is not a frontier shoot-em-up or an exercise in the metaphysics of Indian-hating. The role of Catholicism in settlement of the Old Southwest is viewed as ultimately menacing and disadvantageous but for the moment culturally useful. Anglo-Americans seek out their commonalities with French and Spanish Americans. Even in the cosmopolitan precincts of New Orleans, the enemy English become reconciled once again to their New World compatriots.

At a closer political focus, the work speaks uniquely both of the Indian wars of the Old Southwest and about the Southern War of 1812 in a fictional literature that says little about either of these. It also reminds us that American history of the era was heavily contextualized by the upheavals of England and Europe in the age of Napoleon. That is, at once in the large focus *and* in the small, it proclaims that there was something social and political in America to be written about; and it proves, moreover, that it was being written about, in the forms of a nascent realism attempting to affirm its connections with evolving Anglo-European culture as a whole.

In sum, as to both political and literary constructions of the national character, *The Lost Virgin of the South* provides new information about what our early literature tries to "say." Formed out of the materials of a rude art attempting to assimilate the actualities of local and geopolitical "life," M. Smith's provincial narrative finds its cosmopolitan resolution. In the process, it also forces upon us, through its eclectic regional politics of art—the masculine vein of the historical romance transferred into the precinct of backwoods adventure, and the feminine counterpart of gothic fantasy transferred to the domain of domestic melodrama—a compelling vision of what many Americans in the South at least never doubted as the complementary "social," "political," or—in a word—"realistic" possibilities of the literary subject.

Thus, *The Lost Virgin*, in the way of its Old Southwestern bombast, does make good on its literary and political brag. It reappears on the literary stage as the novelistic rendering of an America in the early nineteenth century extending its frontiers down and outward in the geographical curve of frontier that would redefine the antebellum nation at large, "the first production of the kind, in the South." Like many another rude, slightly fraudulent, patently outrageous frontier production, it got lost looking for an audience which now, again, may be found.

In keeping with our old literary pastime of buying authority in the guise of genealogy and vice versa, we may never know who M. Smith really was. Don Pedro Casender, on the other hand, even as a fiction, possesses at least the logic of textuality deriving from the names of the two brothers. And this problem of literary-historical impersonation also leads us back to the role of that other possible interloper, Wiley Conner, known to have been a journalist-publisher, and, it should be noted, of just an age to have been a personal witness to many of the events described at roughly the age of the young Pedro and Casender. Still, as to those events, "Smith" is often a plagiarized Timothy Flint. On the other hand, Flint is often a plagiarized John Eaton. Hence our M. Smith: a composite figure, at the intersection of life and art, fact and fiction, anecdotal memory and cultural myth, where we have to reconstruct him; or—perhaps, as we now chance upon a famous conversation aboard a literary raft that literarily is yet to happen—find him. It is all, finally, by way of Samuel Clemens's alias Mark Twain's alias Huckleberry Finn's attempt at the great American novel, almost too good to be true:

"Old man," says the young one, "I reckon we might double-team it together, what do you think?"

"I ain't indisposed. What's your line—mainly?"

"Jour printer, by trade," the first answers, and further spins off an impressive list of cognate occupations. Then he returns the honor: "What's your lay?"

The other proves comparably diverse, saving, however, the best for last. "Preachin's my line, too," he says, "and workin' camp-meetin's; and missionaryin' around" (103).

Thus we literarily, before *and* after the fact, reconstruct M. Smith; and in the process, we gain the opportunity, through his text, to reconstruct the literary-cultural "world" he sought to describe. It is a new vision of an old America which recovers a certain kind of history both literary and cultural not hitherto remembered as fully as it ought to be. To be sure, in charting such a recovery, we must admit that M. Smith alias (perhaps) Wiley Conner alias Don Pedro Casender did not nearly write the great American novel. But he tried, and he knew where to put his appeal. At the conclusion, like many another wide-screen American promoter of popular epics, he looks for the smart money. As we heard him first, authenticating, appealing, cajoling, so we hear him at the last, dangling the prospect of an equally ripe and garish sequel.

4

Belles Lettres in a New Country

~

By the standards of more established cultural jurisdictions, the Alabama country had already in effect, however improbably, become the province of belles lettres in the rather traditional sense of the term when a minor territorial functionary, Lewis Sewall, elected for the publication of mock-epic satire as a way of commemorating the misadventures of Colonel James Caller and his ragtag militia band at the infamous Battle of Burnt Corn. Further, as noted, as part of a climate of print production fostered in early cultural development along the Gulf, the new state would likewise shortly boast not only a compendious law and order volume but also, barely a decade after accession to statehood, a backwoods *incognito*'s attempt at a grand literary romance of the forest, styled after such contemporaries as Cooper and Simms, and again focused on the Creek War of 1813–14. And, not surprisingly, as will be seen, particularly during the late antebellum era, it would be to Mobile, the old city by the bay, that a self-conscious literary culture would return to make something of a permanent home. It was there that the state's most influential man of antebellum letters, Alexander Beaufort Meek, would spend the last two decades of his life, itself a period that would see publication of his epic poem, *The Red Eagle*, his book of prose historical sketches, *Romantic Passages in Southwestern History*, and his collection of lyrics entitled *Songs and Poems of the South*. It was there that a young novelist, Augusta Jane Evans, with such early productions as *Inez: A Tale of the*

Alamo and, most notably, *Beulah,* would launch herself upon one of the most visible and lucrative writing careers of the century. And, as important for present purposes, it was also there that Octavia Walton Le Vert would establish herself in the same years as Alabama's most prominent and well-known female belletrist and keeper of one of the South's most famous literary salons.[1]

Meanwhile, however, emanations of the belletristic spirit were beginning to take shape in a number of other locations in the new country as well; and, not surprisingly, some of the most important first flowerings were to be witnessed in the new center of culture at Tuscaloosa, since 1825 the state capital, and since 1831 also the seat of the nascent university. Most prominently, these included the first book of poetry published in Alabama, William R. Smith's *College Musings; or, Twigs from Parnassus,* and A. B. Meek's short-lived but important journal of regional literature and culture, *The Southron.*

Not surprisingly, both were productions of the 1830s; and thereby they surely must be taken as expressions of the confidence and pride of the era in the steady advance of culture that had taken place in the early decades of statehood. Still, as consciously literary productions attempting to stake themselves off into the proper realm of belles lettres, both carefully distanced themselves from the rumbustious boom-and-bust spirit of the era, the rowdy, on-the-make social energy, so to speak, of the flush times that made them possible. For, like most other male figures attaining authorial status in Alabama during the early period, whether in politics, law, journalism, commerce, agriculture, or any other forms of public activity, neither Smith nor Meek would have cared to be known as a professional literary person; nor would they have wished to see their productions carry the taint of commerce in any direct financial sense or as regards any kind of tawdry political involvement. (To be sure, *The Southron* had to be marketed to subscribers; but that dingy matter was left to the publisher. Certainly, it was also to express partisanship as far as the advancement of Southern letters was concerned; but that would have been considered hardly a polemical position.) Rather, they would have preferred to be seen as men of affairs who simply devoted part of their energies to the pursuit of letters as a contribution to the general advancement of culture. To this degree they would conform to images of cultural authority resembling those established by such figures of national stature to the North as Washington Irving, William Cullen Bryant, Henry Wadsworth Longfellow, or, in the immediate region, William Gilmore Simms, in which literary endeavor was in some way overtly connected with a larger career of public service. Certainly, they eschewed the gadfly professionalism, for instance, of their Southern compatriot Edgar A. Poe; if anything, indeed, the careers of Smith and Meek could finally be said to have exemplified the age's emphasis on the relation of literature to some cultural ideal of public-spirited manly gentility.

Smith, besides authoring his book of verse, would briefly edit a literary journal, *The Bachelor's Button*, begun during a short sojourn of the mid-1830s in Mobile and going through a final 1837 number in Tuscaloosa. He would also write verse political satire on such diverse subjects as the Harrison-Tyler campaign of 1840 (*Hard Cider*), U.S. involvement in the Hungarian revolution (*Kossuth Coppered, or, The Banquet at the Capital of Laputa*), and that archfoe of Southern liberty, Abraham Lincoln (*The Royal Ape*); several legal treatises; a novel, *As It Is;* a long philosophical poem, *The Uses of Solitude;* a history of the Alabama secession debates; and an autobiography, *Reminiscences of a Long Life.* Meanwhile, in his public life he had practiced law, raised a company of militia for service in the short-lived Creek uprising of 1836, and served as mayor of Tuscaloosa and judge of the Seventh District. In 1850 he was elected to the U.S. Congress, serving until 1856; and in 1861 he returned to politics as a delegate to the Alabama convention on secession. Despite his anti-secessionist position there, he also served two terms in the Confederate Congress; and after the war he also served as president of the University of Alabama, while pursuing a series of unsuccessful attempts to resume his political career (B. Williams, *Literary History* 28–39; Shields, "Social History" 173–74, 183–84).

As did his friend Smith's book of verse, Meek's editorship of *The Southron* marked an initial venture into the formal domain of letters that would eventuate into other substantive literary production across an impressive range of genre and mode. As detailed in a separate chapter here, the most obvious and visible of Meek's subsequent achievements would be, of course, his verse epic *The Red Eagle;* but, working in competition with his rival Pickett, he would also devote considerable energy to a history of the state. While the larger project never came to pass, much of the material would find publication in the form of orations, sketches, and essays collected under the 1857 title *Romantic Passages in Southwestern History.* And in the same year, Meek would gather for publication the fruits of a long poetic career in his volume *Songs and Poems of the South.* Meanwhile, Meek too had enjoyed an active public career, serving in the 1830s as editor of the Tuscaloosa newspaper *Flag of the Union,* as a volunteer in the Seminole war, and briefly upon return as attorney general of Alabama. After editorship of *The Southron,* he continued to combine work as an orator, essayist, and poet with compilation of a legal digest, until 1844, when he became law clerk to the solicitor of the United States Treasury; and in 1846 he was appointed federal attorney for the Southern District of Alabama. Editorship of the *Mobile Register* followed, and after that, election to the state legislature, where Meek gained credit for authoring the bill establishing a public school system in the state. At the end of the decade he became probate judge of Mobile County, and was reelected to the legislature, where in 1859 he was chosen speaker of the house. Like Smith, he opposed secession; and upon the onset of war he retired from active participation in political and military affairs. He did, however, serve as a trustee of the university, living long enough to see it burned to the ground in 1865, the year in which he died in November (B. Williams, *Literary History* 39–54; Shields, "Social History" 177–81).

It seems only appropriate to the literary emphasis of the discussion at hand that, in a biographical survey of the careers of Smith and Meek, both should be noted as finding place late in their lives to become important figures in the life of the University of Alabama, in the first instance as a president and in the second as a trustee. For the single institutional feature of culture that likely made possible the important literary dimensions of the lives so described was surely in both cases their early relationship with the infant state university, that seminary of learning, as it had been called in its initial 1819 charter, and buzzing in the 1830s with an influx of academic and intellectual talent. Indeed, both young authors, as noted by Johanna Nicol Shields, were likely present at the 1832 celebration of the university's Erosophic Society at which Professor Henry Hilliard, himself an aspirant after renown as one of the age's great men of public affairs, had exhorted the members to "Suffer not the current of the age to pass you by," but rather to "Ride on the foremost billow; your country has claims on you" ("Social History" 168).

Smith had arrived at the pursuit of letters as he had arrived in the capital itself: as a student in the first class registered at the infant university. There, like many another literary undergraduate of poetic inclinations, he found the freedom to get drunk on poetry. He obviously found Byron, Shakespeare, Wordsworth, Coleridge, Homer, Pindar, Walter Scott. He also found a friend, Burwell Boykin, to whom he dedicated a volume of his own highly imitative, albeit earnest, emanations. To be sure, he made every gentlemanly attempt to pass them off as juvenilia. On the title page, he quoted Byron: "A schoolboy freak, unworthy of praise or blame, / I'll print—for older children do the same." Likewise, in the dedicatory remarks to Boykin, he laid great stress on the poems' values less as any attempt to secure "laurels in the world of letters, where there are now so many champions of genius and erudition," than as attempts to recall their early years of friendship in "the joyous groves of Academus" where "first our young fancies were taught to soar above the bounded visions of the vulgar" (viii). And as if he had not protested enough his derivativeness and immaturity, a preface went at it again: "It will little affect me," he concluded, "if this book should 'strut at once out into obscurity,' for indeed I have no other expectations."

The critics say that these *school boy freaks,* are all soon lost amid the crowd of other unfortunate bundles of paper that glitter in the dust of oblivion; and of course what they say must be true—But I have seen it somewhere remarked, that Criticism disdained to follow the school boy to his common place book—I hope that she will not forget her dignity on the present occasion—but that she will suffer my little bird to go forth without a weight around its neck to bear it down;—with equally balanced pinions; with a joyous look, a cloudless eye, and a wildly beating heart. (x)

On all these grounds, even on an early antebellum literary landscape where freestanding volumes of poetry were notably rare, the book is perhaps too easy to put down in several senses.[2] The litany of protestation has led us to expect, between the embossed ivory boards, in keeping with the pale, demure title, a pale, demure volume, the work of a callow eighteen-year-old full of lyric poetry and doing his best not to seem full of himself. In fact, it turns out to be not at all a conventional collection of lyrics, but rather more, as with the Walter Scott and Wordsworth-Coleridge models, but rather a book of lays and/or lyrical ballads. The opening works, for instance, turn out to be two ambitious long poems. The first, in fact, "Shakespeare," is nearly four hundred lines long, a full twenty-three pages in this book of slightly more than a hundred leaves. Accordingly, it is in every sense a properly Parnassian poem, with stanzas of widely varying line lengths composed in heroic couplets and recording an allegory of the birth of the genius of the poet, the Bard of Avon contemplated at his mythic origins upon Helicon. There then follows "Jenny Lee," a ballad, in eight-line stanzas of alternating hexameter and pentameter lines, and running to ten cantos. Next is "The Little Orphan Boy," again a ballad, this time in fourteen octaves of alternating octameter and hexamater. And of comparable dexterity is "Laura," with its eight-line stanzas divided into an opening trimeter couplet and then an octameter sestet. Then comes a section entitled "Fugitive Pieces," mainly shorter poems. But even here one finds a challenging variety of forms and technical approaches. Notable for their variety of theme and mood, for instance, as well as their diversified craftsmanship, are "The Lover's Dream," a ballad in the conventional quatrain form alternating tetrameter-trimeter line but with anapestic feet, and "Advice to a Friend," a blank-verse meditation. There is even a somewhat humorous poem, "The School Girl's Petition." And then there is the concluding feature of the text: a dense, florid, extended prose eulogium entitled "Lament of Waverley" and decrying the recent death of Walter Scott, and poignant testimony to a severe local literary infestation of what Mark Twain called the Sir Walter disease. "The oracle of chivalry now slumbers beneath the cold and silent dust!" the youthful devotee proclaims. "The star of the literary world has gone down into the chaos of eternity; but the beams of his living splendour have flashed over the regions of civilized humanity, and lighted up the Promethean watchtowers of immortality" (103). If nothing else, here we have evidence of the genuine depths of response struck by Scott in the Southern literary temperament even on the nineteenth-century frontier. On the other hand, in structural terms, the piece also brings to the larger text a kind of contextualizing symmetry, a balancing of the opening celebration of the genius of one master with a lament over the passing of another.

Meek had likewise begun his literary pursuits amidst the flourishing literary circumstances of the new center of politics and culture. Having previously studied at the University of Georgia, he too had chosen to become a matriculant in the new student body at Alabama, and had then remained in Tuscaloosa as editor of the *Flag of the Union,* a newspaper that he also used as a venue for his own verse and that of the local literary community, familiarly known as the Tuskaloosa Bards.

These journalistic endeavors in turn eventuated in Meeks's attempt to found a new, specifically Southern, specifically literary publication. *The Southron,* he decided to call it, apparently sharing his friend Smith's enthusiasm for the Author of Waverly, after the archaic Scots phrasing; and from the opening lines onward of a first rousing piece, entitled "Introduction Salutatory," one truly could sense something of an annunciation, a new implanting of the honored spirit of letters "in a region hitherto, but rarely trodden." "THE SOUTHRON," its author boldly announced, would devote itself to the great "purpose of promoting the Literature of the South" (1) in full anticipation of, it went on, "for our section of the Union, a proud pre-eminence in the higher attributes and attainments of the human intellect" (2).[3] At the same time, one might have noted, as a prudent hedge against the financial vagaries of the late 1830s, a subscription fee of five dollars a year was posted as "payable INVARIABLY IN ADVANCE." Still, it boasted an impressive array of contributors, most of them local to be sure, but of substantial reputation. In addition to Meek, clearly the author of the opening essay, as well as a poem and a lengthy historical piece, one could find a sketch by Smith, "Christmas in the Country: A Glimpse at Rural Life in Alabama," and an atmospheric travel piece, "An Evening in Athens," by their mentor Hilliard. Professor F. A. P. Barnard, also an eminent faculty member at the university, was represented by an allegorical dialogue, "Love and Reason," and Caroline Lee Hentz, shortly to become famous as a popular novelist, by "The Father's Vow," a narrative poem about the biblical legend of Jeptha. A local cleric and highly regarded member of the Tuscaloosa literary circle, A. A. Muller, D.D., permitted a reprinting of his renowned "Sunset at

Rome," with the notation of its being "*Revised* and corrected, by the author, expressly for 'The Southron'" (44–45).[4] And a review of Simms's *Richard Hurdis, or, the Avenger of Blood: A Tale of Alabama,* nailed down the appreciation of one of the border romances of that esteemed author in an explicit local connection.

The magazine would last but six issues. But there would be a continuing attempt to maintain a high standard of literary visibility. The second number, for instance, would include fiction by Hentz, "A Legend of the Silver Wave: A Romance of Southern History." The third, attempting to play down its delight over contributions from the mighty Simms, would showcase "River Serenade: Stanzas by the author of 'Guy Rivers,' 'Pelayo, the Goth,' 'Atalantis,' &c. &c." and "Southern Literature: A Letter from the author of 'The Yemassee,' &c." Along the way, Meek and Smith would remain indefatigable contributors. And in sections of "Reviews and Criticism" and "Literary Intelligence" and "Scientific Intelligence" the magazine would attempt to project a cosmopolitan interest in matters of intellectual inquiry, printing everything from reviews of Cooper's *Homeward Bound* and *Home as Found* to "Meteorological and Barometrical Registers, for 1838: Kept by the Rev. O. T. Hammond, of Irwinton, AL."

Issues appeared more or less on schedule for the first five numbers. The sixth was ominously late. For this, an explanation was given in a note from the publisher, R. A. Eaton, dated 1 October 1839. Surely less expected in the same note, on the other hand, was the announcement of the demise of the publication. Subscribers were duly informed that they would receive for their remaining numbers a different paper, Mobile's *Literary Gazette,* a magazine of equal quality which it was hoped would prove a worthy substitute. With that, *The Southron* passed from existence.

In any event, by now the center of political gravity proper was already beginning to shift away from Tuscaloosa. And as it did, so did literary production. As to matters of culture social and intellectual, the old capital and university town would maintain its grip. The Tuskaloosa Bards would continue to flourish, eventually numbering among them such locally prominent figures as Benjamin F. Porter, Bakus T. Huntington, and the merchant-poet Thomas Maxwell, author of the local epic *King Bee's Dream.* The memoirist Virginia Clay Clopton would become famous for her reminiscences of prewar life in *A Belle of the Fifties.* And in the sketches and stories of John Gorman Barr, William T. Porter, editor of *The Spirit of the Times,* would find an Alabama humorist in many ways the equal of more famous contemporaries such as Johnson Jones Hooper and Joseph Glover Baldwin. But as politics moved southward into the Black Belt stretching across the state's rich agricultural midsection from west-central Georgia into northeast Mississippi, so in the main did current literary production. Its new place of quasi-official centering quickly came to be the region surrounding the new capital of Montgomery. Hooper, having begun his career in the town of La Fayette, in Chambers County, continued to mix law and journalistic enterprise in various East Alabama locations, including stints of newspaper editorship in the capital at the *Alabama Journal* and the *Montgomery Weekly Mail*. The historian Albert J. Pickett, likewise active in politics and letters, lived at a plantation in Autauga County, just to the north of the city. Caroline Lee Hentz, having followed her educator-husband from Florence to Tuscaloosa, moved to Tuskegee in 1845 and then in 1848 to Columbus, just across the Chattahoochee River in Georgia. And at the other end of the Black Belt, first in Gainesville and later in Livingston, lived Joseph Glover Baldwin, like Hooper, an active figure in Montgomery politics and in the 1840s a member of the legislature. The 1840s and 1850s themselves were tremendously political decades; and literary activity also proved political in the fullest sense, with popular forms including Southwestern humor, the anti-abolitionist novel, the verse epic, and the history. In all cases, these were the work of literary people, but for the moment eschewing the idea of belles lettres. And it would only be at the end of the antebellum period, as if signaling a certain nostalgia for a vanishing cultural order, that belles lettres would make one final appearance, for a center of activity electing in the process to find its way back down to where it began, in the hospitable, moss-draped, faintly decadent cosmopolitanism of Mobile. By now, for instance, A. B. Meek had migrated there, spending nearly two decades. And among rising younger literary figures was Augusta Jane Evans, to reign after the war as the queen empress of Southern fiction. But belles lettres had also found a home in Mobile now in the sense of their elevated possibilities as an expression of nineteenth-century American literary refinement; and out of that happy conjunction of letters and genteel culture came Alabama's last book of the antebellum belletristic breed, not to mention surely its most well-remembered. That, of course, would be Octavia Walton Le Vert's celebrated *Souvenirs of Travel*.

In terms of the importance of Le Vert's book as a contribution to the growth of antebellum Alabama literary culture, this may seem a large claim to be making for what must now seem—even down to its title—as essentially a minor two-volume travel diary of a socially well-connected woman of literary inclinations now little remembered outside the city where her memory is still cherished or at most the state and region that once numbered her among its leading cultural figures; or, in the broader spectrum of nineteenth-century genteel print production, as an equally minor contribution of that socially well-connected woman of literary inclinations quickly swallowed up in the sheer bulk of a flourishing and plenitudinous, but finally peripheral, antique genre, negligible in its relation to mainstream nineteenth-century American life and culture, and of appeal mainly to an audience themselves numbering upon the socially and/or literarily well placed and well traveled. On both counts, however, we would be the anachronism. For if we may imagine ourselves to be living in the great age of jet-setting travel and tourism, we should know that in terms of sheer literary output, books recording the experience of traveling in print in fact comprised a genre that captivated the American reading public for much of the nineteenth century, again traversing a vast range of social and literary demography, and proving all the rage from the provincial stay-at-home to the practiced cosmopolitan. The most obvious literary evidence of this—albeit then as now, precisely because it seems so obvious, often the most decidedly overlooked—is the degree to which one of the great and recurrent themes among the vast preponderance of the acknowledged major literary figures of the era, frequently occupying large proportions of their textual output, was the idea of Americans abroad. Among such figures would have surely been numbered, for example, Irving, Cooper, Hawthorne, Longfellow, Emerson, Twain, James. Frequently, to be sure, there seemed the propensity, for literary and cultural reasons, to fixate on England, thereby confirming the generic title chosen by Hawthorne: Our Old Home. But travel narratives also celebrated France, Spain, Portugal, Italy, Switzerland, the German states, Austria-Hungary, Russia, Greece, Turkey, the Holy Land. And bookshelves also filled with the counter-migratory accounts of Europeans and English in America: Tocqueville, Dickens, Mrs. Trollope, Harriet Martineau, Philip Gosse.[5]

For traveling Americans especially, however, it was the great age of the grand tour; and so it also proved a great age of the corresponding phenomenon, with motives ranging from the utilitarian and commercial to the most lofty instincts of belletristic appreciation, of putting one's experience of traveling in print so that one less favored or less mobile might have the experience of that travel vicariously as a reader. The result was an avalanche of titles and books. Trying to restrict their view mainly to dedicated book-length examples of the genre, one study of the field pre-1900 finds at least 1,822 titles, and another notes that even before 1868, with the onset of the great rush of Gilded Age travel, the figure already stood at an imposing 691 (Stowe 4).[6] Thus travel scribbling flourished in its obvious vicarious appeal to an American audience too busy or insufficiently leisured and/or affluent to go. It reminded them of European splendors still lacking in their own unformed culture. It appealed to their curiosity, their imagination, and their American wanderlust—in this case by extension as a form of cultural nostalgia taking them into older, exquisitely civilized precincts not nearly so raw or dangerous as the mainly savage new ones available on the vast, as yet largely unsettled and unexplored expanses of the home continent. In this connection, certainly it also appealed to a more general appetite for the "culture" in which so many visitors and complainants among their major literary figures alleged the new nation to be so woefully deficient; and in the alternative, it could also appeal to their biases, their spread-eagle chauvinisms and preferences for the bigger and better, new and improved, as opposed to the smaller and degenerated, older and less advanced.

As with the various appeals travel literature had for its audience, an equally complex set of motivations obtained for its authors. Especially among the well-to-do, who traveled as a consequence of leisure-class status and the general unnecessariness of working for a living, a way of justifying one's position as a cultural nonproducer in any conventional, homebound sense was to produce a text (Stowe 10). To be sure, this was not always the rule. Bayard Taylor, for instance, perhaps the most visible working American travel writer of the century, was a poor boy who took traveling and writing about it as a literal calling, his appointed vocation (Stowe 12–13; Caesar 22). Still, travel in the manner of the grand tour, or, in the less frequent instance, exploration of the regions of the largely unpenetrated and exotic, remained largely a province of the well-to-do. In the North these proved mainly Eastern urban establishmentarians: Bostonians, New Yorkers, Philadelphians. In the South, the grand tour presented itself as an option of desirable cultural broadening mainly to those of the great seaport cities and of the planter classes. The same impulse that impelled a Black Belt planter to import marble mantles or rosewood furniture from Italy and France found a reciprocal urge to send a son to Europe. And, as with their sisters to the north, such well-heeled pilgrims also frequently included Southern wives and daughters.

The combined enterprises of travel and travel writing proved a particularly favored outlet for the well-to-do woman (Stowe 10). While it has been deemed significant by some writers, for instance, that of the pre-1868 figure cited earlier, marking the new onset of Gilded Age travel, of 691 titles, only 35 had been by women (Schriber, "Julia Ward Howe" 269), William Stowe and Terry Caesar are probably accurate in saying that simple numbers misrepresent their impact (Stowe 4; Caesar 54). For a substantial core of the volumes so numbered were in fact highly visible, and often in ways many a male counterpart would have deeply admired. Fanny W. Hall's *Rambles in Europe; or, A Tour through France, Italy, Switzerland, Great Britain, and Ireland, in 1836*, for instance, quickly became a landmark popular women's book, proof that the grand tour could be done in practical terms *and* written about by an American woman for the practical edification of her countrymen, male and female. To be sure, Hall advanced no claims of great novelty in making her appearance on the travel scene or of originality in the recording of her adventures (Stowe 12). Having traveled, she now simply took a turn as author, she averred, to "furnish a telescope, through which [her] home-staying friend, sitting at ease in his elbow-chair, may reconnoitre, and at his leisure trace the course of the wayfarer, and enjoy with him the elegancies of foreign cities, or the exciting vicissitudes of adventurous travel" (qtd. in Stowe 12). At the other end of the philosophical spectrum, Margaret Fuller's travel letters, the work of New England's most prominent female cultural intellectual, surprisingly vied for newspaper popularity with those of Bayard Taylor and likewise gained additional attention when published in book form in 1856 under the title *At Home and Abroad; or, Things and Thoughts in America and Europe* (Caesar 180). Most important, however, and probably regarded by Le Vert as the competition, were contemporary women writers more visible in the popular sphere such as Grace Greenwood and Fanny Fern, both of whom had weighed in with travel narratives. Then there was the indefatigable Lydia Huntley Sigourney, intending with her *Pleasant Memories of Pleasant Lands* (1842) to "please" her readers in the sense of "promoting good and pleasant feelings"—entertainment, that is, which can still qualify as inspirationally edifying (Stowe 12). And finally there was that particular bête noire of Southern culture in general and Southern letters in particular, Harriet Beecher Stowe, whose *Sunny Memories of Foreign Lands* (1854) attempted the spirit of family letters written with a fireside intimacy.

Among these, it can be established that Le Vert's 1857 contribution, especially in her native regions, gained her something of an overnight writing celebrity. But again—considering, for instance, the alacrity with which it was given an immediate postwar reprinting by the New York firm of G. W. Carleton—one would be wrong to underplay its national appeal. Rather, like her Mobile townswoman Augusta Evans, she seems to have found the strategic opening, a female author at the right place at the right time, a Southern woman of obviously cosmopolitan interests writing to a national audience and thereby distanced from the taint of political hostilities attached to male figures actively involved in sectional political discourse.[7] But most importantly here, she rode the crest of one last wave of the antebellum mania for going abroad (and writing back about it), especially among the literary-cultural intelligentsia, that saw even the American Civil War as a bothersome interruption. (It had been railed about, for instance, by Emerson in "Self-Reliance" as "a fool's paradise" and the carrying of "ruins to ruins" [164]). And she also caught the new one that formed in 1865 and peaked with a vengeance in the 1870s and 1880s. Indeed, the immense visibility and popularity of a text such as Twain's *The Innocents Abroad*, for instance, was made possible precisely because of its status as a send-up of the cultural status-seeking of newly rich Gilded Age pilgrims following the trail to Europe traced out by their antebellum betters.

And if anybody ever knew the mid-nineteenth-century culture on both sides of the war that Mark Twain styled the "select," it was Le Vert. Mobile may have been her salon, but she also enjoyed a lifetime of being welcomed in count-less other antebellum and postwar centers of culture and power, where the mighty gathered from home and abroad. Born Octavia Walton on a plantation in Georgia, she spent most of her early life, for instance, in Pensacola, where her father's duties as acting territorial governor brought frequent visits by politi-cal dignitaries of various nations and fostered competency in at least three lan-guages besides English, with the obvious French and Spanish of the region's co-lonial origins enhanced by the acquisition of Italian. And by age fifteen she was apparently so accomplished socially that, allowed to represent an infirm grand-mother, a friend of Lafayette's during the Revolution, when that dignitary made his heralded American tour in 1825, she elicited from him an effusive prediction of "brilliant" future accomplishment (B. Williams, *Literary History* 60). A de-cade later she was given her own tour of the major cities and social gathering places of the new nation, including Washington, D.C., where she met Henry Clay, John C. Calhoun, and Daniel Webster, forming a lifelong correspondence with the first, and also Washington Irving's estate Sunnyside, where she likewise began an extended correspondence with that author. Finally taking up residence in Mobile, she married distinguished physician Henry Strachey Le Vert in 1836 and set out upon the career as hostess and keeper of a literary salon that would occupy her for nearly four more decades, bringing her into constant contact with the great and near-great, and winning her praise in an Alabama newspaper two years before her death as "beyond question . . . the most famous woman the South has yet produced" (66).

In all this, the production of her travel book seems to have had origins al-most incidental. For the paired journeys that spawned it, in fact, were a response to grief over the 1849 deaths of a beloved brother and two of her four children. On the other hand, the writing truly did become a simultaneous way of com-memorating the zenith of her public celebrity. Her second journey, for instance, was widely remarked upon for a meeting with the pope in which she availed herself of the knowledge of all three of the languages of her youth, allegedly persuading the pontiff to speak mainly in his native Italian for the beauty of it (B. Williams, *Literary History* 64). In Paris it found her escorted to the opera by a former American president, Millard Fillmore, on the night when attendance was made by Queen Victoria and the Emperor of France. And in Florence it would also include meetings with the Brownings, crowned by the honor of a rare appearance by Mrs. Browning at her going-away party. Back in Amer-ica, the celebrity-circuiting continued as Le Vert became one of the most visible leaders in the movement to preserve Washington's Mount Vernon as a national shrine. And in 1856, after her return to Mobile, she shortly traveled by new in-vitation to deliver the dedicatory address for the Henry Clay monument in New

Orleans. To crown her success, she was urged by friends and the Mobile publishing house of S. H. Goetzel to gather her travel notes, as well as letters written home to her mother during her European sojourns, into a book.

The problem was, of course, that by now even to set foot in the domain of travel writing was to enter a vast dumping ground of cliché piled upon cliché. Already writers apologized endlessly, male and female alike, for lack of improvement on earlier models. At the same time, looking for a hook, Le Vert was perspicacious enough a surveyor of the literary scene to see that women still had a ready-made one. And that, as pointed out by Stowe, was the travel memoir with the confiding, intimate quality of the letter treating *domestic* detail, playing off from the intimacy of the bourgeois family, and benefiting from the security of quick, reliable international postal service (Stowe 10). Further, Le Vert's letters would have the particular selling point of being a function of her noblesse, of what in a Southern male would have been called condescension (Wyatt-Brown, *Southern Honor* 63–64): of her ability, that is, to speak to lesser mortals through a sense of the naturalness of her own genteel well-connectedness, assuming a class role, albeit without hauteur or ostentation, and affording the privacy, the intimacy, the sense of firsthand glimpses into the glittering European scene of society and culture. It may have been one thing, as noted by Stowe, to *use* "European travel" and, by implication, the writing about it, as "a way of affirming the respectability of one's race, class, or gender. Through travel newly rich Americans could simultaneously claim membership in a superior social class and justify the privileges of that class by demonstrating its 'inherent' sensitivity and refinement" (5). But here, in the case of a figure who had already "arrived" at the free and natural enjoyment of intercourse on a footing of social equality with many of the personages described, status and entrée could be wielded with a far more becoming modesty to produce information at once unavailable to the everyday traveler yet also untainted by the anxieties of the arriviste or pretensions of the parvenu. Or, as a publisher's preface put it, the author's "social position at home, and an extensive acquaintance with the highest circles abroad, gave her familiar access to scenes and personages and conditions of life not ordinarily within the reach of the foreign traveller." Accordingly, "The mystic veil which hides the *penetralia* of courtly and aristocratic society, was lifted for her eyes, and she was facilitated in her observations and experiences to a degree seldom awarded to an American before." And to this degree, "with the readiest and keenest power of perception, with a mind fully informed historically to all the localities she visited, and with a wonderfully retentive memory, . . . she combined advantages calculated to make her visits fruitful with fact and view of wide general interest and utility" (v–vi). To be sure, this may strike us now as a fairly conventional come-on, something of "Lives of the Rich and Famous," complete with dishy nobility and celebrity sightings. But to Madame Le Vert's credit, even in so skeptical an age as our own, it is hard not to feel that we have been vouchsafed intimate glances from a privileged position. Within the first four chapters, for instance, a space of roughly thirty pages, among the conventional place and site naming—Liverpool, London, Haymarket Theater, Westminster Abbey, Covent Garden—has been developed the sense of an imposing celebrity circle of personal acquaintance: Lord Campbell, Fanny Haworth, the Rutland family, Lord and Lady John Manners, the Misses Pyne and Mr. Harrison, Prince Czarstorisky, Lord and Lady Wharncliffe, the Star family, the American minister. By chapter 5 the Queen herself has made a personal entrance, along with Prince Albert, the King and Queen of Hanover, Count and Countess Walewski, the Duchess of Sutherland, and the Duke of Wellington. In a visit to Parliament, D'Israeli is described as "not a very eloquent speaker" and debate in general noted as possessing nothing like "the quick nervous style of Calhoun, the massive grandeur of Webster, or the irresistably God-like eloquence of Clay" (1: 47). An entire chapter is reserved for a reception given the honored American guest by Lady Emmeline Wortley. And more than five hundred pages later, with a first voyage followed by the second, we are still going at it. In Florence it is the Pitti Palace *and* Elizabeth Barrett Browning. In Vienna it is the Wienerwald and the Imperial Library *and* the American minister, the Emperor and Empress of Austria, Prince Esterházy, Lady Westmorland, and the Duke of Reichstadt. In Paris it is, of course, Paris, plus Lamartine, Alexandre Dumas, former president Millard Fillmore. The Countess Walewski gives a ball. There is a happy reunion with Lady Emmeline Wortley. And Queen Victoria appears again, this time attended by the Emperor of France.

To be sure, at the more pedestrian level of diaristic page-filling, the text remains awash in picturesque travel-book detail, all the sights, the principal attractions, but also the local populace, the clothes, the food, the dwellings, the domestic rituals. Even before they are launched upon foreign climes proper, with fellow sojourners at sea there is sweet domestic interlude. Wrapped in a long buffalo robe, she fends off seasickness on deck by telling Indian legends of the Alabama. "Braham, the excellent English singer, and Dodworth, the admirable cornet a piston player," present an evening musicale "for the benefit of the Sailors' Home on Staten Island" (1: 2–3). Once arrived in England, she looks happily upon "the thatched cottage, half covered with rose-vines in full blossom,—the fields of new-cut hay, where the women and children were tossing it into great high-wheeled carts,—the far-off castle with turrets,—the little lakes, where the cows calmly stood in the placid waters,—the myriad sheep upon the hills,—the stalwart peasants at their daily toil; and they seemed pictures we had looked upon in some other period of existence, all were so familiar to our eyes" (1: 8).

In Spain, traveling companions include "an aged man, frightfully ill, accompanied by a young and buxom wife, and his father confessor, a learned monk from a convent near Granada" (2: 7–8). "The wife of the aged invalid" also turns out to be "his niece," apparently part of the national custom, she tells us without visible shock, "to keep all the wealth in the family" by mating "youth and loveliness . . . with age and ugliness" (2: 8). She concludes: "The poor old man was going to Madrid for medical aid, saying 'A few weeks will quite restore me.' Never was the shadow of death more visible upon any face. His lustrous-eyed young wife was tenderly watchful of him, as though he were her father" (2: 8). In Italy, her daughter's recalling to her the words of a song Le Vert has sung to her "in her baby-days" finds an echo in the street below. "We ran out to look," she goes on, "and a fantastically dressed minstrel, fluttering with rags, was singing, playing, and jumping about in a sort of 'Jim Crow' manner, while a large audience of beggars were around him, not listening, but gazing up at us with hungry eyes." She concludes: "We seized all the breakfast from the table, and threw it down to them. What a scramble for it there was, to be sure! Presently our waiter came in, and seeing all the dishes, plates, and sugar-bowl empty, he gravely inquired, 'Will the *two* signoras require more breakfast?'" (2: 180).

At the same time, in the renderings of the great sights and scenes and in such evocations of the quaint and fond atmospherics of everyday life abroad, the narrative is punctuated by surprisingly frequent effusions of national pride. "Everywhere in Italy," she writes, for instance, "has the word *American* been as a 'spell of power' to elevate us by kind and cordial attentions. With honest pride have our hearts glowed, when we have seen the effect produced by the mention of our dear native land. The wish to hear of America and to speak of it was universal" (1: 225). And homeward bound, she waxes similarly effusive. "As I looked upon our dear flag floating from the mast-head," she notes in retrospect, "the beautiful words of Willis came to my mind. "Bright flag, at yonder topping mast / Fling out your field of azure blue! / Let star and stripe be westward cast, / and point as freedom's eagle flew! / Strain home, oh! lithe and quivering spars! / Point home, my country's flag of stars" (1: 281).

Especially in the work of a literary Mobilian writing on the eve of Civil War, we may be surprised here by such patriotic emotionality. In any event, it was sincere. Until the day hostilities began, Le Vert was a committed Unionist. On the other hand, the voice is hardly the chauvinist yawp of the spread eagle that we would associate with someone like the journalist Henrietta Stackpole caricatured in Henry James's *Portrait of a Lady*. The poetic lines adduced by Le Vert, after all, are from N. P. Willis; and, as with the report of the affection demonstrated by everyday Italians for the national character, the sentiment displayed is all part of a proper and demure cultural nationalism that embraced the upwelling of patriotic pride in the American abroad as a natural response to the broadening experience of travel. To put it simply, it was Le Vert's way of saying to her countrymen that she was one of them, high-flown cosmopolitan contacts and connections notwithstanding. Here, as in all of her endeavors, the spirit was one of modest fellow feeling on the part of a writer who, her publisher's preface asserted, had now returned from her travels to undertake the happy work of conveying "to others the pleasure received from wandering amid the storied scenes of the Old World and holding social communion with personages whose names are 'whispered by the lips of fame.'" Indeed, "one pervading charm they will find in these volumes," they concluded, "that will stir and keep fresh their own patriotism": and this would be the observation "that in all her wanderings, whether at the refined court of St James in the imperial presence of Louis Napoleon, or under the consecrated tapestries of the Papal palace, our accomplished countrywoman was ever staunchly true to her republican lineage, and came back home American in heart and mind" (ix). Accordingly, it was in exactly this spirit of the proper patriotism of the true cosmopolite, they concluded, that the work—however "full of valuable information, . . . rich in brilliant descriptions, and . . . picturesque and glowing in style and arrangement of particulars" (viii–xi)—could be recommended to their readership in fullest confidence "that they have made a valuable contribution to a most interesting branch of the rising literature of our country" (ix).

That contribution to "a most interesting branch of the rising literature of our country," of course, would shortly get lost in the new torrent of postwar production. Apace, one of the great American contributions to progress would be the turning of the traveler into the tourist. And in travel writing, the coterie atmospherics of the social and literary salons and their fostering of a genteel belletristic culture would yield to the grandstanding of literary celebrities like Mark Twain and others. That would make Le Vert seem quaint. But to the degree that she had anticipated the fad of the notable and nobility-studded tour and developed a model of information to which all others would, whether they liked it or not, find some way to respond, it would hardly render her inconsequential.

5

Antebellum Alabama History in the Planter Style

∼

The Example of Albert J. Pickett

The title chosen by David Levin for his groundbreaking study of the great nineteenth-century American historians Bancroft, Prescott, Motley, and Parkman aptly imaged his sense of a new national genre they had helped to create: *History as Romantic Art*.[1] In each case, Levin proposed, as with the American romantic fiction of the era by Brown, Cooper, Simms, Irving, Hawthorne, and others, the style of history had been a distinct function of the heightened literary atmospherics of the age, with the historian as exemplar of the romantic man of letters. Had he addressed a contemporary production—grandly entitled *History of Alabama, and Incidentally of Georgia and Mississippi, from the Earliest Period*—by the first epic historian of Alabama, a gifted literary amateur by the name of Albert J. Pickett, the thesis would still have worked. Further, as with the standard "literary" historians, it would have worked concerning American nineteenth-century romantic historiography as a movement away from seventeenth- and eighteenth-century Anglo-European rational models, with romantic inspiration frequently prompted further by new access to the vivid documents of New World empire serving as a direct source. In Pickett and his contemporaries North *and* South, that is, the school of "philosophical" or classicist historiography of such enlightenment figures as Bolingbroke, Hume, and Voltaire could be seen gradually giving way to new romantic conceptions of "narrative" history laying far much less emphasis on fact and reason—the idea of what Bolingbroke had described as "philosophy teaching by example"—and much more, to use William Hedges's terms, "upon structural and stylistic devices which would induce in the reader more vivid impressions of the flavor and color of a certain period in history" (111–12).[2] But for Pickett's addiction to orotund narrative exposition and gaudy dramatic spectacle; his undisguised regional patriotism and fondness for ripsnorting adventure; and his equally Southern predilections for the political excursus, the interminable genealogy, and the anecdote of dubious origin: the modern interpreter would surely have had to come up with something more lurid by way of entitling. And for some of the more specific layerings of inheritance both literary and historical, he would also have had to delve further into the set of complex cultural archaeologies peculiar to the region of the lower South—now encompassing the states of Georgia, Alabama, Mississippi, and Louisiana, but at the time known as the Old Southwest. To put this into the form of explicit argument, the style of Pickett's *History*—with a force of authority attested to, as will be shown, both by his own contemporaries and by generations of writers to come—may now be seen as the direct function of a distinctly literary historiography; and if that historiography clearly partook of general nineteenth-century romantic currents,[3] it also bore equally the discrete signature of the author's active political participation in power, class, and race relationships of a very particular time and place. As romantic art, that is, it also carried the stamp of Pickett's conscious, albeit in many ways ambivalent, identification of himself as a member of the planter class in antebellum Alabama in the years when the great removals of native inhabitants coincided exactly with the accelerated introduction of mass chattel slavery.

In just these terms of time, place, and individual positioning as determinants of shaping his own historiographic perspective, Pickett rightly saw his own formative experiences as an Alabamian as living history, a kind of personalized abstract or epitome of the region's overnight journey from territory to statehood, particularly as it related to the planter and professional classes. To begin with, like many early Alabamians of his background and station, he had made the customary journey in the literal sense. Born in Anson County, North Carolina, on 13 August 1810, the son of Colonel William Raiford Pickett and Frances Dickinson Pickett, he arrived with his family in Autauga County, near Montgomery, on the eve of statehood in 1818. His father, acquiring a large plantation and many slaves, became wealthy and influential and served thirteen years in the Alabama legislature and three times as a Democratic presidential elector.

In his turn, the younger Pickett eventually worked out his own admixture of the planter life with involvement in local politics. Although educated in the law, he never practiced, instead in 1832 marrying Sarah Smith Harris, herself the daughter of a wealthy landowner, and settling on a large estate near Montgomery. Similarly, although politically active, he did not seek or hold office as had his father and his brother William, preferring rather an informal career as a speaker and newspaper writer, and gaining a certain prominence in the 1830s and 1840s for his pronouncements on various states' rights and slavery issues.[4]

It was between 1846 and 1851 that Pickett began actively assembling materials for a history and concentrating apace on writing mainly historical sketches for the newspapers (Owsley, "Pickett" 33). In this, no one should have been surprised, however. If Pickett rightly saw his own experience as a settler, planter, author, and political worthy as something of a contemporary case study in the life of the public-spirited man of affairs during the formative period in Alabama statehood, he had also from the outset been drawn to see his life and those of his contemporaries as part of an era forming a fascinating bridge between present and past.

His first memories of arrival in Alabama, in fact, as he notes in the preface to the *History,* had been inextricably wedded to his fascination with the old inhabitants of the Creek regions, descendants of the war chiefs and frequently elderly whites who had lived among them. With these he conversed, learning of the "green corn dances, ball plays, war ceremonies, and manners and customs" (10). There were tales of the Revolutionary era, of the early decades of settlement, of the momentous and bloody Creek War of 1813–14, the pivotal event in the state's territorial history, concluded a bare five years earlier. Also, during the brief Creek uprising of 1836, Pickett had partaken of his own brief military experience of Indian warfare, serving as aide-de-camp to Governor Clement Clay.

Pickett's political prominence and that of his family gave him access to important living historical figures in the state, many of them having personal experience as pioneers, soldiers, territorial administrators, jurists, and elected officials (Owsley, "Pickett" 37). His wealth allowed him to amass a substantial library, rich in materials of the French and Spanish periods, and to collect printed and manuscript materials from various sources throughout the South. As regards the oral and archaeological records of native peoples, Pickett's leisure and mobility—of which he was somewhat inclined to boast in his preface and at various points in the *History*—similarly allowed him to visit and consult authorities and to examine innumerable geographic and historic sites.[5]

The product of Pickett's labors came to a dense, teeming 669 pages and covered an astounding range of chronology, extending basically from the pre-Columbian period to the earliest years of statehood. In two volumes, handsomely printed and illustrated, it appeared initially in early summer 1851, from the prominent Charleston, South Carolina, publisher Walker & James. It took until September for copies to go on sale in Alabama. In part, however, because

Pickett throughout the composition process had cannily paced his popular writing endeavors to keep his project in the public eye,[6] it quickly gained attention from readers and reviewers, including mainly favorable response from fellow historians and literary professionals. Two editions were reprinted in Alabama before the year's end. Governor Henry W. Collier secured funds from the legislature to place a volume in the official library of every state in the Union (Owsley, "Pickett" 31–32). As a work of scholarship, it eventually gained a regional prominence similar to that of analogous texts of the era such as J. F. H. Claiborne's *Mississippi as a Province, Territory, and State* and William Gilmore Simms's *History of South Carolina*. More importantly, as a popular classic it became a staple of the Alabama library and schoolroom. Generations of textbook writers depended on it for pre-1820 materials.[7] And, as noted by novelist Harper Lee, among others, generations of schoolchildren grew up on its strange admixture of amateur pedantry, impassioned regional patriotism, and thrill-a-minute melodrama.[8]

As to our own assessments of historiographic and literary attitude in the present case, were we to attempt something in the vein of Levin, the closest we could now come to a comparable designation of Pickett's peculiar hybridizing of history as romantic art with the grand and gentlemanly, if on occasion somewhat gaudy, style of the Southwest planter would now probably be something like history as Whig pageant: or, to seize upon more localized forms of popular-culture example, something of an anticipatory merging of the florid, voice-over, elaborately narratorial style of Southern storytelling with the latter-day form of historical spectacle that would be come to be known as outdoor festival drama.[9] To be sure, as with most American historians of Pickett's time, the overall scheme of the enterprise could have been said to partake, in regional version, of the basic national scenario: the epic adventure, upon the breathtaking stage of the New World landscape, of westward-moving Anglo-European civilization; and the concomitant rise of the American nation out of a grand, operatic clash of cultures, savage and civilized, all blessed with their full panoply of larger-than-life heroes *and* villains. As to immediate narrative and dramatic particulars, on the other hand, Pickett's frontier materials even now strike us as standing in a class by themselves, with their sheer garish plenitude *and* variety frequently upping the romantic ante in ways undreamed even by a Prescott or a Parkman, not to mention a Simms or a Cooper. There was the clash of empires, for instance. As in the North, much of the colonial history of the Southern frontier could equally be seen as a playing out of the great geopolitical drama Parkman called France and England in North America. But here, that action had to find *its* foregrounding in accounts of the prior explorations and conquests of Spain, and further, in much of the ensuing narrative, with all three colonial powers maintaining active presences through the formative years of the Republic and well into the recent territorial history of the present century.[10] As to native peoples, here too the spotlighted materials proved notably spectacular and exotic, harking back to the archaeological record of the great mound-building pre-Columbian civilizations and then moving forward through the histories of such diverse and colorful successors as the Mobilians, Chatots, Thomes, Tensas, Natchez, and Alabamas. Most notably configured, however, as befitted their role in recent history, were the five great Southern nations—the Creeks, Cherokees, Choctaws, Chickasaws, and Seminoles—with an allure fully equal to that of the forest peoples of the North, and with their immense romantic appeal to the historical imagination also significantly coupled in this case with contemporary visibility as the latest sacrifices to the new religion of national expansionism.[11]

With such abundance of heroic resources, it virtually became impossible for Pickett not to write history without having to work his narrative *and* dramatic way through a whole panoply of legendary figures, all standing astride their particular sections of the text and frequently jostling for dominion with others of nearly equal stature. Further, such focal imagings of historical process frequently create their own complex dynamics of conflict, with issues of light and darkness, heroism and villainy, and good and evil less often providing the moral theme of history than its unfolding dialectical content. The conquistador Hernando de Soto comes to stand configured against the legendary Mobilian chief Tuskaloosa, the giant Black Warrior; the bravely pertinacious French explorer Bienville survives battle after battle with native enemies while managing an endless warfare of political survival against local cabals and the machinations of his scheming adversaries at court; the Creek chieftain McGillivray, carrying in his veins the blood of the Scotch, the French, and the Indian, conducts a long royalist holding action of blood and intrigue amidst the byzantine frontier politics of Revolutionary struggle and early national consolidation; and early in the nineteenth century, a new succession of climactic battles between native peoples and settlers compels the last of the great war chiefs, William Weatherford, the Red Eagle, to bow before the might of the stern, pitiless conqueror, Andrew Jackson.[12]

Meanwhile, hordes of attendant *dramatis personae* breed endless further intricacies of plot and historical complication. Indigenous tribes, one after another, abet their downfall at the hands of whites through the attempts to marry ad hoc strategies of political survival with ancient patterns of internecine hatred and rivalry. New pioneer breeds—Georgians, Mississippians, Louisianians—frequently obtrude their own competing social interests. The landscape teems with traders, land speculators, government agents; native princesses and mixed-blood chiefs; circuit-riding evangelicals and conspiratorial Jesuits; re-deemed captives and lawless renegades; utopians, profiteers, intriguers, turn-coats, and cutthroats of nearly every degree of savage and civilized stripe. John and Charles Wesley, with hopes of new conversions among the Indians, find their efforts balked by the crudities and gross immoralities of their own fron-tier flocks. The celebrated naturalist William Bartram records his experiences among the Creek Nation as part of a walking tour taking him from West Florida through lower Alabama and Mississippi, and finally into Louisiana. The traitor Aaron Burr, murderer of Hamilton, the arch-intriguer of the Republic, is ar-rested in solitary flight through the backwoods he so recently intended to make his wilderness imperium. An exotic band of Napoleonic exiles, cocked hats and swords, parasols and ballgowns, struggles unsuccessfully to transform an up-river canebrake into a vine and olive colony. There is the pious Indian chroni-cler Adair, convinced that such priestly ejaculations as "*Haleu! Halelu!*" and "*Haleluiah! Haleluyah!*" confirm his theory of native peoples as descendants of the lost tribes of Israel (104–5). There is a displaced Russian princess, allegedly the wife of "the Czarowitz Alexis Petrowitz, son of Peter the Great" (225). There is a literal wandering Jew, the dauntless trader Abraham Mordecai, still unkill-able after five decades in the wilderness, although in one late appearance an ear, a boat, and a cotton gin short after an ill-considered liaison with an amorous squaw (470). The text fills with all the other legendary names: Iberville, Cadil-lac, Crozat, Sehoy, Tecumseh, the Prophet, Pushmatahaw, MacIntosh, Galvez. The array of nefarious talent alone is so star-studded that so feckless a back-woods *miles gloriosus* as Colonel James Caller, responsible for the ignominious rout of the militia by a Creek war party at Burnt Corn, or so thoroughgoing a military scoundrel on the national horizon as General James Wilkinson, rates but a brief mention.

As to material presence, all this is further enhanced by its distinct sense, as "territorial" record, of being unmediated by intervening colonial and early re-publican tradition. Like the culture of the region itself, that is, history in the Old Southwest somehow aggregates itself for Pickett directly out of a colorful formative past always visible just under the surface of an equally rumbustious, teeming present. As with the landscape and its people, it all seems raw, uncut, just-created. Accordingly, even for chronicles of Old World empire, Pickett can attest to direct access and firsthand familiarity with original Spanish and French documents and ancient maps of the region in his personal possession.[13] For co-lonial and territorial materials, and for records of the years of early statehood, he likewise notes his painstaking and laborious work of gaining direct access to primary archival resources and, as a matter of regional pride, on his ability to enlist the support and active collaboration of other Southern men of letters and public affairs—fellow Alabamians, to be sure, such as William Lowndes Yancey, Burwell Boykin, Basil Manly, Clement C. Clay, A. B. Meek, and numerous others; but also outside luminaries including John H. F. Claiborne and John W. Monette of Mississippi, Arthur P. Hayne, Francis W. Pickens, and William Gilmore Simms of South Carolina, Charles Gayarre of Louisiana, and even Theodore Irving of New York.[14] As importantly, in local matters, he claims on occasion after occasion the immediate authority of oral tradition, with resources ranging from popular legend to family and village anecdote, not to mention his own memories of encounters and conversations with Indian inhabitants and older settlers and their descendants. Within the text and without—in footnote, parenthesis, and narrative aside—Pickett's account literally teems with accounts of transmission, corroboration, and verification, frequently involving accounts of interviews with persons still living or attestations of journeys made to ensure factual accuracy.[15] "I have sought materials for a correct history of my country," he tells us straightforwardly, "wherever they were to be procured, whether in Europe or America, and without regard to cost or trouble." Moreover, he continues, this has been his effort as an Alabamian notwithstanding that "all the Atlantic States have historical societies," where "books and manuscripts relating to those States have been collected," or that "agents have been sent to Europe by different Legislatures, who have transcribed the colonial records which relate to their history." "I have had none of these aids," he says. Rather, "I have been compelled to hunt up and buy books and manuscripts connected with the history of Alabama, and to collect oral information in all directions" (9).

A corresponding sense of rhetorical immediacy is supplied through Pickett's insistence on his own distinctly unprofessional status. "About four years since," he simply tells us, "feeling impressed with the fact that it was the duty of every man to make himself, in some way, useful to his race, I looked around for some object, in the pursuit of which I could benefit my fellow citizens; for, although much interested in agriculture, that did not occupy one-fourth of my time." Further, he confesses, "having no taste for politics, and having never studied for a profession," he likewise found those traditional avenues of his class foreclosed. And it was thus, he concludes, "I determined to write a history" (10).

Thinking "it would serve to amuse my leisure hours," he has been surprised, he confesses, to have found it "the hardest work of my life"—a project, indeed, that he has more than once despaired of completing. Still, he has persevered; and, if nothing else, he concludes, he can thus present the text as at least the earnest production of his own sense of political and rhetorical noblesse oblige, the scrupulosity of the historian as the public-spirited Southern man of property *and* letters. Or, to put it more directly in the hierarchical context at hand, the rhetorical assertion of the status of the gentleman-amateur here becomes itself the most trustworthy of all authorial credentials, the assurance of a history written at once as a matter of rigorous truth-telling *and* of the preserving of gentlemanly honor. "Believing that the historian ought to be the most conscientious of men," he thus asserts, "writing as he does not only for the present age but for posterity, I have endeavored to divest myself of all prejudices, and speak the truth in all cases." Or, at the very least, he goes on, "if it should be found, by the most scrutinizing reader, that any of my statements are incorrect, let me say in advance, that when I penned those statements I believed them to be true." Indeed, he says, in every case "so anxious have I been to record each incident as it really occurred, that upon several occasions I have traveled over four hundred miles to learn merely a few facts" (9–10).

The stylistic payoff in the text—as with the ease of tonal command frequently distinguishing the work of the region's self-controlled Whig humorists and gentleman-historians—is a historical prose that is itself a demonstration of public-spirited social authority, political realism in a familiar magisterial and patriarchal key. As with many another teeming, rumbustious Southwestern tale, that is, by perhaps a lawyer, a judge, a newspaper editor; a doctor, an educator, a legislative worthy; or some other spokesman for the region's professional and literary-cultural intelligentsia, Pickett's history is framed by the voice of political authority—here, that of the planter aristocrat, sure of himself and his place in the world, with historical truth a function of a distinctly Southern code of moral and political honor.

It is the style, then, of gentlemanly veracity itself, albeit again, as with regional compatriots, with plenty of time amidst all the grandiloquence and dramatic spectacle for political opinionizing; and again, it is the distinctly class-bound ideological quality of the literary rhetoric that is the key to cultural authority. Veracity? Of course: a gentleman always tells the truth. Moral and political neutrality? Hardly: for gentlemanly honor equally demands a truth of manly conviction as well, especially when matters of local and regional reputation are at stake. Or, to put it more succinctly, Pickett seems to assume that any honorable man who has worked this hard to find out the essential facts of history and to bring them alive again in narrative and dramatic re-creation is surely entitled to the occasional informed opinion.[16]

To be sure, Pickett often takes visible pains to let himself appear as a writer of something close to actual "objective" history. On verification of the site of the ancient Indian capital of Coosa (30), existing data are simply compiled in a note from various written and oral relations, as well as from maps. On the mysterious origins of brass and copper plates held sacred by native tribes of the modern era, Pickett explores all opinions on the subject. They may well be relics of de Soto; they may have been bought from British traders; they may represent advances in primitive metallurgy. He has done his duty, he says, by assembling the body of speculation for the reader to judge (83–85). Similarly, widely conflicting archival accounts are adduced on numbers of natives killed at Maubila (42). Pickett smoothly reminds the reader that one record specifies body count within the walls while the other seems to take in the larger battlefield. Still, he suggests, one might not be misguided in splitting the difference. As to the fate of the legendary Black Warrior himself, the author, again having attested to a consultation of all existing accounts, concludes nothing, simply resting with the suggestion that one might reasonably infer a desire to die fighting at the head of his people.

More characteristic demonstrations of what Pickett actually means by words such as "veracity" and "objectivity," however, occur in those innumerable other cases when the historian not only assembles complex evidence but also makes it clear to us that he finds it something of a matter of personal or political honor that he supply a firm and forthright conclusion. In full candor of empirical investigation, he seems to tell us, finders of historical fact often do have to make findings, after all; and in equally full candor of political honor, makers of historical judgments are often compelled to judge. For the author of Pickett's *History* to hedge on any such account would be to renounce all one's claims to cultural authority in any of its forms—personal, political, literary, and historiographic.

Thus, on particular points of archival record, the narrator confidently announces his preference for one source over another (20, 348). A dispute in native traditions over a historical location is simply deemed "not important" once it has been dovetailed with more reliable European sources (23). With the right records in hand, as Pickett demonstrates at considerable length late in the text, one may confidently adjudicate even a matter so involuted as the welter of unresolved treaty claims still perplexing American relations with all three previous colonial powers. It is simply, he shows us, a matter of working carefully through the evidence (427).

When a figure considered something of an authority shows himself to be significantly crackbrained, as in the case of the pious Adair, Pickett makes it clear that he thinks so and that we ought to think so as well (104–6). When blame for a historical disaster may be laid at the feet of a notable poltroon or fool, as with Colonel James Caller at the Battle of Burnt Corn (521–25), or with the negligently incautious Major Daniel Beasley at Fort Mims (529–32), Pickett does not hesitate to name the party.

Similarly, when prior history has shown someone significantly maligned, that figure, no matter how controversial, is relentlessly rehabilitated. Bienville, although convicted of the occasional misjudgment, recurrently reaps designation as "the great and good"; and for all his alternating loyalist and revolutionary intrigues, the indefatigable McGillivray, the author argues, must still be accounted as deserving the epithet "Talleyrand of Alabama" (432).

When a noble historical example calls out for comparison with some shabby analogue in contemporary behavior, Pickett does not hesitate. There is the equanimity, for instance, of Bienville, finally removed from colonial leadership after years of tireless struggle. How poorly this compares, Pickett declaims, with the tireless whining of cashiered political functionaries in the current Republic! (300–301). And as easily Pickett can extrapolate from historical example to future desideratum. The brave, independent Chickasaws, he enjoins us, to the end unbroken and unbowed, must now inspire Alabamians and Mississippians who may similarly find their native regions threatened with invasion (298).

As might be expected, on other such great current issues of regional pride—particularly Negro slavery—history provides rich meat for an impassioned defense. Let it be known after all, Pickett reminds us, that it was the French, their current denunciations notwithstanding of "the Southern States for their mild and beneficent system of domestic slavery" (225), who actually authorized their great India and Mississippi Company to introduce the first African slaves into the region (221–22). And so also did England, he continues, "with her men-of-war, at the same time, plant her American colonies with slaves, also captured in Africa." Next, "the Puritan fathers of New England received them, paid for them, and put them to hard labor, sold and re-sold them for many years" (225). What sheer Yankee self-righteousness must be at bottom, he thus polemically concludes, when the latter's descendants so readily "profess to be shocked at the sight of Southern slaveholder, and denounce Southern slavery as 'a damning sin before God!'" (225).

Yet for all the melodramatic adventure and political hectoring, as noted by fellow Alabamian Harper Lee, to read Pickett's *History* even now is still to sense one's self in the presence of genuine literary *and* historiographic achievement; and the source of that achievement she likewise identifies, with the unerring novelist's eye, in Pickett's profoundly artistic sense of fictional construction.[17] How easy would it have been, she notes, in writing New World history, to have begun with de Soto's legendary *entrada*—as Pickett himself does—but then to have simply jumped ahead a century or so to the next surge of colonization brought about by the French? Instead, as she observes, Pickett seizes both the fictionally creative *and* the historically contextualizing option available to the true frontier chronicler. He goes back, that is, to the archeological record and the ensuing histories of a succession of native peoples as a way of working his way forward again into the modern era—with the result being, to this date, still one of the most well-documented and continuous accounts of the evolution of indigenous cultures from prehistoric times to the present.

And how confidently and firmly, we might add, does Pickett then undertake his chronological march through the ensuing major structural divisions of the narrative. The early materials described, for instance, accounting for the first 150 pages or so in the text, are followed by a section of roughly equal size—with a brief caesura midway noting English activities in Georgia—devoted to the French. And a third, again of roughly the same length, propels early English settlers into what becomes the ongoing clash of three empires for ascendancy over the landscape and the native tribes. Only then, somewhere between two-thirds and three-quarters of the way through the text, come the Americans—traders, settlers, and eventually a territorial establishment. Government occupies a series of early seats of political authority: St. Stephens, Huntsville, Cahaba. Meanwhile, as if writing a tragic counterpoint to the extensive discussion of native cultures supplied in the beginning, nearly half of the American narrative is devoted to the Creek War of 1813–14, at once the determining event in Alabama's passage toward statehood and the single most decisive step toward final removal of all the great Southern tribes from their lands east of the Mississippi.[18]

A few remaining pages write vivid new chapters. Short histories follow of the exotic French Vine and Olive colony; of the momentous Huntsville constitutional convention; of the groundbreaking work of the first legislature; and of the administration of the first governor, William Wyatt Bibb.

From the start, one has continued to sense the firm authority of a structuring intelligence. The narrative cadence remains, as Harper Lee aptly puts it, that of "a prose style that falls somewhere between Macaulay and Bulwer-Lytton" (15). Yet at the same time, it is a style that has no fear of the anecdote, the excursus, the forensic disquisition, the patriotic essay. Most importantly, as if the author had properly taken a lesson from Cooper or Simms, it is also a style of narrative control cemented exactly by its dramatic pacing.[19] As in Cooper, action scenes involve us in the skirmish, the siege, the set-piece battle; in other dramatic moments, we are equally the beneficiaries of the dialogue, the tableau, the vignette. Further, also through a kind of Cooper-like, equal-opportunity heroism clause, one colorful figure's moment in the spotlight actually does seem as good as another's. De Soto at Tuskaloosa's court shares equal time with Sam Dale and the Canoe Fight of Creek War legend. Aaron Burr and his frontier plots of empire play off against Abraham Mordecai and his backwoods amours. That is, if Pickett possesses what Melville described as the midcentury American's romantic passion for the mighty pageant creature, as with many other frontier chroniclers of the era, he also betrays an equally lively fascination with the renegade, the charlatan, the rapscallion, the social outsider.

To some degree, as new characters and events propel us toward the present, one may legitimately sense a certain decline in historiographic and stylistic energies. Still, nothing quite prepares us for what Pickett decides abruptly to do in the vicinity of 1820: and that is simply to declare personal victory over the project as conceived and quit. Of events of the last three decades—on the eve of the Civil War arguably the most important to date in the formative era of the state and the region—Pickett flatly says he defers to chroniclers able to satisfy themselves with the dullish and politically sordid business of workaday statehood. Or, as the author himself phrases it, in a characteristic, if departing flourish of syntactical hauteur, "to some other person fonder than we are of the dry details of state legislation and fierce party spirit, we leave the task of bringing the history down to the later period" (669).

For this concluding masterpiece of condescension and evasion, several reasons may be inferred. Perhaps an obvious answer was simple writerly fatigue. Another, equally plausible, might have been the natural feeling of anyone, historian or not, who has actually lived through a particular historical epoch: it may eventually be history; but for us, epochal as it may turn out to be, it can't ever really seem like history. Further, in terms of current governmental affairs, one also infers easily Pickett's real disdain for the ascendancy of a new professional political class.[20] The small men of recent affairs, he seems to tell us, not only suffer by comparison with larger figures of the past; they are also unlikely to prove of requisite stature, he implies, in any future crisis of Union (611).

But, most importantly, for the gentleman chronicler and the regional patriot, we also see here an Alabama historian in particular clearly not wishing to cross a distinct historical fault line: and that line, of course, is the one marking the post-1820 ascendancy of the antebellum planter elite of which Pickett clearly deemed himself an exemplary member. For to cross that line, in turn, would also have required him to detail the staggering growth over the decades in question of the literal slave empire on which that same class founded its claims to authority—or, to be exact, from the 42,450 Africans recorded as having been brought into the state between 1812 and 1820 to the 435,080 eventually to be counted in the census of 1860.[21] And this time, of course, there would be no French or English or hypocritical Yankees to blame. Without excuse or apology, that is, writing at the height of the slavery controversy in America, Pickett would have been forced to address the peculiar—if not downright headlong and intransigent—investment of his fellow Alabamians in "the peculiar institution" as just that.

Accordingly, then, on race, Pickett the historian finally takes recourse to the same built-in literary-historical escape valve devised by virtually all other fellow Alabama writers of the era: the intense, even obsessive contemplation of one vision of sociopolitical tragedy—the subjection and eventual extirpation of native peoples—as a way of not contemplating the other comprised in the newer racial curse.[22] And to this degree, again to cite Harper Lee, perhaps Pickett probably did leave his heart at Horseshoe Bend. At the same time, one must insist, deeply in the vein of most of Alabama's other first books, he also probably did it on purpose. Like others of his class and racial and regional outlook, by constructing the past largely in terms of the great racial tragedy arising out of the struggle of native peoples against the westward-marching forces of Anglo-European and American civilization, and thereby dodging a present in which, through the literal overnight institutionalization of mass chattel slavery, that tragedy had been compounded by one even greater, Pickett may indeed have written history as he saw it. But in using the prospect of the trail of tears as a detour away from the issue of chattel slavery, he also carefully chose to write history as he didn't see it.

6

A. B. Meek's Great American Epic Poem of 1855; or, the Curious Career of *The Red Eagle*

~

At least three major poetic texts published in 1855 could claim status as original American epics based on the large-scale treatment of native materials. Of these, surely the best-known and most widely appreciated at the time was Henry W. Longfellow's *Song of Hiawatha*.[1] Twentieth-century readers, on the other hand, would now readily identify the great epic "original" of 1855 as that arty, enigmatic collocation of prefatory manifesto and twelve untitled poems— including the debut of the one eventually called "Song of Myself"—comprising the first edition of Walt Whitman's *Leaves of Grass*.[2] Less known then and now, although achieving considerable literary and historical recognition in the author's native Deep South, was a third production, corresponding visibly in poetic subject and attitude with the first, but with important political and historical affinities to the second. This was A. B. Meek's *The Red Eagle*.

To be sure, then *or* now, there will be no confusing the importance to literary futurity of *The Red Eagle* with that of either *Hiawatha* or *Leaves of Grass*. Nor, even within a historical frame of reference, is one tempted to a scholarly reflex of long critical habit and accreditation in wishing to claim for Meek's *Red Eagle* the status of neglected or lost classic, popular masterpiece, etc. On the other hand, as already suggested, it does provide an opportunity to reexamine conventional accounts of literary history, North and South, in a number of significant ways. Certainly, the text itself provides yet another scholarly opening in current reconsiderations of nineteenth-century literary and cultural categories. From a national perspective, for instance, a consideration of Meek's poem and its cultural visibility challenges conventional notions of a literary flowering of the 1850s as taking place predominantly within the philosophical orbit of American transcendentalism; and, at the very least, in the dimension of epic poetry of the era, it certainly forces us out of the convenient 1855 juxtaposition of Longfellow versus Whitman as genteel versus subversive, paleface versus red-skin, conventional versus avant-garde, and the like. As importantly, however, it further impels us to a particular consideration of the nineteenth-century liter-ary politics of region, in this case with many of the century's very real questions of social ideology—here, most pointedly, the complex cultural politics of class and race in the antebellum frontier South—brought into very specific contexts of historical relief. Accordingly, in an examination both of the circumstances of its composition and reception and, as will be seen, of its subsequent career as a staple of the library and classroom, *The Red Eagle* thereby becomes a deeply historicized case study in the forms and processes of cultural mythmaking, of what truly might be called ideology in a new country. As a political text, like many another popular epic of the era, North and South, it once again becomes important for what it attempts to say about the groundbreaking work of social organization; and, particularly in its relationship to regional counterparts, it also becomes equally important, as a distinct kind of compensatory history, for what it carefully attempts not to say about cultural origins—in this case by exploit-ing a conventional tendency to use tragic accounts of the treatment of native peoples as an equally conventional way of sublimating the larger racial guilt of chattel slavery.

To put this for the moment back into the context of 1855, Meek, like Long-fellow, chose, then, to weave his homegrown epic out of a romantic tale of Native American culture, steeped in aboriginal lore and sounding an elegiac lament—as had contemporaries as diverse as James Fenimore Cooper and William Gilmore Simms, Catherine Maria Sedgwick and Lydia Maria Child—for the passing of a great indigenous race.[3] Further, here, too, the scale of the action was large, centering ultimately on a pair of fated lovers, with that love placed against the backdrop of savage myth and heroic conflict; and here, like-wise, as if in formal recognition of the grandness of the topic, the poetic tones and cadences were replete with quaint atmospherics.

On the other hand, unlike Longfellow's attempt at deep literary primitiv-ism—unapologetically imitative in its attempt to approximate the vaporous mythicality of the great Finnish national poem, the *Kaelevala*[4]—Meek's epic was also deeply political in a way that Whitman, and before him, Emerson, would have grasped readily. Although grandly stylized and replete with the air of legend, for instance, Meek's version of history was also local and concrete, having its basis in actual events of the relatively recent Alabama Creek War of 1813–14; and—as in Whitman's interpolated vignettes in "Song of Myself" of the massacre at Goliad or the sea battle between the *Bonhomme Richard* and the *Serapis*—it thus could be said to partake of a political realism emphasizing the epic potential of roughly contemporary historical events.[5] In Meek's case, a collection of actual wartime episodes formed the core of his epic plot, and included the Creek massacre of several hundred settlers at Fort Mims; the advance into the region of militia armies under Claiborne of Mississippi and Jackson of Tennessee; various battles including the Canoe Fight of the heroic Sam Dale and the penultimate defeat of insurgent forces at Holy Ground; after the war's deciding engagement at Horseshoe Bend, the bold, unflinching appearance of Creek leader William Weatherford before Andrew Jackson to plead for his people; and, by dint of the young hero's rare majesty and eloquence, the great warrior's famous decision to spare his life.[6]

Similarly, Meek's central characters—to the degree that characters in any nineteenth-century American romance of the forest could be so—were for the most part historically real. As importantly, within the poem there was at least the attempt to make them actual, of allowing them to exist, that is, within living tradition and to act and speak in at least some poetic approximation of their historical roles. The titular character is, for instance, the actual William Weatherford, the last of the great mixed-race Creek political leaders in the lineage of McGillivray, McQueen, and McIntosh. His great love is Lilla Beazeley, a forest maiden, and herself a person of mixed racial descent. A character of the author's imagination, in a careful Montague-Capulet touch, she is cast as the daughter of a frontiersman attached to the Fort Mims garrison;[7] and the latter, known to his former Creek kindred as the White Wolf, as one of the few survivors of the massacre, thereby also continues to figure importantly—by some contemporary evaluations, too importantly—as the vengeful antagonist.[8]

Most real of all is the actual Andrew Jackson, the Indian fighter and hero of New Orleans ultimately to become the seventh president of the United States. Here, he becomes the central historical presence, by virtue of both his role in local events and his subsequent stature in regional and national politics. So, too, the historical events recounted, those of the Creek War of 1813–14, possess the same kind of multi-leveled political reality. They comprise local, historical tragedy while proving as well a crucial arena for the making of Andrew Jackson as a frontier military hero; and they can now be seen also as prophesying the larger design of regional and national expansion eventuating over the next quarter-century in the great and final removals of native peoples from the antebellum Southwest.

As to the traditional stylistics associated with mid-nineteenth-century poetry, although heavily belletristic and mannered in its reliance on genteel poetic convention—and thus hardly to be mistaken for Whitman's free verse—Meek's epic assemblage nevertheless reveals a remarkable variety and musical heterogeneity. It certainly avoids the drumbeat monotony of Longfellow's pounding tetrameter trochees—alleged in most accounts to be the author's improbably native-sounding attempt to approximate epic formula, albeit arising out of transliteration of a German rendering of the Finnish original. To be sure, in Meek's poem there is a conventional iambic tetrameter core advancing the main narrative in the vein of much long poetry of the era, British and American; and if not as deadly as Longfellow's simulation of native song, a kind of homegrown quantitative, for the majority of the poem it does its craftsmanly work mainly by staying out of the way. At the same time, however, in accord with the various requirements of plot, character, setting, tone, and theme, one also finds in *The Red Eagle* considerable formal variation not only at the level of rhyme, meter, and stanza pattern, but also at times involving leaps and shifts of categories of poetic mode and even genre. The poem, so to speak—albeit, again, hardly any Whitmanesque heterotopia—still becomes something like a poem of poems. Narrative mixes with lyric, and lyric with dramatic. Rhyme, meter, and stanza join, along with subdivision of individual cantos, into discrete formal units, creating a succession of tones and moods. Strung along a main strand of tetrameter exposition, iamb mixes with dactyl and anapest, sonnet with song, song with ballad, ballad with dramatic dialogue, and dramatic dialogue with blank-verse oratory.

To choose just the poem's opening passages, for instance, a prefatory sonnet leads off, claiming in its first measures, "Voluptuous Spring!—in this soft southern clime, / With prodigality of birds and flowers! / Not Guido, in his rosy Dream of Hours, / Framed in Arcadian vales, a lovelier time!" (11). This yields in the first section of Canto I to several pages of tetrameter exposition, in a mixture of successive and alternating rhyme—"Few days agone, the song of peace / Was heard amid these woodland homes, / The sounding axe smote forest trees, / And upward sprang new rustic domes" (18); or, "Along the stream, the light bark bore / Young commerce to the opening shore, / And rosy children strolled away, / With bees and birds through woodlands gay" (18)—and concluding with a couplet of stately pentameter: "And now while all the West in radiance swims, / The sun's last glory lingers on FORT MIMMS!" (19). A second section provides an interlude of natural description rendered in more conventional ballad pattern of alternating tetrameter and trimeter, albeit again with flexible rhyme. Section three, introducing the heroine, lightens the tone into tetrameter anapestic and shortly, in the voice of the "Woodland Flower" herself, yields into pure song. "The blue-bird is whistling in Hillibee grove,—" she sings, "*Terra-re! Terra-re!*"

> His mate is repeating the tale of his love,—
> *Terra-re!*
> But never that song,
> As its notes fleet along,
> So sweet and so soft in its raptures can be,
> As thy low whispered words, young chieftain, to me. (21)

Then, as the lovers meet and the plot begins to advance, ensuing sections again take up the basic exposition, albeit even here with the iamb in appropriate cases replaced by the anapest, and the octasyllabic line by the more stately pentameter couplet.

To be sure, here and elsewhere within the formal hodgepodge, one finds the inevitable excess of a forced meter or stretched rhyme, most frequently originating in some clank of the lofty and the vernacular that a genteel critic of the era would have described as the occasional poetic "fault." Still, in diction, rhyme, meter, and stanza pattern, Meek reveals a laudable, even adventurous willingness to let the music go where it needs to: to create a sudden couplet, for instance, where the rhyme has been alternating; to allow a couplet to spawn a triplet; to break from tetrameter into a concluding pentameter and even the occasional alexandrine. Technically, it may not be up to the grandstanding of Poe, but certainly Meek maintains a musical quality equal to that of Southern contemporaries Simms and Hayne, Lanier and Chivers.[9]

In the traditional sense, of course, Meek in these respects is certainly much closer to Longfellow than to Whitman. But even here regionality is pronounced in a distinctly Southern kind of direct, Arcadian simplicity—albeit, ironically, with much of the sensuosity and musicality that seems to have so influenced Whitman on his Southern sojourn, but also in this case coupled with a local traditional of frontier storytelling, a kind of narrative poetic realism. Further, as to the visible influence of Anglo-European poetic models, these too seem to have been largely favorites of the South, with pronounced emphasis on Scott and, in particular, Thomas Moore's wildly popular *Lallah Rookh.*

Further, even with so literarily establishmentarian a figure as Meek, one also detects a distinctly Southern concept of the profession of authorship. He is the poet as learned, genteel man of letters, to be sure, but with an emphasis placed on his prize standing as the gifted aristocratic amateur. This is to say, like such fellow Alabama literati as Johnson Jones Hooper, Joseph Glover Baldwin, and Albert J. Pickett, not to mention countless regional figures including

William Gilmore Simms and others, he embodies that expressly Southern image of the cultural patriot and man of affairs who counts among the many features of his reputation significant status as a literary author. As a member of such a regional comitatus, Meek, indeed, seemed to take a kind of perverse pleasure in remarking on an "indolence" that he described to Simms in a letter of 18 May 1847 as "the God of my nature" (Williams, *Literary History* 40). Accordingly, his literary remains even now strike us as notable for projects of many genres in varying degrees of incompletion.

Finally, as will be seen, distinct evidence of the importance of Meeks's poem as a literary-cultural property would also be apparent in its history of reception. Further, in the present case, this would be uniquely twofold. Widely noticed and approvingly read at the time of its initial publication, *The Red Eagle* was given new impetus and substantial public visibility nearly six decades later by a cultural intelligentsia wishing to make it serve the historical and educational politics of a new century as well.

On the first point, if nothing else, it should be realized that, in a substantial portion of the antebellum Republic about to recognize itself as a separate nation—and, accordingly, at a zenith of regional patriotism both political and literary—Meek's poem was an important literary-cultural production of its day. Billing itself explicitly in a subtitle as "A Poem of the South," it could and did claim major visibility and popularity, that is, as an distinctly Southern achievement, albeit in what was recognized to be one of the most important *national* literary-cultural projects of the antebellum era—the breakneck quest of a new generation of romantics in poetry and prose to come forth with a bona fide original American epic. The author certainly affirmed such a purpose on his own part in a historical preface. "The love-life of Weatherford," he claimed, "his dauntless gallantry, his marvellous personal adventures and hairbreadth escapes, and, chief of all, his wonderful eloquence, which eventually saved his life, when all other means would have failed, afford as fine a theme for the poet as any in American history" (9). And to emphasize what Meek hoped to be both the regional and the national appeal of the text, he had it published simultaneously by D. Appleton Company of New York and S. H. Goetzel and Company of Mobile.

Such efforts were rewarded for the moment at least by six printings in the first year and mainly approving reviews in major publications North and South. The December 1855 *Harper's* praised the poet's "frequent vivid pictures of nature" as manifesting "an enviable power of accurate description" and concluded, "we know of few more faithful delineations of Southern scenery than are given in many passages of this poem." It also praised the plot as "one of varied interest" being "well sustained throughout" (118). In Richmond, the *Southern*

Literary Messenger of the same month rhapsodized, "Mr. Meek is one of the truest poets in the country, and has that deep sense of the beautiful that finds its proper utterance in song. His gift is one from nature, and can no more fail to declare itself than the melody of birds." It went on: "We regret that we have not the space to do justice here to 'The Red Eagle,' a poem which abounds in striking incident and vivid representations of life and character. . . . At present we can only say that it is a most delightful addition to the literature of the South and shows that Poesy yet loves to linger in the dread haunted dells and glorious forests of the Southern land" (674).[10] Meanwhile, over in Charleston, the current hotbed of Southern patriotism literary and political, the estimable William Gilmore Simms, who had risked a review of Meek's epic-in-the-making a full decade earlier while it was still in manuscript,[11] took to task the editors of the *Mercury* for not reviewing the work at sufficient length. "I do not like to see our native authors, even in their crude beginnings, passed over neglectfully in our domestic courts of criticism," he wrote. "Mr. Meek has a fine imagination, a lively fancy, an excursive thought, and a grace and force of expression which with proper pains-taking must assure him of the highest excellence in style" (qtd. in Parks 129).

Augmenting the visibility of the text and the approving response among the literary-cultural cognoscenti was the fact that Meek himself was acknowledged as a figure of considerable consequence in antebellum Southern letters, mentioned in the same breath with Simms, Poe, Kennedy, Chivers, John Esten Cooke, Hayne, Timrod, and Bagby.[12] As a critical arbiter and literary patriot, he was certainly considered a worthy contemporary of most of these, having made something of a name for himself in a career in law, politics, oratory, and general public affairs notable in many eyes for how little effort had actually been expended in the service of literature. Among his achievements had been the creation of the short-lived but influential literary magazine *The Southron*, with big-name contributors during the first half of 1839 including Simms and A. B. Longstreet, as well as Alabama worthies W. R. Smith, F. A. P. Barnard, and H. W. Hilliard. In the same year he published an essay entitled "Southern Literature" and delivered an oration at the Erosophic Society of the University of Alabama on "The Southwest, Its History, Character, and Prospects." Other such productions followed, including "Jack Cadeism and Its Prospects" and "Americanism in Literature."[13] In turn, some of these were reprinted, along with other essays and poems from Meek, by Simms in periodicals and collections of the 1840s and 1850s appearing under his editorship. As noted above, Simms also gave favorable notice to Meek's work, and the two engaged in an extensive correspondence during the 1840s on matters cultural and literary. Meek returned the favor by "cordially" dedicating *The Red Eagle*—as had Alabama historian Albert J.

Pickett his 1851 volume—to "W. Gilmore Simms, LL. D., the Historian, Novelist, and Poet."

For all this, as noted by Benjamin Williams, 1855 proved hardly the most propitious year for a work staking its quest after enduring renown on self-advertisement as an epic poem of the South; and during the post–Civil War era it largely sank from view to become an object of appreciation mainly among literary antiquarians and cultural nostalgists. Meek himself died in 1865; and what local reputation he retained became increasingly associated with popular lyrics such as those contained in his 1857 volume, *Songs and Poems of the South*, and a collection of prose historical sketches and essays, many of them reprinted orations, published in the same year and entitled *Romantic Passages in Southwestern History*. By late in the century, in Sutton S. Scott's *The Mobilians*,[14] a devotee of the merits of *The Red Eagle* had to content himself with the hope that the poem might once again shine "as the finest production of the kind which the Gulf States have given to the world"—or, as he phrased it, "when the South shall turn her attention to the literature in which her particular history and characteristics are set forth, [it would] not only be highly regarded, but lastingly as well as affectionately cherished" (123).

Ironically, what neither Scott nor his fictionalized commentator could have known was that shortly, across the entire region, just such an articulated campaign of general remembering in Southern literature and history would soon be under way; and that, in Alabama particularly, the single text benefiting most directly from such efforts at cultural recovery would be none other than A. B. Meek's *The Red Eagle*. Yet such was the case as a new century beckoned, and a New South cast about accordingly in search of occasions to reconnect past and future. To be sure, among cultural heralds pushing ahead toward twentieth-century topics, there remained plantation nostalgists and celebrants of the lost cause; but in most cases, such an atmosphere of historical and literary renewal called for a turning away from slavery, secession, war, military defeat and devastation, and enforced political reconstruction[15]—or at least the attempt to look beyond recent historical tragedy and find a means of reconnection with what might be termed a usable past. And in Alabama, especially, that meant recourse to the same built-in literary-historical escape valve devised by virtually all major writers of the state in the decades before the Civil War: the intense, even obsessive contemplation of one vision of sociopolitical tragedy—the subjection and eventual extirpation of native peoples—as a way of not contemplating the other comprised in the succeeding racial curse of chattel slavery. Accordingly, in the new century as in the old, there was a return by history-minded Alabamians to the twinned legacies of frontier heroics and Native American lore, with emphasis on accounts of early settlers and records of aboriginal inhabitants; territorial development and constitutional deliberation; early statehood and accomplishments of founding political figures; and works dealing in such topics by pioneering figures of literature.[16]

In terms of institutional specifics, certainly such a purpose of reconnection seemed the thrust of the activities of the State Historical Society at the turn of the century,[17] and, from 1905 onward, of the newly founded State Department of Archives and History, both under the leadership of Thomas McAdory Owen. Similarly, the newly organized Alabama Library Association actively promoted the productions of important early Alabama figures. Again, with Owen in the lead as author of a massive four-volume history and biographical encyclopedia, and through the continuing efforts of the latter's wife, Marie Bankhead Owen, and the textbook author Albert B. Moore, such a reconnection was also emphasized in the writing of Alabama history and the distribution of texts to the schools and libraries. The cause of local culture would be abetted by folklorists such as Ruby Pickens Tartt, educationists such as Julia Tutwiler, and literati such as the state's official poet, Samuel Minturn Peck; and through various state agencies there would be a serious refocusing of public interest on Native American history and archaeology, with such efforts eventually abetted further by depression-era WPA support.

Amidst all this, in 1914 a celebrated literary-cultural touchstone of the effort would turn out to be an attractive, new, custom-printed edition of A. B. Meek's *The Red Eagle,* published by Montgomery's Paragon Press and timed to coincide with well-publicized public celebrations of the centenary of the great Battle of Horseshoe Bend. Accordingly, with due historical reverence, in size, jacket color, and textual layout, it presented itself as essentially a facsimile of the slim octavo original, but with important gift-book features accentuating its commemorative status. Meek's dedication, introduction, poetic text, and explanatory notes were faithfully reproduced, this time on high-quality uncut stock; in the frontispiece and interleaved at the beginnings of separate cantos were engravings of several period illustrations; and the original embossed red cover was updated with full title and likeness of the hero in gilt decoration.[18] A most important new addition, however, was an introductory essay, credited to Geo. T. Bayzer and Will T. Sheehan, the latter the editor in chief of the *Montgomery Advertiser* and well known as a promoter of early Alabama history and literature.[19] In it, Meek was lauded for his innumerable contributions to early Alabama life and culture: as poet, orator, editor, critic, and historian. Further, paralleling Meek's own textual commentary, a renewed attempt was also made to set various matters of the historical record straight concerning the work's titular hero and the essential nobility of his character and actions.[20] But from start to finish, the main object of the new preface was clearly literary promotion of the text itself as a recovered touchstone of cultural memory. Here was a book, the authors strenuously asserted, of epic importance in the fullest sense—a testament to the misfortune "that the school children of Alabama should be so familiar with the exploits of King Phillip and Tecumseh, and other Indian leaders, and be kept in ignorance of the deeds of Weatherford and Osceola, Indian leaders of their own state"; or that Longfellow's *Hiawatha* enjoys continuing renown at the expense of "a poem of Indian life in Alabama, and of equal merit" (5–6). Left to "dusty places in old libraries" or quotation by an elder "with kindling eye," they concluded, here was Alabama's true contribution to the world in the very definition of epic: "a poem which to the South should be as Scott's *Lady of the Lake* to Scotland" (9); a text whose loss would truly be that of history itself.

The obvious curricular thrust of republication paid important cultural dividends, some immediate and some longer-range. With new copies widely distributed to schools and libraries, simple availability led to a modest twentieth-century popular revival of the text as a staple of classroom reading and recitation. At present, it is a rare college or university library in the state that does not have multiple copies in the stacks or as part of special collections. Most educated Alabamians to this day know something of Weatherford. Some, mostly of the pre–World War II era, can still recollect a classroom encounter with the poem. And, *pace* Bayzer and Sheehan, there are still even a few elders around who can recite "stirring passages." To be sure, in the popular or literary canon, on the other hand, fate has once again dealt *The Red Eagle* a renewed verdict of critical oblivion.[21] Yet, from the grave, Meek—as an artist, frequently disparaged at the time for not devoting himself sufficiently to a purely literary career—surely must have enjoyed some small literary and political triumph, if for nothing else on the basis of the multifariousness of his talents. For besides all his literary achievements, he had also been, as was well known from biographical accounts, a political figure of some consequence, with a record including service as a federal attorney and a probate judge, and several terms as a state representative. And it is in the latter role, no doubt, that Meek the politician would surely have enjoyed seeing the epic volume by Meek the poet reissued in a commemorative edition clearly intended for classrooms and libraries. For, even though he had presided as speaker of the house during the so-called "secession convention" of 1859–60, the legislative achievement most visibly associated with his name over the years had always been his sponsorship of the 1854 Alabama Education Act, whereby the state had officially established its system of public schools. Even as the poet had prepared to publish his mid-nineteenth-century epic, then, the politician was already helping to create the twentieth-century reading constituency who would ultimately serve him most widely and affectionately.

Thus Meek's *The Red Eagle*—the last of Alabama's premier literary productions to occur before the Civil War—became in new popular and educational incarnations among its most culturally cherished; and thus, as well, a production by an antebellum Alabama writer became as important once again for the subject of racial tragedy it depicted as for the one it allowed Alabamians to evade. In 1855 *The Red Eagle* had been an epic poem of a South standing at the crisis of Union and yet insisting for all the world that chattel slavery was not the central fact of its history; in 1914 it had been resurrected for a South styling itself "New" but knowing full well that it was a savage, segregated South to be feared and disparaged for endless decades to come. The curse of race lying upon the land remained the curse of race arising out of chattel slavery. As to the literary celebration of history and the celebration of literary history, on the other hand, the frontier and native associations of the Old Southwest could be made to serve once again. For a new educational class of twentieth-century readers, the world of the forest wars in America—in this case, that of early-nineteenth-century Alabama—could once more be made distinctly prelapsarian in a general sense as it had been in other contexts by Cooper or, in a more directly Southern connection, Simms: as a living Whig explanation of history—a world, that is, before the fall into politics, law, and the need for governments. But for Alabamians, a particular attraction of that world would remain its identification as a world before the fall into slavery as well. With the resurrection of Meek's poem, the epic celebration of the past would be allowed to rework its old politics of racial substitution into a new politics of cultural affirmation and reassurance.

7

Historicizing Alabama's Southwestern Humorists; or, How the Times Were Served by Johnson J. Hooper and Joseph G. Baldwin

~

As a working laboratory of social experiment on the antebellum frontier, early Alabama could hardly have been expected not to prove hospitable literary ground for corresponding developments in the raffish new regional genre of politico-economic realism called Southwestern humor. To put this more directly, in a world of flush times and fast characters where self-making was the name of the game, it seemed only natural that such ebullient existential exercise of creative individuality would find comic literary celebration as well. In this, readers of the era at both the regional and national levels were not disappointed by premier antebellum Alabama practitioners of the form, from whose hands they received at least two acknowledged classics.[1] These were Johnson Jones Hooper's *Adventures of Captain Simon Suggs* and Joseph Glover Baldwin's *The Flush Times of Alabama and Mississippi*. The first, with prominent episodes published initially in the *La Fayette East Alabamian* and reprinted in William T. Porter's influential New York sporting journal, *The Spirit of the Times,* appeared in book form in 1845. The second, with most of its contents having been published as individual pieces in the prestigious *Southern Literary Messenger,* came out as a collection in 1853.

Further, in the domain of literary history, the work of both of these Alabama authors has continued to earn their texts not only enshrinement in the canon of an important nineteenth-century American genre but also independent critical recognition as works of distinctly original genius. In the domain of cultural archetype, *Adventures of Simon Suggs* has regularly been invoked by critics as a reigning early representation of the confidence-man archetype in American myth and literature. It has rightly been called one of the most skilled parodies ever concocted of American campaign biography.[2] And in its complex politics of narration—what Kenneth Lynn has memorably analyzed as the style of the "self-controlled gentleman"—it has been held up as an exemplary document of Whig critique in its battle against Jacksonian mobocracy. Similarly, as social representation, in Baldwin's expanding on the standard cast of "hunters, hog-merchants, ring-tailed roarers, gamblers, circuit riders," and the like rendered familiar by the genre (Justus xviii), *The Flush Times*, in its colorful survey of the frontier bench and bar, has been celebrated as a great, teeming gallery of period authentics and originals, a kind of living legal archaeology of the rumbustious era described in its title.[3] And likewise stylistically, precisely in its eschewing much of the vernacular experimentation common to the Southwestern genre for a more traditional comic realism in the grand manner, it has been singled out for an almost Dickensian robustness of rhetorical and representational vigor.

On the other hand, exactly in these various forms of celebration as literary classics, both have frequently earned institutional status in studies emphasizing their uniqueness and/or difference rather than their common political origin as deeply historicized *local* achievements in the fullest sense of that term; and as a result, critics have continued over the years to make large cultural claims about Hooper's and Baldwin's classic volumes—albeit in many cases just and supportable ones—in increasing dissociation of the two texts not only from each other but also from the virtually identical contexts of political and economic circumstance that brought them into being in the first place as cultural representations. Or, to put this in the context of my present purpose, if no one has ever really debated that Hooper's and Baldwin's books were, as explicitly as any written in the era, quite literally about what Mills Thornton has called power and politics in early Alabama, the time has also probably come for us to take the trouble of reading them together again in exactly that way in order to reattach claims we have made about their humor in the domain of cultural myth to explicit issues of cultural formation. We need to see again, that is, despite their visible differences in style and outlook, as well as their times and places of composition, what these texts actually say about Alabama life and culture in the period that became in both cases their focal, even obsessive concern—by no coincidence, in both cases, the crucial years of 1835–37 investment boom and bust that might properly be called Alabama's age of speculation; and, as will be shown, we also as importantly need to see what they go to great pains, as political and economic texts, not to say—in this case, almost astoundingly, given their common concern with wildfire economic growth and investment—about chattel slavery.

The age of speculation: mid-1830s Alabama was truly a world where any door could be opened, as Hooper's hero clearly understood, for a man named "Cash"; or, as Baldwin called it up front, these were truly the flush times. The place was pervaded, to use James Justus's brilliant phrasing, by a sense of "promissory atmosphere" without limit, a view of material profit and possibility derived of "an economic system based on paper money, credit, confidence, and unrestrained speculation" (xvii). Especially in the Black Belt territory stretching into Alabama from west Georgia and then hooking upward into east and north-central Mississippi, during the years in question it was a brave new world in which the economic action persistently outstripped even etymology. This was no arena of mere investment, of calculated capital risk for anticipated gain. Rather, it was a time and a place in which the very idea of speculation seemed to require some bizarre new yoking of concepts, as if specie—portable wealth—and peculation—fraudulent transfer—had contrived to join forces in their own original synergy of creative misappropriation. Or, in an appropriate coinage, with apologies to Karl Marx by way of P. T. Barnum, here the name of the game was not capital so much as pure capitalization. To cite an expression common to both texts, "making a raise"—either the ad hoc generation of actual capital or, in the more likely alternative, the producing of at least the appearance thereof—was the quintessential flush times phrasing that meant exactly what it said.

To apply the principle directly to both texts at hand, if the confidence-man hero of Hooper's world for good or ill was a man who seemed capable of endlessly making money out of nowhere, parlaying the self into the latest batch of what he called the old spizarinctum, the legal gladhanders springing up at every courthouse crossroads in Baldwin's texts were denizens of a new country who equally found such a world "made to order for them" (xvii) as well. For every Simon Suggs or Suggs Jr. making money, that is, there would always be at least one Ovid Bolus or Cave Burton standing by to help him keep it and make it grow, while also happily helping himself to the proceeds; or if, as was decidedly more often the case, whirlwind gain suddenly found itself converted to loss, still other lawyers were likely standing by, as Baldwin made a point to show, not unlike "the wreckers near the Florida Keys," waiting admirably to profit by the disaster (240).

As to political and economic facts themselves, students of the era fortunately find themselves amply supplied with materials to construct a historical overview, with the main events of the period rendered distinct enough in outline to be fairly summarized. Overall, as Johanna Nicol Shields concisely puts it in her introduction to Hooper's work, there was "the boom of the mid-thirties, the Panic of 1837, and the depression that followed it" (xxiv). Further, thanks to the work of various scholars, constituent activities may likewise be examined in terms of relatively discrete, although interrelated, subcategories.

As a catalyst of political and economic activity, first in local importance early in the decade, surely, was rampant land speculation, turned loose in many cases by the last native removals. Specifically visible, for instance, in Hooper's text, was the celebrated east and south-central Alabama episode in the era's flurry of land speculation known as the "certification" of sales of Creek lands. Occurring mainly during the early to mid-1830s, and enacted through meetings of Creek Indians and the government, such was the quasi-legal procedure whereby eager speculators were enabled to grab up individual properties of soon-to-be displaced natives at bargain rates. As might be expected, spectacular frauds were perpetrated against native owners, and often as well by white purchasers upon each other as a result of the machinations of contending cartels.[4] Further, new complications were often induced into the practical politics of such land grabbing by an influx of settlement, both authorized and otherwise. Hostilities grew among settlers and remaining Creeks, and clashes also took place between white citizens and local militias and U.S. government troops detailed to evict unlawful intruders. Despite the intervention of government mediators and investigative functionaries, the frauds continued, coming to a head in 1835, with various Creek bands along the Chattahoochee River agreeing to close matters but with others farther west on the Coosa and Tallapoosa more resistant. Meanwhile, violence broke out between remaining Creeks and white settlers, with young braves reduced to the brigandage of roving bands, stealing cattle and burning houses and barns. It was also alleged that others were incited by agents of competing land cartels. Resistance was quickly put down in the so-called Creek War of 1836, when, as Leah Rawls Atkins records, "several thousand militiamen tracked down" the last native bands and defeated them "at Hoby's Bridge on the Pea River" (Rogers et al. 138).

Meanwhile, to the west, as imaged repeatedly in Baldwin's pages, the hapless Choctaws were being steamrolled by both state and federal authorities toward a similar fate, with native and settler alike plunged into a welter of so-called "cultivation," "contingency," and "pre-emption" claims, and with the resultant legal chaos eagerly abetted by the courts and their myriad functionaries. Again, the jumble of transactions was nothing short of byzantine, with disagreement between settler and native frequently exacerbated by machinations of groups of rival speculators. No less than three public offerings of Choctaw land had been conducted by 1835, and the remaining years of the decade saw a welter of confusing property and payment claims growing more complicated at every turn. Well into the late 1840s and early 1850s matters were still being sorted out, with the primary losers in what came to be called the great "Choctaw Speculation" naturally, as with the "Creek Fraud" to the east, the tribe in question.[5]

All such speculation, however, was but a function of the even grander orgy of individual self-seeking being played out in the domain of money and banking, with economic crisis on both the national and the regional level being played out in an series of speculative restructurings of the relationships among wealth and currency, notes, bonds, deeds, and other instruments of credit and indebtedness. Nationally, of course, these were the years of the great Jacksonian bank crisis, involving the struggle between the president and his adversary Nicholas Biddle. Jackson's veto of a bill for rechartering the existing Bank of the United States (technically the second) had occurred in 1832; in 1833 he had followed with the removal of government deposits and their resettling in "pet banks"; this maneuver had been countered with machinations by Biddle to protect his shareholders, including the abandonment of former loan controls and curtailment policies, and the general fostering of a speculative atmosphere in the absence of any real centralizing authority. In turn, Jackson had been forced into an attempt to halt the inflation of paper currency with the Specie Circular of 1836, which limited acceptance of payment on federal lands to gold and silver; and the resultant currency collapse fostered the more general crisis of economic faith that came to be known as the Panic of 1837.[6]

Leah Rawls Atkins, among others, is surely correct in observing that it was the specie matter that quickly put the brakes on the flush times of Alabama and Mississippi, forcing prices of land, cotton, and slaves rapidly downward (Rogers et al. 137). As might be expected, outstanding loans precipitated an anxious flurry of attempted collection and consolidation among financial institutions in the state. Meanwhile, however, an equally serious Alabama bank crisis had been building, itself born of a history of rivalry between a bank of the United States established in Mobile and a state bank, with a directorship created by legislative and gubernatorial appointment, seated first in Cahaba, and then in Tuscaloosa, with eventual branches in Decatur, Montgomery, Mobile, and Huntsville. And although thereby, as Albert Moore writes, the state tried, and managed with some success, to avoid the speculative wildcatting fostered by "spurious private banks" around the country, "no one would contend that it escaped the evils of a 'rag money' currency," with "the issues of the state" far outstripping "their ability to reclaim" (221–22). It proved simply inevitable, he goes on, that "speculation begat bank notes and loans, and notes and loans begat speculation" (222). By 1837 an estimated ten billion dollars in notes had found themselves in circulation. Meanwhile, "there were numerous rumors of irregularities, excessive loans and collusions between bank directors and members of the legislature that corroborated the findings of the legislative committee" (223). Still, Moore concludes with an appropriate flourish, "as well one might have attacked the hosts of Belshazzar's Feast as to have assailed the State banks, which were accredited with the prosperous days that had come upon the land" (223).

Shortly, of course, came the crash, with the national economic crisis rendered locally all the more damaging by the state's own grievous mismanagement of the relationship between actual wealth and proliferating currency. To put it simply, when the Bank of the United States came down, it was simply a matter of time until the Alabama banking system turned into the financial equivalent of a black hole in space. Money wealth suddenly turned out be what it had been all along: numbers and paper; and with its basis likewise in paper instruments of indebtedness and no purchasers in sight, property wealth—land, slaves, mercantile establishments and inventories—plummeted accordingly. Specie payment was suspended by the banks after a run in the spring of 1837 (Moore 224). But by June of the same year, as detailed by Mills Thornton, the "disastrous" acts of a special legislative session forced them anew "to increase their already bloated note circulation by $5 million and to suspend the collection of $5 million of their debts" (79). Further efforts at specie redemption followed in 1838, but these in turn were forestalled by another suspension made necessary in the following year by the failure of the Philadelphia descendant of the Bank of the United States. Meanwhile, Whig and Democrat traded predictable accusations of mismanagement and corruption involving everything from directorial incompetence to legislative swilling at the trough. In 1842 the bank was finally placed in liquidation—but not before all parties had stored up grievances sufficient to make the egregious mishandling of the crisis a mother lode of political opprobrium for years to come.[7]

The events described, in *Adventures of Simon Suggs* and *The Flush Times of Alabama and Mississippi,* comprise the literal center of mass around which both texts coalesce. In Hooper, they provide something like a chronological backbone, with highly visible "satires about land speculation, about 'rag' paper money, and about state-sponsored banking" (xxxiv), as Johanna Nicol Shields points out, strung prominently along the picaresque line of adventure. In Baldwin, explicit reference weaves in and out of the social panorama, with the times themselves distinctly part and fabric of the play of character, scene, and event in virtually every sketch.

Suggs's first "adult" adventures, for instance—following a Parson Weems-like boyhood chronicle of the hero's apprentice lying and cardsharping—place him in east Alabama during early adventures explicitly dated in the year 1833, where he successfully outrides and outwits a fellow sharper en route to Montgomery attempting to corner a choice purchase of Creek lands. Shortly, we also find him aboard a stagecoach to Tuscaloosa—putatively to do battle with the Faro Bank, but also probably to avail himself of whatever pickings may avail themselves during a new legislative session; accordingly, while en route, he is mistaken by a candidate for a bank directorship as the "member from Tallapoosa" and quickly finds himself on the receiving end of a generous bribe. In turn, by 1835 we find him back in the Creek territories profiting once more at the hands of greedy rivals for public lands, this time capitalizing on their foolhardy lip-smacking over the prospect of hard currency—a pair of saddlebags, allegedly full of "Mexicans" (117), but in fact stuffed with "rocks and old iron" (120)—rather than paper money to turn the deed. By the following year—carefully noted by the narrator as being one both "of grace" and of "excessive bank issues," he finds himself in the midst of the spurious Second Creek War, where he earns his equally spurious captaincy (123). And in the last of his sharp dealings we hear of—through a valedictory letter scrawled by the hero himself—he happily describes himself as back into currency manipulation, this time with shinplaster paper provided by a cartel wishing him to seed it into the slave market.

And so, in Baldwin, the atmospherics of the titular epoch permeate the action from the first word of the first page onward. The sketch at hand may be ostensibly about Ovid Bolus Esq., Attorney at Law, Solicitor in Chancery, and liar extraordinaire; but thereby it can only be equally, the narrator insists, of "the history of that halcyon period, ranging from the year of Grace 1835, to 1837; that golden era, when shinplasters were the sole currency; when bank-bills were 'as thick as Autumn leaves in Vallambrosa,' and credit was a franchise" (1). As easily, he asserts, one might "write the biography of Prince Hal and forbear all mention of Falstaff" (1)—or in a host of proximate cases, one presently sees, detail the lives of the new American nobility of frontier free enterprise without their hordes of attendant lawyers. Indeed, throughout the texts, litigation is the air that democracy breathes; and money for fees and awards, not to mention as a source of the claims and disputes that get matters moving in the first place, is as near as any convenient printing press. As related by the narrator, a "smutted rag" simply became "money," "was money," the miracle growth of "a sort of financial biology, which made, at night, the thing conjured for, the thing that was seen, so far as the patient was concerned" (82). Thus, we are told, "Commerce was king," or at least declared itself so; "and Rags, Tag, and Bobtail his cabinet council. Rags was treasurer" (87).

Accordingly, as in Hooper, when the king and council find themselves in need of raw material for major money and property swindles, it is the long-suffering original inhabitants of the place who supply most of the real estate. "INDIAN affairs!—" the narrator rhapsodizes at one point: "the very mention is suggestive of the poetry of theft—the romance of a wild and weird larceny! What sublime conceptions of super-Spartan roguery! Swindling Indians by the nation! (*Spirit of Falstaff, rap!*) Stealing their land by the township! (*Dick Turpin and Jonathan Wild! tip the table!*) Conducting the nation to the Mississippi River, stripping them to the flap, and bidding them God speed as they went howling into the Western wilderness to the friendly agency of some sheltering Suggs duly empowered to receive their coming annuities and back rations" (238).[8]

As to banking and finance, the situation is identical to that depicted by Hooper: it is a sheer saturnalia of frauds, mendacities, and chicaneries—invariably abetted, one might add, by the customary combination of governmental incompetence and corruption. "State banks," the narrator tells us, "were issuing their bills by the sheet, like a patent steam printing-press *its* issues; and no other showing was asked of the applicant for the loan than an authentication of his great distress for money. Finance, even in its most exclusive quarter, had thus already got, in this wonderful revolution, to work upon the principles of the charity hospital" (83). Apace, he goes on, "the old rules of business and the calculations of prudence were alike disregarded, and profligacy, in all the departments of the *crimen falsi*, held riotous carnival. Larceny grew not only respectable, but genteel, and ruffled it in all the pomp of purple and fine linen. Swindling was raised to the dignity of the fine arts. Felony came forth from its covert, put on more seemly habiliments, and took its seat with unabashed front in the upper places of the synagogue" (87). In public and private life alike, "avarice and hope joined partnership," with "the reptile arts of humanity, as at a faro table," being "warmed into life beneath their heat. The *cacoethes accrescendi* became epidemic. It seized upon the universal community" (87).[9]

And it is through this vision of capital fever as a kind of collective madness that we come back again and again, whether following the decidedly miscellaneous course of Suggsian "adventure" or making our way through Baldwin's equally various gallery of sharpers and rapscallions, to the very particular kind of historicity that finally endows both works with common, almost Aristotelian unity of theme and event. And that historicity is, of course, of an America fully launched into its first great age of speculation, with the Old Southwest an abstract or epitome of an entire nation trying to "make a raise," trying to come up with the specie to underwrite its own expansionist promise. And for good *and* ill, as both Hooper and Baldwin profoundly understood, along an ever expanding frontier, that was going to require a kind of politico-economic effrontery, both material and spiritual, unprecedented in the national experience, indeed an egalitarian marriage of capital and confidence never before attempted in the history of humankind. The great theme of the linked chicaneries lies in their composite function as a primer on the art of "capitalization"—how to create capital or the appearance of capital; or as likely, in alternative, at least how to pretend to create it, to give the appearance of just having created it, or to exude the aura of being about to create it. This truly is the ideological content of these texts, what William T. Porter famously called "the spirit of the times." Whatever the proximate topic, episode, or adventure, everything seems ultimately converted to a running allegory of boom and bust.

To say this of Simon Suggs, political economist, given the number of sketches in which some highly visible form of politico-economic swindle is itself the central action, might at least seem on the face of it to belabor the obvious. What one must notice in addition, however, is how relentlessly his capital legerdemain continues to exert itself even while he seems to be doing *something else*. Even in the first sketch, for instance, as the young Simon and a slave confederate hastily break up a card game and attempt to conceal the evidence in fear of punishment from Suggs's approaching father, the avaricious, hypocritical Elder Jedidiah (17), the clever boy busies himself with making sure that his fellow sufferer gets euchred out of the original pot; and by the time he has finished with Suggs Sr.—having shortly seduced the latter into a renewal of the game on the pretext of wagering his way out of an anticipated punishment—he has managed not only to avoid his appointment with the parental rod but also to add a profit of twenty dollars and a horse. And so as the ensuing chapters unfold, whatever the ostensible business of the adventure at hand, the connecting thread of character in the book, if it may be so called, remains the hero's indefatigable energy for converting nearly any occasion into an opportunity for ad hoc fundraising. During a legislative sojourn in Tuscaloosa, for instance, seed capital of a twenty-dollar bribe provided by the candidate for a bank directorship transmutes itself into a fortune at the faro tables, only to evaporate as quickly as it has come, only to find itself shortly rematerialized in the form of a new stake gained by Suggs's impersonation of a visiting Kentucky tycoon hog drover. Meanwhile, that worthy's hapless nephew has also been plied for $250 in cash and left holding the bill for an immense champagne and oyster supper. Similarly, if the 1836 Creek War heroics earning the hero his coveted captaincy at the defense of Fort Suggs provide occasion to fleece a widow over a trumped-up violation of "martial law," this fortune too comes to be lost as quickly as it has been won; and it is this newest capital depletion crisis that in turn generates the celebrated affair of the camp meeting. So at every turn, this Simon Magus of a new country works his magic of making money. He makes it appear and he makes it vanish; he sees it coming and he sees it going; he conjures it up out of nowhere and expresses little surprise or regret when it is reclaimed into the void. The only sure thing about the new Suggsian political economy is the inevitability of its flowering within moments of the newest arrival of the Suggsian person.

In Baldwin, likewise, the fine art of capitalization, for a representative figure, if less pronounced as a focal attribute of character, is still deemed in most cases a basic skill, like numeracy or literacy, something simply assumed, present at the creation, a bedrock component of individuality. To this degree, for instance, Ovid Bolus, as lawyer *and* liar, is a model citizen, with some of his most expert mendacity, as the narrator notes, invariably reserved for profitable exercise in some fiduciary dimension. "He was as free with his own money," we are told almost offhandedly, "—if he ever had any of his own—as with yours. If he never paid borrowed money, he never asked payment of others. If you wished him to loan you any, he would hand you a handful without counting it: if you handed him any, you were losing time in counting it, for you never saw any thing of it again: Shallow's funded debt of Falstaff were as safe an investment: this would have been an equal commerce, but, unfortunately for Bolus's friends, the proportion between his disbursements and receipts was something scant" (7). Thus the highest accolade afforded Bolus by the narrator: that "such a spendthrift never made a track even in the flush times of 1836" (7). And thus his rueful notation of the lowest moment of his subject's lying career, the swindling of Ben O. It is not so much that he did it, we are told, but that it was so easy, and thereby so degrading to his talents (10–11). For like an American Dickens or Bulwer, the narrator concludes, this frontier prevaricator has truly become the laureate of the lie, turning fiction at once into both a literally capital activity and a signature art (16–17). In fact, when we see him last in the sketch he still plies the writer's trade, attaching yet another autograph to yet another instrument of credit and thereby beginning the newest chapter in an exemplary Southwestern life.

Conversely, in "How the Times Served the Virginians," justly cited by critics as a touchstone of the work's political vision, it is exactly the fatal flaw of those worthies in a new country that they prove unable to adapt to a new system of creative finance in which capital itself has become completely democratized, where every man is a self-created nabob, as good *and/or* as bad as his word. Or, as the narrator puts it, "the new nation was making" its own "second great experiment of independence: the experiment, namely, of credit without capital, and enterprise without honesty" (81); and thereby it became in those parts a crucial principle of democracy "to make, for all purposes of trade, credit and enjoyment of wealth, the man that had *no* money a little richer, if anything, than the man that had a million" (82). In fact, he goes on, if anything, "money, or what passed for money, was the only cheap thing to be had. Every cross-road and every avocation presented an opening—through which fortune was seen by the adventurer in near perspective." Equally "credit was a thing of course"; and "to refuse it—if the thing was ever done—were an insult for which a bowie-knife were not a too summary or exemplary a means of address" (83).

Thus in Baldwin, as in Hooper, we are also persistently brought back to the unifying subtext of the flush times: Making a raise, to put it simply, has become the measure of a man, and the test of a judicious gamble or a jury award the Suggsian knack of knowing how to size a pot.

Even down to the last sketch, we should probably see that we are continuing to get the message. Ostensibly one of the lighter exercises in the book, something of a throwaway item, it seems to be just one more legal piece, the humorous examination of yet another greenhorn candidate for the bar. On the other hand, not surprisingly, it turns out to be exclusively about property law, albeit in a nice raffish touch, with one penultimate libel question thrown in for free. As we begin to leave the book, the candidate is straining to elucidate the distinction between "trespass"—an offense against person or property—and "case"—a more abstract or metaphorical form of trespass involving violation of a contract, a prior agreement, or an obligation. As the hapless examinee slouches his way toward disaster, the joke may seem to be on the candidate. But if, as Baldwin probably suspected, we too have taken the hook and gone to the trouble of looking the matter up, we also find the joke damnably comprehensive in a book and a world where, as matters of property and law, the material and the metaphorical have become completely interchangeable. When it comes to the "Virginians" versus the "times," in literature and life alike, it is still mainly business as usual.[10] And so Baldwin shows us by way of a parting vignette. The candidate, named "Jefferson," it turns out, "walked slowly out of the grocery," the narrator tells us, "and, after getting about thirty yards off on the green beckoned me to him." He goes on:

> As I came towards him, he drew himself up with some dignity, took aim at a chip, about fifteen feet off, and squirted a stream of tobacco juice at it with remarkable precision. Said he, slowly and with marked gravity, "B_____, you needn't make any report of this thing to the Judge. I believe I won't go in. I don't know as it's any harder than I took it at the fust—but, then, B_____, ther's, so, d——, much, more, of, it." (330)

To be sure, then, it will always be important that any discussion of the confidence man in American literature will at some point invoke the Suggsian apothegm, "IT IS GOOD TO BE SHIFTY IN A NEW COUNTRY"; or more directly, that in any study of Mark Twain's *Huckleberry Finn,* the King's fleecing of a revival crowd will be noted as drawing directly on Hooper's uproarious chapter entitled "The Captain Attends a Camp Meeting." Accordingly, it will always be good to remember that the incomparable Twain also accorded equal reverence to Baldwin's Ovid Bolus as a presiding deity of American literary *and* lawyerly lying; or that in fiction about lawyers generally, particularly in the Southern manner, Baldwin's bitterly humorous swindlers, hypocrites, and cheats would remain the measure of the breed, albeit with the occasional happy flowering of the genealogy into the odd Gavin Stevens or Atticus Finch.

Further, in the domain of cultural myth, such a body of observation will remain useful in continuing to define the genuine importance of *Adventures of Simon Suggs* and *The Flush Times of Mississippi and Alabama* as major nineteenth-century American literary and—in the broadest sense of that term—political texts. On the other hand, as suggested at the outset, it also deprives Hooper and Baldwin of much of the richest and deepest part of their achievement, which lay in the shared quality of political imagination allowing them to identify, frequently even down to place and date, a sense of the importantly, even crucially *local* relationship between literary representation and the concrete workings of cultural ideology.

And this is true, finally, of the two books, even down to the historicity of composition. In both cases, albeit with Hooper writing in the early 1840s and Baldwin nearly a decade later, the prevailing mood of authorship might be best described as Whig nostalgia. For Hooper, this came of his relinquishing his law practice for the editorship of the *LaFayette East Alabamian,* a staunchly Whig newspaper in which he found himself as a writer turning increasingly away from present political controversy and back toward the colorful events of the previous decade when he, like Baldwin, had come into the state as a young candidate for the bar. A first production, entitled "Taking the Census in Alabama" and signed "By a Chicken Man of 1840," derived of his own experiences doing such work in Tallapoosa County. It was quickly picked up by William T. Porter's *New York Spirit of the Times.* And shortly, he began to produce the Simon Suggs sketches, most of them likewise republished by Porter as rapidly as they appeared, and collected finally in the 1845 book. For Baldwin, such nostalgia was even more emphatically the product of a frustrated Whiggery in that it included actual political disappointment. Like Hooper, as a candidate for the bar, he too had come into the state in the mid-1830s when, as he observed in the *Flush Times,* "practicing law, like shinplaster banking or a fight, was pretty much a free thing" (324). And, one suspects, he too just never really got over the general fun. During the 1840s he prospered in a legal partnership, gained election to the state legislature, and served as a delegate to the 1848 national convention. In 1849, however, he suffered a narrow defeat in a congressional race that by all accounts weighed heavily on both his personal and political morale. And it seems directly in consequence of such political disappointment that he turned to the writing that would eventuate over the next few years in the *Flush Times* sketches and a shortly ensuing volume entitled *Party Leaders: Sketches of Thomas Jefferson, Alex'r Hamilton, Andrew Jackson, Henry Clay, John Randolph of Roanoke,* a more serious book of history and politics, but equally nostalgic in its concentration on what Baldwin clearly meant to be seen as the golden age of American domestic statesmanship.

Further, given the emphasis in *Simon Suggs* and *The Flush Times* on the runaway rapacity and folly of the era, for both writers, the chief developments in economic politics of the era could hardly have been cheering, centered as they were on the almost willful perpetuation of the state banking crisis. With abolition of the state bank in 1842, Whigs had favored a conversion to a system of private chartered banks, while Democrats had continued to seek improvement in the existing bank as public servant (Thornton 47). Neither had gotten their wish. Between 1842 and 1848 there had remained only one bank in the state—the Bank of Mobile (Thornton 47). By the mid-1840s, Black Belt financiers had become the state's major lenders (Thornton 40). Thornton summarizes:

> The Bank of Alabama had been placed in liquidation in 1842 by the votes of those Democrats who had opposed all banks as intrinsically corrupting and of the Whigs, who wished to create a private banking system in place of the public one. But the Democratic proponents of public banking joined with the Democratic opponents of all banks to defeat the private bank charters offered by the Whigs. Thus, from 1842 to 1850, the state was without banks entirely, except for the small and shaky bank of Mobile, whose charter, granted in 1818, could not constitutionally be repealed. But throughout the forties, the pressure for some form of banking facilities grew. (281–82)

At the same time, "The absence of banks did not give the state a wholly specie currency as the orthodox opponents of banks had hoped it would. . . . The commercial demands of the community were simply too great to be carried on within the confines of so constricted a circulation. Rather, the absence of local notes attracted to Alabama the notes of banks in neighboring states—many of them of rather dubious reliability, accepted in Alabama largely out of necessity" (282–83).

To put it succinctly, as to any resolution of the political and economic catastrophes of the late 1830s, events of the 1840s and 1850s proved a major disappointment. The ongoing corrupt implications of electoral politics in the process did not help. In 1845, for instance, the gubernatorial election would wind up turning on the call of a Democratic candidate—himself deeply in debt to the bank—for repeal of the newly adopted Debt Collection Act of that year. The situation was somewhat alleviated only in the 1850s, when a new statewide system of private banks came into being (Thornton 47).

Finally, given the focal, even obsessive concerns of the age with property relationships, what then really are we to make of the missing matter in both texts of chattel slavery? Or, more properly, what are we to make of it especially here in books explicitly about the flush times of the region when, as a matter of historical fact, no one could deny then or later that surely their "most pronounced feature," in the words of Albert Moore, "was the expansion of the slavery regime." Moore goes on: "There seemed to be no limits to the profitable production of cotton, and there was a mad scramble for lands and slaves, which resulted in a very marked appreciation in the value of both. The mania for lands and slaves made large demands upon capital and invoked a very extensive use of credit" (221).

Here, in both cases, when slavery even merits mention, it seems a simple given of political and economic circumstance. Both texts, to be sure, are filled with what might be called a slavery residual of endemic racism.[11] Still, almost nobody seems to own a slave; and the exceptions depicted strike us as morally suspect, if not downright disreputable. In Hooper's text, the only "real" slaveowners we ever see, for instance, are both Suggses. And Daddy, apparently, owns just one, thus marking his social status as dirt farmer, while in a last sketch, as noted earlier, Simon is shown branching out into market speculation—with that enterprise, appropriately, even further sullied by his attempt to circulate worthless currency with which he has been equipped by a syndicate of shady investors.[12]

As to Baldwin, given his titular subject *and* focal concern in sketch after sketch with relationships between law and property, he can hardly avoid the occasional admission that the *other* major speculative commodity of the era besides land was, in fact, slaves (237). Still, here too one finds virtually no actual depictions of slavery. The one set of serious references to the "system"—a detailing by Samuel Hele of the ghastly tortures administered to slave miscreants and of the frequent forcible separations of mothers from their children—turns out, for instance, to be not serious at all, but rather scary gossip purveyed by that dyspeptic Democrat and village curmudgeon, playacting an abolitionist's worst nightmare, in an attempt to run off a starchy New England schoolmistress.[13]

Regarding the relation of both texts to other prominent ones of the era, our most obvious answer to the question posed above must be simply to remark on their partaking of the standard quality of denial generally characterizing the literary works of the period—and again the tendency, albeit here in rather cruel forms of humor, to sublimate racial guilt out of slavery and into contemplation of the injustices done native tribes. But here too, given especially the class and party biases of the authors, one might also assert a more pressing political motive as well. To put it simply, large planter-slaveowners and other members of the legal, financial, and political elites with a sincere interest in perpetuating the "peculiar institution" would almost all have been, like Hooper and Baldwin, either Whigs or Democrats deeply identified with planter interests. Accordingly, to depict flush times slavery would have been of necessity to depict the wild-fire flush times slave speculation that was almost exclusively the province of the large planters and their legal and political hangers-on; and that in turn would have forced both writers to include in their galleries of rogues and rapscallions not a few portraits drawn from their own class.[14]

One suspects finally, however, for two ebullient Whig humorists at the height of their talents, that even fear of class disloyalty finally had less to do with the matter of avoidance in question than simple unwillingness to betray their beloved form. That is, Whigs they were, to be sure; and in its origins, Southwestern humor had likewise been an essentially Whig form, a conservative, upper-class critique of Jacksonian frontier democracy. Yet, as detailed by Kenneth Lynn, at the same time it frequently became almost against its will a celebration of the prospects and possibilities of mid-nineteenth-century American personality in the great age of democratic individualism, with satire of the backwoods buffoon frequently tinged with a genuine admiration of his vitality, strength, and joie de vivre.[15] Accordingly—as the writers in question could have known only too well—during the very years in which the genre had come to flourish, chattel slavery had increasingly come to be seen as the most glaring imaginable betrayal of that promise, even as the flush times planters arrogantly sought to drive the dying institution through one last lucrative burst of exponential expansion. And that, in any humorous depiction of the era, would have been a truth far too oppressive for satire. Better, then, they both seem to have decided, that it stay unsaid. Like the historian Pickett or the epic poet Meek, on the matter of the well-documented explosive growth of slavery into Alabama as the fundamental demographic fact of the state's early history, Hooper and Baldwin made the choice of simple avoidance. As gentleman humorists, they wrote political realism as they saw it; and they also wrote it as they didn't see it.

8

Caroline Lee Hentz's Anti-Abolitionist Double Feature and Augusta Jane Evans's New and Improved Novel of Female Education

~

Outshining *and* outselling in the literary marketplace even the double-barreled contributions of the humorists Hooper and Baldwin to a muscular new genre of vernacular realism, two antebellum Alabama women novelists, both practitioners of a domestic realism enjoying immense popular visibility, helped ensconce Alabama even more firmly on the national map. One, Caroline Lee Hentz, had already made something of a name for herself in the late 1840s and early 1850s, having emerged amidst a flurry of productions of popular novels and story collections—sometimes as many as two or three a year; the other, Augusta Jane Evans, beginning to publish her fiction in the years just before the Civil War and finding major Southern popularity during the great conflict, would go on afterward to become one of the nation's best-selling novelists of the late nineteenth century. Both became famous in the decade just before the outbreak of war, however, largely on the basis of a single book. For Hentz, the novel in question would be *The Planter's Northern Bride;* for Evans, the crucial text would be *Beulah.*

Hentz's *The Planter's Northern Bride,* an 1854 novel achieving considerable visibility in its own era as a major Southern riposte to Harriet Beecher Stowe's *Uncle Tom's Cabin,* continues to this day to be regarded by scholars and historians as the most artful and literarily significant of the texts—the genre of "anti-Toms," as they came to be called—devised in that capacity.[1] The problem is that no one, then or now, seems to have been greatly able to explain the secret of its success.[2] As noted, for instance, it was hardly the first novel of Hentz's to bring her national attention; or, to put this another way, its popularity could easily be said to have been as much a function of its status as a new novel by Caroline Lee Hentz as a novel written in explicit response to Stowe.

Indeed, if anything, in direct contrast to Stowe's plunge as inspired neophyte (divinely, she alleged) into best-selling authorship, *The Planter's Northern Bride,* in spite of the boost it surely gained from its own topical notoriety, actually built on a well-established literary popularity of Hentz's among readers North and South. Further, success had been the result of serious literary apprenticeship. Having moved from one location to another in the South as wife of the French-born schoolmaster Nicholas Hentz, in the 1830s she wrote several dramas that made their way into production; late in the decade she published in Alexander Beaufort Meek's short-lived but influential literary magazine, *The Southron;* and in 1846 she also exhibited a ready talent for longer sentimental formula writing in the novelette *Aunt Patty's Scrap Bag.* Then, in 1849, like many another writing woman of the era, she was officially ushered by family misfortune into the pursuit of a literary livelihood; and in short order she parlayed a spate of ensuing works of the early 1850s into a reputation competitive with that of other worthies including E. D. E. N. Southworth and others. These included such popular novels as *Linda; or, the Young Pilot of the Belle Creole* (1850); *Rena; or, the Snow Bird: A Tale of Real Life* (1851); *Marcus Warland; or the Long Moss Spring* (1852); and *Eoline; or, the Magnolia Vale; or, the Heiress of Glenmore* (1852). In 1853 alone, a year in which her book sales were estimated at ninety-three thousand, she published the novel *Helen and Arthur; or Miss Thusa's Spinning-Wheel* and two collections of short stories, *The Victim of Excitement* and *Wild Jack; or the Stolen Child;* and in the following year, *The Planter's Northern Bride* proved but one more in a sequence of rapid productions concluding only with the author's death in 1856.

Even as to the genre in question, *The Planter's Northern Bride* was also rather a late arrival in a field that came to number between twenty and thirty.[3] Nor, in the latter context, as will be shown as well, did it seem to depart markedly in various standard conventions of plot, character, setting, and theme from others in the anti-Tom breed. The cross-regional love story in which the Southern suitor is forbidden the hand of the Yankee maiden by the abolitionist father; the comparison of the happy lot of the Southern servant with that of the used-up, discarded Northern working poor; the introduction of the Northern bride into salubrious planter life South of the Mason-Dixon Line, where she finds happy slaves and benignant masters in abundance; the deceit practiced upon a faithful servant, induced to abscond, by Northern philanthropists; the machinations of the sinister abolitionist, traveling under false colors, who foments slave revolt on the plantation: all of these elements of Hentz's story would themselves have been encountered—and more often than not, as here, in a variety of dexterous combinations—by practiced readers of anti-antislavery fiction.

What made the difference in Hentz's book, I will propose, was the way in which the author, herself a Massachusetts native converted by long residence in the South to her adopted region's views, disposed her anti-antislavery materials into a two-volume *anti-abolitionist* structure—thereby writing the cannily titrated equivalent of a political double feature that thus secured the attention of an established popular audience North and South. To put this more directly, the secret ingredient of Hentz's anti-Tom was a calculated trans-sectional appeal strategically underwritten by its focus on the generalized cultural unpopularity—North and South—of the fanatic abolitionist. And to this day, a reader acquainted with the history of slavery debate in general and abolitionist agitation in particular remains stunned in both cases by the degree to which she understood the distinct regional configurings of the specific cultural prejudice addressed. Setting the story of volume one in the North and centering it on the awakening love of the visiting Southern planter for the New England village maiden, she could first depict the abolitionist in terms of humorous and derisive caricature familiar to many of his Yankee brethren.[4] Then, turning southward in the second, and focusing mainly on a dark melodrama of abolitionist-incited slave insurrection, through a portraiture menacingly familiar in her adopted region, she could show the same figure in the colors of present, palpable evil.[5]

In all cases, Hentz's chief advantage lay in her possession of the novelistic wherewithal to hit readers where they lived politically by drawing them into those familiar precincts literarily. To borrow another current phrase, especially in the first volume—centered on the quest of the gallant Southern planter and wealthy slaveowner Moreland to win the love of the New England maiden Eulalia Hastings, daughter of the village abolitionist—one is tempted to call the book something of a stealth anti-Tom. To be sure, there has been a prefatory appeal to Northern countrymen to forego their anti-Southern prejudices and their automatic tendency to believe the worst of any member of the slaveowning class. All she asks, says the author, as in the book that follows, is that they too may seize "the abundant opportunities we have had of judging" and thereby arrive comparably at their own "honest belief, that the negroes of the South"—presumably by implication with their own wretched masses of wage slaves—"are the happiest laboring class on the face of the globe" (1: v–vi).[6]

Accordingly, although the bucolic environs of a New England village to which the Southern agriculturalist Moreland has retired after doing business with "the merchant princes of Boston" (1: 13) may seem a world away from the plantation, they quickly prove fertile ground for a dramatized rendering of North-South agon precisely in terms of the labor issues so conceived. Moreland, for instance, has brought along his adoring, handsome, articulate mulatto servant, Albert, albeit against the advice of friends who fear the latter's "superior intelligence and cultivation" as traits making him uncommonly "accessible to the arguments which would probably be brought forth to lure him from his allegiance" (1: 15). To their warnings, Moreland has responded at the time, "I defy all the eloquence of the North to induce Albert to leave me"; and he has quickly found the sentiment eagerly seconded by the servant himself. This has done nothing, of course, once the two have arrived at the New England village tavern where they are to be lodged, to prevent an almost immediate run-in with local idlers who insist on Albert's being served as an equal of his master. The event is then crowned by some particularly ugly anti-Southern speechifying on the part of the dour, self-righteous innkeeper, Mr. Grimby. Fortunately, a walk abroad with one of the more reasonable members of the company provides Moreland the occasion for more enlightened discussion of basic sectional issues. But at the same time, it also ensues in Moreland's charitable assistance homeward of a young woman, Nancy Brown, an obviously sickly and worn-out member of the local working poor just dismissed from her job—dismissed, as it happens, and summarily cast out of doors by the same taverner who has so vociferously insisted on his abolitionist passion for human equality. This, naturally, allows for reflections on the "contrast . . . between the Northern and Southern laborer, when reduced to a state of sickness and dependence" (1: 27), and how stark indeed must be the sufferings of "the thousand toiling operatives of the Northern manufactories" (1: 28) when measured against the happier prospect of "the sick and dying negro, retained under his master's roof, kindly nursed and ministered unto, with no sad, anxious lookings forward into the morrow for the supply of nature's wants" (1: 27).

At the same time, artfully induced touches of more general romantic plot intrigue begin to make irresistible claims on readerly attention. Or, to put this in an appropriate agricultural metaphor, if the New England of the opening chapters is for our hero a hostile political landscape, Hentz ensures that it is also made ripe ground for a love story. Moreland, we increasingly infer, is a mystery man. Although an obviously virtuous individual, he is also a character with a past, someone looking for something, someone who has suffered for love, who carries "a widowhood of the heart" (1: 36). Apace, there also come first hints at the promise of solace. During attendance at services in the local church, the handsome visitor attends to the radiantly apparitional introduction of Eulalia, angelic of both voice and feature, "the Flower," as she is called, "of the village"

(1: 39). Further, he is undaunted by information that her father is the local abolitionist crackbrain, investing his hobbyhorse passion for the subject on lecture tours and editorship of a polemical newspaper, *The Emancipator*. Instead, he immediately asks, laying the troubled path of true love directly before him, "You think, then, he would not allow his daughter to marry a Southerner?" (1: 40).

With the central terms of romantic conflict thus clearly set in place, a first actual meeting between hero and heroine is shortly facilitated by Moreland's solicitous visit to the cottage of Nancy Brown and her aged mother. For there, of course, he also finds Eulalia present, herself an indefatigable benefactress of the village poor. Conversation ensues, predictably on sectional themes, with Moreland once again defending the views of his native South with polite firmness; and by the end of the chapter we witness their second meeting, with Moreland introduced into the Hastings household as a result of seeing Eulalia home, and the romantic plot has been fully joined.

From this juncture, the love story becomes pure vintage Hentz. The characteristic male suitor, Moreland proves passionate, assertive, imperious, tempestuously manly in the fullest nineteenth-century sense of that term, but also magnanimous and thoroughgoingly noble.[7] Eulalia, likewise, proves the characteristic Hentz heroine—chaste, pious, fine-minded, charitable, but also possessed of independence, intellectual discrimination, and an invariably strong streak of resolution. Meanwhile, the course of true love also proves characteristically dire and wrenching, in this case running to nearly a hundred roiling, tear-stained pages that culminate, unbelievably, in the near-deaths from fevers— presumably induced as the result of romantic despair—of both principals. Fortunately, both make miraculous recoveries; and, given the depth and fidelity of their love, assent is quickly gained for their marriage. To be sure, we have more cameo appearances by the faithful valet, alternately bemused and aghast at Yankee attempts to cleave him from his beloved master. Endless dialogue likewise ensues on various sectional matters between the Southern suitor and the blustering abolitionist father, best described as a kind of Garrisonian Quixote, who along the way also manages to pry out the information that Moreland is divorced (1: 97). On the other hand, the focal love plot increasingly tends to subsume everything within its emotional magnetism, with cultural politics backgrounded for the moment into a kind of early American North-South version of Montague-Capulet. Accordingly, our reward in the last 120 pages of the first volume, after a journey southward, concentrates on the happy establishment of Eulalia as mistress and cynosure of the Moreland domestic establishment, complete with the faithful slave cast, the froward daughter of the previous marriage, and the adored sister and clever but sickly brother-in-law.

To be sure, with the geographical movement, especially, the distinctly

Southern anti-Tom quality of the text becomes decidedly more pronounced. Aboard a riverboat while journeying southward, for instance, Moreland courageously rescues from drowning a huge, muscular Negro. While he is being revived, Eulalia recognizes him as Nat the Giant, an impostor once taken into the Hastings household by her gullible father and later revealed by Moreland's researches to have been in flight after the attempted murder of his master. And shortly, as a consequence of Albert's faithful attendance upon his master while still in free territory, the couple is forced to endure more bouts of abolitionist speechifying on the part of a shipboard reformer.

Further, as to specific character parallels, upon the early scenes of arrival in the South, the novel for the first time seems to take on a distinct sense of mirror-image correspondence with Stowe's text in particular. Among the slaves, for instance, the doting Aunt Kizzie, although later to be succeeded at the Moreland plantation proper by the even more grandly matriarchal Dilsey, is an obvious Aunt Chloe prototype. Crissy, the restive house servant of Moreland's sister Ildegerte and her dying husband, Richard Laurens, likewise strongly calls up the image of Stowe's Eliza.

Albert, once returned to the South, in his household airs and amours suddenly proves more than reminiscent of Augustine St. Clair's foppish mulatto valet Adolph. And the spirit of St. Clair himself—albeit, as Rhoda Coleman Ellison remarks, with a far more worthy species of appropriately manly "condescension"[8]—is suggested in Moreland's relations with Claudia, his spoiled, selfish, willful ex-wife, and Effie, his beloved daughter. In the same connection, Eulalia herself provides an obviously welcome evolution of Stowe's Ophelia, the transplanted Northerner, in this case instantly loving and beloved of white and black alike. At the same time, in an especially tricky turn, Effie, the frequently moody and ungovernable stepdaughter, seems cast here in the Topsy role.

It is especially at this point, however, in the Ildegerte–Richard Laurens subplot that the *Uncle Tom* plot *and* character parallels become most unavoidably announced at least for the moment; and they do so, moreover, in a daring invasion of Stowe's own well-publicized autobiographical turf—as it turns out, at least briefly shared by the two authors—that could have hardly gone unnoticed. For the two, it turns out, have traveled to Cincinnati, where, in a last hope of cure, they intend to seek the medical wisdom of Richard's beloved schoolmate, the skilled Dr. Darley.[9] And it is there, at the hotel where they are lodged, that their faithful servant Crissy falls under the sway of Mr. and Mrs. Softly, two wheedling, solicitous antislavery agitators by whom she is persuaded to escape Eliza-like into the free territory just across the river. This she does, of course, opening up the plot terrain of what is obviously meant to be a correlative to Stowe's charitable depictions of border-state activity in support of fugitive slaves. And eventually, the parallel will result in a rewarding depiction of the return of the penitent runaway, whose happiness in "freedom" will have proven predictably short-lived after her alleged benefactors—in contrast to Stowe's saintly Quakers, iron-willed matrons, and other backwoods stalwarts—have quickly re-enslaved her to their own political and economic ends. Even at the moment, however, the instigation of her faithless act alone seems tragedy enough. For her alleged rescuers have literally seduced her into violation of a trust precisely in her mistress's moment of greatest heartbreak. Ildegerte, rising from her vigil at a husband's deathbed, seeks the sympathy of her faithful bond-woman companion. Instead, she finds herself abandoned in the first moments of widowhood.

All these new developments notwithstanding, it is only in the second volume, once the Morelands have arrived at the plantation proper, that the novel truly seems to start earning its anti-Tom appellation with interest. Indeed, upon their arrival, fictional refutation of Stowe's portrait of planter-servant relationship seems to become the primary order of the day. Upon arrival, the slaves gather about their master in adoration. To his wife, he seems "more like a father welcomed by his children than a king greeted by his subjects." The narrator continues, "Eulalia thought she had never seen him look so handsome, so noble, so good" (2: 34).

Next, she is escorted to the cabin of Aunt Dilsey, "the most ancient and honored matron of the establishment" (2: 36), whose evocation of Stowe's plantation matriarch Chloe is ingeniously compounded by a shortly ensuing death scene in which she evinces vociferously and at considerable length a rapturous piety fully the equal in Stowe's book of the final passion of the dying Tom himself. Meanwhile, among the living, for new plot purposes soon to be revealed, Hentz has also supplied a more obvious correlative to Stowe's titular protagonist in the person of the pious but somewhat slow-witted slave preacher Uncle Paul.

On the other hand, equally intriguing elements of the romance plot continue their development apace. We meet for the first time the vain, willful Claudia, who comes to demand custody of the daughter Effie, and this appearance in turn allows the narrator to fill us in on the career of vain self-indulgence that has led to the divorce. Concurrently, in Cincinnati, we witness the return of the chastened Crissy from an abortive fling at freedom and the forgiveness she receives from Ildegerte.

Meanwhile, back at the plantation, the anti-abolitionist cast of the novel takes an explicitly Southern turn toward the sinister with the arrival of the unctuous Yankee preacher Brainard—from the outset a distinctly Legree-like figure in the impression he gives off of a sheer, protean, palpable evil. The latter purports to be an evangelizing divine bent on converting the souls of humble,

striving Africans; he is actually, of course, an abolitionist agitator, bent on in-
filtrating himself into the slave community in search of co-revolutionists. And
thereby Hentz introduces, to extend the earlier stealth metaphor, the plot
equivalent of the smart missile designed to strike directly at the deepest nightmare fears of the Southern imagination: the chilling specter—in absolute con-
tradistinction to Stowe's insistence on the final triumph of right through the
absolute power of Christian love—of abolitionist-organized and -instigated
slave insurrection in which whites will be literally butchered in their beds.

Nor, should it be added, is Hentz merely content to leave us with just an impression. We are made privy, for instance, to the deepest bloodthirsty thoughts
of the miscreant Brainard, a shape-shifting criminal personality having enjoyed
a career of evil genius, we are further informed, extending backward to the earliest days of his youth; we also witness by night, at the plantation forge of the
blacksmith Vulcan, the corrupted slave ringleader, the fashioning of crude, bru-
tal weapons of bloody execution; and, as the crisis approaches its culmination,
in a local jail, we overhear, along with the sharp-eared jailer's wife, the gleefully
sanguinary conversation of other slave plotters—captured, it turns out, during
a bank robbery intended to help finance what is clearly a great, general rising.
Fortunately, at the moment all hell is about to break loose, that good woman
proves astute and intrepid enough not only to beard the miscreants at their game
but also to manage an escape with the maximum amount of information.

In response, Moreland travels alone to the plantation where, in a characteristic display of manly resolve and eloquence, he singlehandedly puts an end
to the threat. As might be expected, the shifty Brainard has just made good
an escape, leaving Moreland to confront only the local ringleader Vulcan and
his halfhearted accomplice, the gullible slave preacher Uncle Paul, seduced by
Brainard's rhetoric, who now, presumably in "good" Uncle Tom fashion, pros-
trates himself at Moreland's feet, begging forgiveness and swearing everlasting
fealty. (In a nice extra touch, he then has to be restrained from killing his quon-
dam fellow conspirator, whom he has knocked unconscious with a blow to the
back of the head while the latter has struggled with Moreland to resist capture
[2: 209].)

Eventually, of course, Moreland also gets to show his manly mettle in personal confrontation with Brainard as well, whom he has trapped. The latter,
however, brandishing a concealed bowie knife, manages to get away, as does
Vulcan, we are shortly told, from the makeshift jail where he has been kept.

As these crucial events have progressed, various other strands of attendant
domestic plot develop and move toward resolution. There has been the sudden
disappearance of Effie, for instance, a suspiciously short time after the imperious Claudia's visit with Eulalia.[10] This mystery is unriddled by a summons of

Moreland to the bed of the dying ex-wife, who has of course been her own child's kidnapper. She begs Moreland's loving forgiveness, which is readily and manfully granted. Meanwhile, Moreland's sister Ildegerte has been rescued from the grief of early widowhood by a deepening friendship with her husband's old comrade and physician, Dr. Darley. And by novel's end, in a family visit, the story has come full circle with the return of the happy Morelands to the New England village where their romantic saga began.

Yet even here, back in the heart of the Yankee abolitionist bastion from which she has made bold to begin, Hentz has still reserved for her audience one last anti-Tom surprise; and, to the everlasting credit of her novelistic ingenuity, it is a rattlingly good one. For now, as it turns out, Moreland will still get one more chance at heroic face-off not only with his old nemesis Brainard but also with the treacherous Vulcan, with whom the preacher has again spliced acts, the former impersonating "Mr. Howard, a distinguished philanthropist" scheduled to give a village antislavery lecture, and the latter "a fugitive slave who would relate some of the most startling and thrilling incidents of the horrible system from which he had recently escaped" (2: 257). To be sure, when the announced evening arrives, Moreland is at pains to attend. He is also accompanied by Darley, who by chance happens to have traveled to the same place while attending Ildegerte on a pleasure trip. Together the planter and physician work a gorgeously complete and ignominious unmasking of the shabby pair. Vulcan, for his part, immediately repents and casts himself on Moreland's mercy, which is generously extended. But Brainard, on the other hand, tries to brazen it out with the customary diabolical ingenuity. Fortunately, however, this time Darley is on the scene also to recognize him as "Hiram Cootes," a notorious Cincinnati forger; and this discovery is further tallied with the villain's simultaneous identification by an audience member as "Ichabod Jenkins"—the latter being the youthful appellation under which he had begun his nefarious career of crime (2: 269–71).

Bringing the novel and its political message directly back home in the most literal fashion, Hentz thus concocts a laughably delicious denouement. Before his adoring brethren, the latest star on the abolitionist lecture circuit is revealed to be a notoriously chameleonic career charlatan; and—to the delight, no doubt, of skeptics North *and* South—so the customary platform companion, the heroic slave, escaped to retail the usual litany of horrors, is unmasked in the role of medicine-show accomplice.

The usually undemonstrative Darley, by temperament a man of science, and by virtue of his cosmopolitan medical career conversant at one time or another with life in all the regions of America, seizes upon the moment to deliver an impassioned, ad hoc two-hour oration on national unity. Accordingly, among the auditors most affected is the deeply chastened Mr. Hastings. From that day onward, he seems no longer to care to ride his former hobbyhorse; nor, it is important to note, does he attempt to mount any other. Rather, his is now a more general spirit of passionate justice, in which he frequently speaks out "with great bitterness against one-sided and prejudiced people" (2: 277). Moreover, during a subsequent visit to the plantation of his beloved daughter and admired son-in-law, the once laughable chauvinist know-it-all is also seen taking copious notes in "a memorandum-book" to serve "as materials for a new course of lectures, with which he intended to illuminate the prejudices of the Northern people" (2: 280).

To be sure, the author concludes, there are others who will remain, unlike Mr. Hastings, unconverted, alleging that the pages just completed "give false and exaggerated views of Southern life" (2: 280). To these, she says, as one who likewise has seen life North and South, she can only offer earnest testimony of her own abundant love of each of the regions, and the hope that they may equally avert the horrific consequences, "should the burning lava of anarchy and servile war roll over the plains of the South," that would surely accrue to both. "The North and the South are branches of the same parent tree," she reminds us in closing, "and the lightning bolt that shivers the one, must scorch and wither the other" (2: 281).

Thus Hentz concludes her anti-abolitionist double feature, at once playing out the vein of comic geniality adopted to attract Northern audiences and striking a final tone of apocalyptic admonition equally devised to elicit the cheers of her own adoptive Southern compatriots. And thus the novelist, one might further claim, capitalizing precisely on the gendered capacities of her form, finds it possible to dispense in both directions certain literary gratifications of moral closure unavailable in more strictly political, and by definition male, forms of discourse. To the North, on one hand, domestic comedy has cast the abolitionist in a variety of humorous caricatures—the canting hypocrite, the quixotic ideologue, the platform charlatan. To the South, on the other, sentimental melodrama has allowed for development of the figure into the lurid colors of a truly satanic villainy. In both cases, popular emotion over sectional issues has been able to invade areas of debate that more rational forms of argument must eschew. The Northerner may confirm what a vast majority of his compatriots actually feel to be so but cannot say for fear of being soft on slavery: that the preening, self-righteous, abolitionist fanatic is a laughable cultural aberration, at best a fool and at worst a poltroon. Correspondingly, the Southerner, having seen dramatized the prospect of abolitionist-inspired slave violence, has been allowed to address in complex imaginative projection an equally pervasive sectional belief that, were it expressed aloud, would subject the speaker to accusations of being unnecessarily inflammatory or of succumbing to a bad case of cultural nerves.[11] To put this simply, she returns Stowe's favor by doing it herself as only a novelist could do it: through forms of fiction unavailable to male participants in formal political debate on sectional issues, to have a voice in the debate by being able to say what formal political discourse must leave unsaid.[12]

Traditional criticism has thus been essentially correct in the autobiographical inference invited by Hentz's title: that the success of *The Planter's Northern Bride* among the anti-Toms of the 1850s lies as a thematic consequence of the author's ability to structure her novel as a kind of North-South dialogue along the lines of a unique trans-sectional perspective acquired of her unique and extended experience, as an educator and literary intellectual, of American life and culture North and South. To be sure, Hentz herself was obviously not a planter's Northern bride. But, for her literary purposes, she was probably something even better—the Northern bride and full working partner of a cosmopolitan critical intellectual and traveling educator in the traditional mold, the missionary of classic philological learning, undertaking his labors initially in the North, and then eventually called to a series of outposts across the South. Accordingly, that extended opportunity to experience the domestic and intellectual politics of both regions empowered Hentz the novelistic observer and recorder as one of the few members of the antebellum American literary-cultural intelligentsia with unique trans-sectional credentials.[13] Deeply acquainted with Northern ways, and brought up on the clichés and commonplaces of anti-Southern bias, as a cultural cosmopolitan she could claim, as she often did, both an abiding affection for her native region and a unique ability to see through native prejudice. Accordingly, in the text at hand, Hentz genuinely does seem to have meant what she said in an early paragraph of her introduction by averring, as had been "said in the preface of a former work, that we were born at the North, and though destiny has removed us far from our native scenes, we cherish for them a sacred regard, and undying attachment" (iii). Her novel certainly bears this out in the depiction of her "good" Northerners, and especially her spotless heroine, who shines in both precincts. At the same time, as a literary intellectual and an educator ministering to the offspring of the South's planter, merchant, and professional classes, she had also now spent the better part of her adult life viewing the work of Northern antislavery activism through the mythic imagination of her adopted region's social and political elites. And as a novelist considerably skilled and experienced in manipulating popular-culture conventions of the comic and melodramatic, she was thus uniquely qualified to capitalize on the pairing of the figure of the antislavery fanatic so frequently the subject of political derision in the North with its precise demonological correlative in the Southern image of the abolitionist as slave insurrectionist. Hence, it was probably with equal sincerity of literary conviction that she spoke in the sentence directly following of her hope that the distinguishing feature of the novel at hand would be readily recognized as its attempt, from the outset, not so much to exploit "hostility or prejudice" as to defuse them within a larger figure of consensus; or, as she phrased it, "to represent the unhappy consequences of that intolerant and fanatical spirit, whose fatal influence we so deeply deplore" (iv).

The "we" is telling. For it is, after all, she goes on, quickly extending narratorial privilege into the political plural, the "*national* honour" that becomes at issue "when a portion of our country is held up to public disgrace and foreign insult, by those, too, whom every feeling of patriotism should lead to defend it and shield it from dishonour" (iv). That is, even at this late date, she tries to tell us, and on this dreadfully complicated and divisive matter, here at least, while controversy follows controversy, and compromise follows compromise; while politicians pontificate and polemicists threaten and bluster—here at least is something a community of sensible readers North and South can agree on: that in the long, ongoing, arduous search for national conciliation, the work of the abolitionist fanatic does absolutely no one any good anywhere. And so, by reading her novel, she proposes, fellow citizens will find this demonstrated.

Let the compromises and controversies come and go, she seems to say, and let the politicians pontificate and the polemicists threaten and bluster. Thus far, North and South, the nation seems to have survived it all, save for that single radical constituency persisting in the attempt to turn sectional controversy into open sectional strife. Accordingly, she goes on, as a national readership, affirming relationships of good sense and goodwill extending across sectional lines, let us now devote our candid attention here to a close, realistic representation of the disruptive and dangerous work actually being carried out in everyday people's lives North and South by that pernicious handful, intent on undoing all civil discourse and polity, who ought to be actively despised by right-thinking persons in both regions.

And so, in fact, by the novel's end, that image of consensus in the readerly imagination has been structurally worked out in a novelistic interplay of carefully paired popular-culture melodramas, first set out against each other in opposing relief and then themselves reconciled at the end. From the New England inn, cottage, church, and parlor, Hentz works her way down to the Southern great house and plantation, and then back northward to one last scene of absurd denouement ingeniously staged on the hallowed Yankee platform of the lyceum hall. Apace, Hentz has thus novelistically delivered on the abstract political premise of her introduction, as the abolitionist fanatic has been revealed in all his protean shades from the satiric to the satanic. At the last, with his traveling fugitive slave accomplice thrown in for good measure, the true villain of

Hentz's anti-abolitionist double feature stands totally unmasked before us, the chameleonic fraud in all his criminal glory.

For literary historians, the career of Alabama's Augusta Jane Evans—or Augusta Jane Evans Wilson, as she eventually came to be known to a large post–Civil War readership nationwide—remains one of the longest and most remarkable, not to mention one of the most commercially successful and remunerative, enjoyed by any American woman novelist of the nineteenth century. Further, among the major works of that career, the early novel *Beulah* remains the touchstone of the author's unique combination of popular and literary appeal—of a synthesizing genius, it might be called, drawing on a mastery of the well-rehearsed conventions of a well-known genre of domestic fiction while frequently reshaping those same conventions to meet the demands of a new women's intellectualism.

Published by the New York firm Derby and Jackson on the eve of the Civil War, *Beulah* was not Evans's first book. That honor would go to a piece of precocious juvenilia, *Inez, a Tale of the Alamo,* allegedly written when the author was sixteen and presented to her father as an 1854 Christmas gift. Neither was it the book that established her as a major heroine of letters and won her the most friends in the Civil War–era South. That would be the 1864 *Macaria; or Altars of Sacrifice,* which brought her fame as a literary spokeswoman for the Southern military cause. Nor was *Beulah* finally her most famous or, perhaps more properly, her most notorious book. That would turn out to be her 1867 novel, *St. Elmo,* described by a literary chronicler early in this century as "the most praised, best abused novel ever written" (Fidler 128). Appearing in between the two, in 1859, *Beulah* was the Evans book that counted, however. As the last of Alabama's first books, selling twenty-two thousand copies in the first nine months and receiving major critical praise (Fox-Genovese xiv), it finally put a native author on the map as a national figure in ways that not even the book's ill-timed publication and the intervening years of war could obscure; and in the process, it introduced into traditional domestic realism a tone of overtly intellectual aspiration new to women's fiction in America. To put this into more explicit terms of definition and argument, *Beulah,* for all its tried-and-true literary reliance on the standard conventions of the novel of female initiation— albeit with its capitalization on the growing popularity of the subgenre called the "psychological" or "subjective" (Fox-Genovese xiv)—in addition flaunted itself quite explicitly in theme and form as an intensely philosophical book: something close, as would be all of the rest of her major fictions, to what we would call a novel of ideas.[14]

To be sure, it has become a commonplace of American literary study that women's fiction of the antebellum era—besides constituting a vigorous genre of native realism written largely by women about women's concerns and issues for women—supplied cultural empowerment as an important popular alternative medium of women's education. Thus, in novels by such major figures as Lydia Maria Child, Catherine Sedgwick, Susan Warner, Maria Cummins, and E. D. E. N. Southworth, we are rightly told, domestic fiction does truly attempt to provide—in the several senses implied by the term—an unauthorized literary version of the official curriculum foreclosed to women by the institutions of learning producing male doctors, ministers, lawyers, educators, and writers. On the other hand, as is equally well known *and* well documented, in the works of the same writers, the terms of such alternative education themselves continued to be carefully monitored and controlled through a kind of gender self-policing. Depictions of female literacy seldom extended beyond socially approved forms of reading and writing; evidence of political concern was generally limited to matters domestic and/or local; sexual decorums remained firmly in place; speculative activity of any sort kept itself firmly within the bounds of issues of conventional morality and orthodox religion.[15]

The secret of Evans's innovative genius in making domestic realism a vehicle for the novel of ideas lay in a single idea that must have come naturally to a young writer accused throughout her career of composing with an encyclopedia by her elbow.[16] And, starting most markedly with *Beulah*, that idea was to write a new, improved formula for the novel of female education as at once a genre and a curriculum, tracing the heroine's conventional progress in a male-dominated world—and thereby, of necessity, frequently affirming traditional social roles—while at the same time increasingly asserting a new relationship of intellectual equality. To put this in terms of conscious literary invention, Evans had basically discovered an ingenious and original way to make the practice of women's writing itself a curricular experiment. While ostensibly keeping with the basic concepts of fictional construction—conventions of genre, plot, character, action, theme (although even there, as will be seen, frequently pushing the curricular envelope)—at the level of the explicit discourse of cultural ideology, she also elected to avail herself boldly, as had male counterparts in American fiction ranging from Brockden Brown and Fenimore Cooper to Nathaniel Hawthorne and Herman Melville, of the discursive potentialities of fictional dialogue as a way of a continuous rewriting and expanding of the cultural curriculum implied by the very conventions of the nineteenth-century women's novel into the speculative realms of the moral, the aesthetic, the religious, the philosophical, even the metaphysical.[17] Or, to enlarge the educational figure, Evans sought to make domestic realism from the ground up an ongoing curricular conversation, perhaps beginning in the "alternative education" standard, and focused thereby within the dramatic situation of a given text through a rather conventional set of specific conditions of plot, character, and action, but finally also linking author and audience in a larger discourse of American and Anglo-European intellectual culture at large. Posited in its conventional sense, the theme remained that of much women's fiction: the attempt to affirm the values of Christian spirituality in an increasingly secularized age of cultural crisis; but here, developed in response to that theme of crisis, the account of resolution became along the way the extended confrontation of such spirituality with a culture's full textual apparatus of metaphysical critique.

Expanding the curriculum: for Evans, this came quickly to be embodied in the idea, basically—from the most obvious elements of genre convention on up to the most recondite matters of speculative metaphysics—of manipulating an assumed capacity on the reader's part between what might be called convention and prediction. Further, at all levels, the object of such manipulation was frequently to bring about a distinct and perhaps unsettling subversion of conventional expectations. An obvious example here would be the reaction of Beulah's male guardian and mentor, the intellectual physician Hartwell, to his dawning awareness of her philosophical propensities: he actively encourages them. On the other hand, at her most characteristic, even the most radical rupture in expectation could equally be trusted to ensue in Evans—to use the phrasing of an appropriately totalitarian political formula—in some ultimate rectification of conventional boundaries. To return to the aspect of the novel just described, for instance, as part of a rather conventional domestic resolution, in the end Beulah does, after all, find true religious affirmation. Evans has frequently been called in these respects ambivalent and self-contradictory, a writer who frequently subverts and retreats (Baym, *Women's Fiction* 278). In *Beulah,* especially, the operative term, according to Anne Goodwyn Jones (Fox-Genovese xix), has been suggested to be "capitulation." The tendency to push the envelope of female heroism is fully matched, Jones alleges (as in their own ways do Beverly Voloshin and G. S. Goshgarian), by the tendency to draw back at the last to resolve complications created as a result of female overreaching by a kind of Dickensian domestic fiat. Further, at the thematic levels of the social and moral as well as the philosophical and/or ideological, this remains an incontrovertible structural objection. In the domestic sphere, woman's destiny is love, marriage, and the reform of men.[18]

On the other hand, one might also come at this tendency in Evans from the domain of a nineteenth-century male analogue, likewise specializing in literary construction as a conservative critique of cultural ideology, who as frequently posits a radical challenge to social orthodoxies and then returns to an essentially conventional resolution; and that, of course, would be Fenimore Cooper. Here, it might be posited, gender roles play something of the equivalent of Cooper's racial theory of "gifts." As there are white gifts and red gifts, so there are women's gifts and men's gifts. Still, as with Cooper, so with Evans: in works of fiction ultimately leaving the races or the sexes in their social roles, there is still the interruptive envisioning of a world in which such limitations might be transcended.[19] In both cases, to put this more simply, between the positing of a challenge to a conventional standard and a fictive resolution achieving the reinstatement of a conventional standard, there is frequently created a large intervening space of alternative possibility that still very much matters. In the case of *Beulah* and its effect on a nineteenth-century audience, Fox-Genovese thus is surely on the mark in invoking a diary entry indicative of one Southern woman's finding Beulah's *struggle* in and of itself inspiring (xix).

In the present case, to be sure, for the antebellum reader versed in American women's fiction of the era, Evans was at pains at least initially to mask the boldness of the curricular experiment about to be attempted with a textbook exercise in convention and prediction. If anything, in the first few pages, she almost makes it seem too easy. By the end of the book's opening sentence alone, "the slanting rays" of a January sun have illuminated "the window panes of a large brick building, bearing on its front in golden letters the inscription 'Orphan Asylum.'" And within the long introductory paragraph so begun, we have been introduced to the customary juvenile *dramatis personae*. The first figure we see is "a slight fairy form, 'a wee winsome thing,' with coral lips, and large, soft blue eyes, set in a frame of short, clustering golden curls," easily recognized, as the narrator shortly tells us, as "the pet of the Asylum" (5). The second, "but a few months older" than the other, "was one whose marvelous beauty riveted the gaze of all those who chanced to see her," with "the brilliant black eyes, the peculiar curve of the dimpled mouth, and long, dark ringlets," endowing "the oval face" with "a maturer and more piquant loveliness" (6). And then, finally, and most decisively, there is also a third, the narrator tells us, "a girl whose age could not have been accurately guessed from her countenance, and whose features contrasted strangely with those of her companions." Indeed, she continues, "at a first casual glance, one thought her rather homely, nay, decidedly ugly; yet to the curious physiognomist, this face presented greater attractions than either of the others" (6). It is, of course, our heroine, as the narrator tells us immediately, further essaying in great detail "the portrait of that quiet little figure whose history is contained in the following pages" (6). She goes on, first describing the visage:

A pair of large gray eyes set beneath an overhanging forehead, a boldly-projecting forehead, broad and smooth; a rather large but finely cut mouth, an irreproachable nose, of the order furthest removed from aquiline, and heavy black eyebrows, which, instead of arching, stretched straight across and nearly met. There was not a vestige of color in her cheeks; face, neck, and hands wore a sickly pallor, and a mass of rippling, jetty hair, drawn smoothly over the temples, rendered this marble-like whiteness more apparent.

In turn, the physiognomy is recapitulated in simple expression and gesture:

> Unlike the younger children, Beulah was busily sewing upon what seemed the counterpart of their aprons; and the sad expression of the countenance, the lips firmly compressed, as if to prevent the utterance of complaint showed that she had become acquainted with cares and sorrows of which they were yet happily ignorant. Her eyes were bent down in her work, and the long, black lashes nearly touched her cold cheeks. (6)

Thus, by now, the reader is persuaded that *Beulah* will be, in fact, not only a certain kind of novel, but also a certain kind of novel already operating in certain kinds of predictable ways. Indeed, having now taken in the scene of the orphanage and the assembled little women, we have already had a number of important fictive choices made for us. Of the two basic choices of female protagonist, for instance, the fallen heiress or the waif ascendant, we have in all likelihood gotten the waif. Anticipating an early glimpse of the extraordinary beauty undone by her charms and the homely intellectual, we get the intellectual. Indeed, in the present case, if the standard of physical attractiveness is to be relied upon, the potential for intellectual development seems likely to be limitless. By her own accounting and that of nearly every other observer in the early portions of the text, the operative term is "ugly."

Shortly, the customary complications begin. The heroine suffers parting from both her angelic sibling, Lilly, and the ravishingly beautiful third member of the orphan sisterhood, Claudia, to whom she is also deeply attached. They are adopted into a wealthy household. She is put out to another as a nurse for a sickly infant. Moral solace is provided by the kindly matron and a noble-souled youth, a fellow orphan, complete, in this case, with a gift volume of Longfellow marked at the pages for "A Psalm of Life." In the ensuing weeks, an epidemic of fever strikes the city. The beloved Lilly is among the victims, with her sister prevented by the child's cruel guardians from a last visit. Claudia too lingers near the brink of death but recovers, as does Beulah's desperately ill charge, the infant Johnny, whom she nurses back to health.

Thus are established, according to the standard conventions of genre, the requisite circumstances—and measured here, as elsewhere, by the cruel spiritual height of the hurdles erected—for the proper education of the heroine in pious forbearance. At the same time, however, certain messages of a decided impiety are already suggesting that this will be no ordinary heroine's progress. When Beulah is prevented from a final visit with her beloved dying sister, for instance, she quickly pronounces a healthy malediction on her tormentors. "A curse on that woman and her husband!" she expostulates. "May God answer their prayers as she has answered mine" (33). (To her horror, at a much later date, it will be fulfilled, albeit even then not eliciting total repentance.) More important as a sign of things to come, however, is a conversation the intellectually precocious thirteen-year-old engages in shortly with a young physician sent to minister to Johnny as the latter's illness reaches its crisis. "Sit down, girl!" he tells the exhausted Beulah, who has spent the night carrying the child and bathing his limbs to ward off fever and convulsions; "you will walk yourself into a shadow." With a shake of her head, she refuses, and again takes up "her measured tread." "What is your name?" he then asks, to which she replies, simply, "Beulah Benton." The conversation continues:

> "Beulah!" repeated the doctor, while a smile flitted over his moustached lip. She observed it, and exclaimed with bitter emphasis:
> "You need not tell me it is unsuitable; I know it; I feel it. Beulah! Beulah! Oh my father! I have neither sunshine nor flowers, nor hear the singing of birds, nor the voice of the turtle. You ought to have called me MARAH." (35)

The young physician pursues at once the biblical and the literary thread: "'You have read "The Pilgrim's Progress" then?' said he, with a searching glance" (36). But by now, Beulah has subsided into a despairing silence.

The mysterious, skeptical physician with the searching glance and the commanding ways is, of course, Dr. Guy Hartwell, soon to become, according to the standard fictional model, Beulah's guardian and mentor. Further, the tone of relationship set by this conversation is likewise in keeping with convention. Hartwell, the archetypal restless, searching intellectual, the man of science and secular learning in a world of conventional piety, has found the perfect protégée to educate as a companion in his quest and, eventually, a wife; the heroine, chafing against the conventions of the same piety and fumbling with the fragments of an incomplete knowledge, has found the perfect master against whose stern rule she will test the limits of her own rebellion and measure the consoling satisfactions of return.[20]

Yet here, too, is exactly where convention ends. For in this case, the intellectual mentor will be actively complicit in launching his protégée on her own intellectual odyssey; and even by the standards of arduous conventional struggle prescribed by the genre, discipline and submission will accordingly be placed a long way off, across a vast minefield of invitations to the spiritual apostate. The central intellectual plot that has begun, initiated in the dialectical sparring of an opening conversational interchange, will shortly become a full-blown education in infidelity.

As if to suggest the unauthorized character of the intellectual odyssey in question, the settings of the opening scenes in what might be called the education of Beulah Benton carry distinct suggestions of sites of literary-philosophical overreaching made familiar in works by well-known male contemporaries. Hartwell's city dwelling, for instance, where he has installed Beulah as protégée and surrogate daughter, is visibly a Rappaccini-like palace and garden. But even there mostly, as in Poe's "Ligeia," with the figure of the passionate intellectual heroine herself explicitly invoked as one of the literary shades presiding over the heroine's progress, most of the significant action takes place in the library.

It is in that bookish precinct, with Hartwell as mentor and intellectual conversationalist cum interlocutor, that a tour is actively undertaken of the major texts of eighteenth- and nineteenth-century transcendentalist metaphysics—with frequent stops along the way as well at the major documents of skepticism. But preferred above all texts are surely those of the great romantic ironists,[21] with their vision of the artist as the creating god of his own universe—Coleridge, Carlyle, Emerson; and then, at the crisis, that darkest and most harrowed American representative of their number, Edgar Poe. Appropriately, given the fictional situation at hand, favored texts include "William Wilson," "Morella," and "Ligeia"; but even more importantly, the literary-philosophical figure invoked is also the Poe of the greatest and most tortured and enigmatic of all American texts of the metaphysics of romantic irony, *Eureka*. "You must not play with such sharp tools just yet," Hartwell admonishes when he finds her reading it. "Go and practice your music lesson." But it is too late for her to be put off from the "methodical madman" whose "philosophy"—in this case the beckoning black hole of metaphysical mystery—becomes "the portal through which she entered the vast Pantheon of Speculation" (121). Shortly, it is on to De Quincy's *Analects from Richter* and then back to the luminous Jean Paul himself; and then it is back and forth through the names, as observed by Fidler, "Emerson, Carlyle, Goethe, Theodore Parker," compounded and re-compounded in turn by "more of Richter, Feuerbach, Kant, and Coleridge" (61); Tennyson's *Palace of Art*; then "Locke, Descartes, Cousin, Sidney Smith, Hume, William Hamilton, Spinoza, and the commentaries upon their works" (62–63).[22] Eventually comes Hamilton's *Philosophy of the Conditioned*, in this case supplied to her by a suitor, the cultivated and intellectual Reginald Lindsay, attracted to her by his reading of essays she has contributed to a prominent intellectual journal (359), and laudably determined to cure her of her grand tour of dangerous books and authors by not scrupling to treat her as anything less than his full intellectual equal. They argue aesthetics. She pronounces her nearest model to be Cousin. He seizes the philosophical opening. "Once admit his theory of the beautiful," he challenges, "and you cannot reject his psychology and ethics; nay, his theodicia?" (355). "Pantheism," he asserts, is surely the object. "No; his whole psychology is opposed to pantheism!" she responds, "pushing aside her drawing materials, and meeting his eyes fixedly" (356). And so, the argument continues. As "Cousin's pet doctrine of the 'Spontaneous Apperception of Absolute Truths' clearly renders man a modification of God," so its results must be "very nearly allied to those of Schelling's 'Intellectual Intuition,'" Lindsay continues; "yet I suppose you would shrink from the 'absolute identity' of the latter?" No, she replies with steadiness. "You have not stated the question fairly, sir. He reiterates that the absolute belongs to us. We perceive truth, but do not create it!" (356).

And so throughout the text, the dense philosophical argumentation and disquisition pass back and forth among a host of skilled intellectual conversationalists, male *and* female, in an imposing array of pairings and sites of interchange. *And virtually never is a figure invoked for the sake of mere name-dropping.* Rather, each is a topic of serious, if not nearly interminable, discussion. With the brilliant, skeptical Cornelia—like Beulah, a female figure fully the equal of such imposing male intellects in the novel as Hartwell, Lindsay, or the venerable freethinker Dr. Asbury—a searching critique is undertaken of Emerson. Does Beulah "accept his 'compensation,'" Cornelia challenges. "Are you prepared to receive his deistic system?" Beulah responds, "Why strive to cloak the truth? I should not term his fragmentary system 'deistic.' He knows not what he believes. There are singular antagonisms existing among his pet theories" (228). If anything, after long study, she goes on, she has sadly determined "that of all Pyrrhonists, he is the prince" (229), backing up her assertion by quoting a representative maxim. Cornelia contests it as spurious. Beulah quickly identifies it from memory as a passage in "Circles." Accordingly, she concludes, she must continue to search elsewhere for spiritual guidance, in need of "something more than an immutability, or continued existence hereafter, in the form of an abstract idea of truth, justice, love or humility" (230).

Similarly, even with the more pious and conventional Clara, Beulah does not scruple to tease out dangerous speculations on art and madness, spinning her reflections over "the frantic madness of Lamb, or the final imbecility of Southey, . . . the morbid melancholy of Cowper, the bitter misanthropy of Poe, the abnormal moodiness and misery of Byron, the unsound and dangerous theories of Shelley, and the strange, fragmentary nature of Coleridge" (177). "Oh, Beulah, I don't know what will become of you!" calls out the sturdily resistant Clara, keeping up her end of the argument at length but at last succumbing to sisterly tears. "Do not be at all uneasy, my dear, dove-eyed Clara," Beulah responds. "I can take care of myself" (181).

And so she does, in full embrace of what she increasingly finds to be her own creative potentialities as romantic ironist, achieving identity precisely as she *becomes* the heroine of speculation. Pushing, probing, ceaselessly exploring, Beulah makes her own journey through philosophy, the working of a frequently cheerless and forbidding way toward the limits of metaphysics through the endless elucidations of texts, authors, and philosophical positions. The result is a text of astonishing intellectual density, frequently proving itself an essayistic tour de force of comparison, contrast, parallel analysis, and dialectical critique; and accordingly, by page and paragraph count alone, Evans has frequently been criticized for this, even lampooned. On the other hand, once more if one makes reference to nineteenth-century male analogy, this seems a queer prejudice. Cooper, again, certainly does much the same thing on virtually any subject of cultural import—political, philosophical, religious—whenever the opportunity presents itself. And once launched in high metaphysical winds, Melville frequently does nothing besides. If anything, by almost exact analogy with a male contemporary in a comparably fictional situation, Evans certainly proves more bold in this respect than the reticent Hawthorne, where with Hester Prynne, for instance, he must leave the ideological content of her feminist speculation unsaid, or with Kenyon, the male protagonist of *The Marble Faun,* who finds his flirtations with infidelity quickly swatted down by the pious riposte of his beloved Hilda.

In a larger sphere, one might also cite the examples of contemporaries as diverse as Flaubert, Dostoyevsky, or George Eliot, all using fictional dialogue as the central way of advancing the novel of ideas. One suspects the real prejudice against Evans in this respect, given that the most active and visible period of her career would take place in the decades after 1865, would derive from the new orthodoxies of late-nineteenth-century realism—with its bias against abstract ideation, its preference for showing versus telling.[23] Even here, Evans acquits herself creditably as a writer of realistic dialogue. Much of the intellectual argument of the novel is ably advanced through conversation as a Socratic medium and personal reflection in the form of interiorized self-debate. Further, one can only admire the degree to which the process of speculative inquiry so devised is completely, patiently, even exhaustively carried out to its argumentative conclusion. If metaphysics in this novel is ultimately found wanting, and insufficient as a substitute for faith, it is because we have truly worked through to the end of metaphysics. And whatever the conclusion, one might propose that the drama-tized possibility of an independent woman's making such an intellectual jour-ney itself may have provided many a nineteenth-century female reader of an analogous philosophical bent with a thrill of proud identification.

Meanwhile, as if to further the identification of her heroine with an intel-lectual readership in a properly literary sphere, Evans had also in the process undertaken a massive gloss on a host of obvious, major literary analogues, in both men's and women's writing, at home and abroad. Overarching by direct reference, for example, are such standard religious and philosophical texts as the Bible and *The Pilgrim's Progress*, *The Rime of the Ancient Mariner* and *Sartor Resartus*. In the women's sphere, a complex set of bold relations is also estab-lished with Brontë's *Jane Eyre*.[24] But again, most of all, on this side of the Atlan-tic one must cite Poe. Often, as that story hovers over the text, Beulah *is* Ligeia, refusing to be Rowena.

As importantly, one also recognizes the direct influence of such important American women's texts as *The Wide, Wide World* and *The Lamplighter*, in which a young girl—frequently taken on as a ward—is adopted by a forceful, passionate, intellectual older man and educated for a wife. Yet even here, the crisis and the departure is in fact in two stages, each more unconventional than the one before: in a first proscribed role, Beulah aspires to live independently as a teacher, thereby recapitulating as a professional educator the pursuit of intel-lectual development—growth of mind, the romantics would have called it—that has been encouraged but also monitored in her by Hartwell in the patriar-chal role of mentor and guardian; and it is only later, once she has boldly sustained herself in this resolution at major financial and emotional cost, that she turns to yet a new, and even more forbidden, career as a writer of intellectual prose. Yet here, in either case, the focal issue of struggle is less vocational than it is in the fullest sense philosophical and spiritual. The issue, to put it simply, is will itself.[25]

In all these respects—and others—Evans persistently proves a jolting ir-regularity, a strange, brilliant, and unsettlingly seditious ride. The faithful or-phan boy, for instance, Eugene Graham, who serves as an early mentor and lov-ing "brother," is predictably sent abroad by his adoptive family for an education. According to the genre, he should eventually return, morally and intellectually ennobled by the experience, to find his boyhood filial affection transformed into mature romantic love. Here he comes back a sordid businessman and a drunkard. According to the genre, along the way his love for the heroine should also have triumphed over the attractions of a rich, beautiful, selfish, and flirta-tious competitor. Here he marries the dreadful person and, until reformed of his confusions late in the novel, lives in misery. By comparison, the novel's established flibbertigibbet, Hartwell's vain, spoiled niece Pauline, mends her ways early on, and only *then* has the fortune to marry a dour, tyrannical, Casaubon-like divine. Then there is the recurrent thread of Beulah's doubled dialogue with the two female alter egos, Clara and Cornelia. Clara, the voice of conventional piety, spiritual belief, domestic faith, would have been a pale spiritual exemplar in many works of the genre; here she is gamely employed as a worthy sounding board for Beulah's infidelities. Meanwhile, at the other extreme, the brilliant, doomed Cornelia Graham, Beulah's frequent companion and true soul mate on her intellectual odyssey, beckons her into the metaphysical black hole of her own irrepressible skepticism, the alternative curriculum of the novel that is more properly an anti-curriculum, even a devil's curriculum. While Beulah attempts to hold on to some slender faith in a theory of the soul, the sick, suffering, bitter Cornelia seeks only death. "If our past and present shadows the future," she complains, "I hope that my last sleep may be unbroken and eternal" (230). And shortly, she is actually seen to die the bitter death of a skeptic carrying her anguished infidelity to a cold, lonely grave.

To be sure, Beulah in the ensuing pages will arise from the depths of grief and solitude engendered by her own perilous questing and questioning to complete her own voyaging to the end of philosophy. And relief, finally, abetted by Lindsay's gift of Sir William Hamilton, finally descends as if in heavenly blessing. "Oh, philosophy!" she cries out: "thou hast mocked my hungry soul; thy gilded fruits have crumbled to ashes in my grasp. In lieu of the holy faith of my girlhood, thou hast given me but dim, doubtful conjecture, cold metaphysical abstractions, intangible shadows, that flit along my path, and lure me on to deeper morasses. Oh what is the shadow of death, in comparison with the starless night which has fallen upon me, even in the morning of my life! My God, save me! Give me light: of myself I can know nothing!" (371).

"Her proud soul was humbled," the narrator goes on, "and falling on her knees, for the first time in many months, a sobbing prayer went up to the throne of the living God; while the vast clockwork of stars looked in on a pale brow and lips, where heavy drops of moisture glistened" (371). Solace has finally arrived. So, conveniently, also does Hartwell shortly, after five years of Rochester-like Oriental wanderings, albeit unbowed and unrepentant. And now, he becomes her new spiritual project. This time he asks for her hand; and this time she as quickly assents, in confidence that God's will must be done. Fortunately, in this she has been supplied by a new female role model who becomes of increasing importance late in the book, the admired and gracious Mrs. Asbury, faithfully, lovingly, and, above all, *firmly* holding out for the conversion of her own household skeptic and infidel, Hartwell's venerable medical colleague.

In this sense, a new comitatus of great-spirited, loving, resolute women thus launch themselves into yet another dimension of spiritual quest, doing battle with philosophy, metaphysics, freethinking, skepticism, unbelief in their own households; apace, reversing institutional educational roles, they now become the new mentors and guides, with the confidence that philosophy will be found wanting demonstrated by a faithful and loving willingness to attend the questioner's voyaging to the end of philosophy. Near the end, Asbury bounds through the door to welcome his old ally in unbelief. "Oh Guy!" he exults. "You heathen! You Philistine! you prodigal." Meanwhile, we are told, "Beulah stole out quickly, and in the solitude of her own room, fell on her knees, and returned thanks to the God who hears and answers prayer" (415). And by the end of a short final chapter, we find her already launched in the new role as spiritual educator, with Hartwell her pupil. "Sir," she expostulates, "can you understand how matter creates mind?" The man of science falls silent. Meanwhile, "she had laid her Bible on his knee; her folded hands rested upon it, and her gray eyes, clear and earnest, looked up reverently into her husband's noble face." In response, "his soft hand wandered over her head, and he seemed pondering her words." Thus, the narrator concludes prayerfully, "may God aid the wife in her holy work of love" (420). And work it will be. Yet so have we been persuaded by Beulah's personal triumph in her own long, desperate, excruciating struggle with intellectual infidelity, that the new project of love cannot finally be unfulfilled.

Much has been said about *Beulah*'s philosophical attributes, as well as its literary relation to major American and English productions of the era. Scant attention, on the other hand, considering the focus of this book, has been given to its political status as regional literature. Here, one has been directed into such a course of cultural reading with good historical and literary reason. For, as was made evident by a reviewer in the *Southern Literary Messenger,* even at the time *Beulah* was instantly identified as one of the "modern" books not identifying itself by place or region. The city was Mobile, obviously. But more importantly here, it exists purposely as a nameless, urban, cosmopolitan center—a rich and culturally advanced seaport city situated on the Gulf. Mainly of interest are the upper classes, the men of professional and political standing, the social matriarchs, the young females who get their grand tours and their social seasons, the dissolute young bloods. Of the promising but orphaned, Beulah and Eugene are gathered into this estate; and a few others of interest to us—mainly attendant to various social and educational duties performed by the main characters—are assembled on the margins in genteel poverty. Aside from Eugene's ill-fated foray into business, or the occasional venture of a male figure to a distant plantation, we hear little of commercial life. We see nothing of the urban poor. And slaves, as observed by Elizabeth Fox-Genovese, who ought to know, simply appear "as necessary but unremarkable features of Southern society" (xiii).

Accordingly, Evans—although an ardent Southern patriot—seems to have been at pains, in this book at least, not to make her regionalism either in the part or the whole an explicit political component of her literary frame of reference. And so she continued to look outward as a writer from her native precincts from 1867 on, beginning with the legendary and notorious *St. Elmo,* when she carried her own boldly problematic concept of women's fiction into the new landscape of postwar realism. As a domestic novelist with a well-established national following, she survived the war and the ensuing realism-naturalism controversies, writing well into the next century. She also survived the parodists and the disparaging critics. And now, it turns out, she may even survive her latest set of champions attempting to rescue her from what are frequently seen as her feminist capitulations. For what Evans the realist, the modernist, and, yes, the feminist, had realized about the relationship between gender and intellectual discourse was that if men usually practiced science and metaphysics and women moral philosophy and religion, it was mainly because people had just been socialized to accept it; and that only in challenging the intellectual climate that underlay such socialization might come a new basis of discursive and ideological relationship. To be sure, Evans hadn't nearly gotten there; but by imagining any kind of intellectual conversation in which men and women could speak as equals, she had surely pointed the way.

9

Alabama's Last First Book

⁓

The Example of Daniel Hundley

In form and theme, not to mention chronology, one could hardly find more fit material for concluding a book on literature and cultural formation in early Alabama than in Alabamian Daniel Hundley's 1860 *Social Relations in Our Southern States*—itself a conflation of social analysis and imaginative myth speaking in strange, defiant coda and reprise on most of the cultural themes already discussed. Indeed, beyond its importance as a social document, the most salient feature of Hundley's text, from both a cultural and a literary standpoint, remains its curiously composite nature. On one hand it was an attempt to configure—and, for the most part, justify—the distinctive sociopolitical patterns of class and race (and to a minor degree gender) it saw as arising out of a world come in the brief space of five decades from the hubbub and bustle of the Old Southwest frontier to slave empire and political heart of a newly formed Confederacy; and on the other it was an endeavor to come to terms, at once in strident defense and tortured apologia, with an increasingly complex myth of Southern identity touching upon the deepest springs of the regional imagination. As a result, it seemed neither history nor literature—or rather, as noted by William J. Cooper and Fred Hobson, it could not help being something of both.[1]

Not surprisingly, the author of this deeply complicated and even divided book was himself a deeply complicated and even divided man. As Hobson suggests, this went even to Hundley's self-image as a native Alabamian, where one discerns frequently from his life and writings something of a wish that he had not been born there, with the place in the 1830s and 1840s still a precinct of frontier rapscallions and showy parvenus not sufficiently refined for "a patrician who believed one's highest calling was to be a gentleman" (63). Descended from Virginians, Hundley was the son of a practitioner of both medicine and law who had emigrated southward to become a landowner in the Tennessee Valley region of upper Alabama; then, in a kind of reverse migration, Hundley's education carried him to undergraduate studies at Bacon College in Kentucky, where he took an A. B. (1850), a year's additional work at the University of Virginia (1852), and finally an LL. B. from Harvard (1853). Subsequently, he combined marriage to a well-born first cousin from Virginia with a business career in Chicago managing his wealthy father-in-law's real estate interests. There in turn he combined his business pursuits with apprentice political writings on a variety of subjects: the dangers of American commercial expansion conducted at the moral expense of the national character; the "pharisaical" status of Northern denunciations of Southern slavery when compared with the human traffic in the British West Indies; the social consequences of unemployment among the urban poor.[2] Although regularly accompanying his family to spend winters in Alabama, he still thought of himself as a dedicated Unionist; and he returned to take up permanent residence in the state only in 1860 when he saw the election of Lincoln as having forced the South to secession as a last-ditch response.

There, on the eve of a political rupture deemed increasingly inevitable, he quickly wrote *Social Relations,* albeit with a timing that could not have been worse; and, as with everything else in this complex man, bad chronology was further compounded by an almost perversely maladroit conceptualizing of rhetorical occasion. For he wrote, he noted insistently, precisely as a result of his living for an extended period in the North, mainly for readers of that region, and especially for those too long exposed to writings of the "Uncle Tom school"— themselves largely the work of "Englishmen, Frenchmen, Down-Eastern men, the Bloomer style of men, as well as countless numbers of female scribblers"— ceaselessly attempting "to drum on the public tympanum (almost to deafness indeed) in praise or blame—generally the latter—of Southern peculiarities, social habits, manners, customs, observances, and domestic institutions."[3] And if, he averred, he elected to present himself as an enthusiastic defender of Southern life and institutions, surely long personal involvement in Northern affairs allowed him to claim a uniquely reasoned perspective on issues of comparative culture. In his education and his subsequent living arrangements he had, after all, evinced "a strong desire to come in contact with the Northern people, and Northern prejudices, on their own soil; to correct his own sectional prejudices, should these require correction" (19). And even as he wrote, such a desire for balanced vision was also buttressed, he was at pains to note, by "pecuniary interests in the North and South" standing roughly "equal" (20). On this basis, he said, he was thus happy to stake out a claim to "strict impartiality." The matter, he suggested, was largely one of perspective. "Indubitably, there is much in the Slave States to call forth either unqualified approbation, or equally unqualified denunciation; owing entirely to the nature of the individual's sympathies who so applauds or denounces." He went on: "We will even go a step further, and declare in all good conscience, that there is much in the South to call forth honest praise from honest men, as well as, much to grieve the spirit of the most rational and conservative of philanthropists. But we have yet to stumble on that community, free or slave, of which the same remark can not be made with equal truth and pointedness" (13). Further, even to the point of offending the sensibilities of his Southern compatriots, he vowed to stick to such unflinching objectivity. He understood the perils, he said: "although we do not deny that we entertain very warm sympathies for all classes of persons in the Slave States— not excepting those who are there held as property and sold as chattels—we are yet perfectly well aware, that many of them are in very bad odor with all honorable men, as they rightly deserve to be." Accordingly, he went on, "when, therefore, we come to speak of such, while we shall take care to set naught down in malice, we shall endeavor nevertheless to state the plain, unvarnished truth; even if, as the great English novelist has suggested, it may occasionally scratch" (20).

Thus Hundley opened his book, published by the New York firm of Henry B. Price, by digging himself both North and South into the rhetorical equivalent of political antigravity. On one hand, he wrote for a Northern audience already essentially deaf to any further argument for Southern values; and on the other, he courted the ire of a Southern constituency too defensive about those same values to admit to even the slightest opening of critical scrutiny.

That, to put it mildly, was a shame. For in the text proper, a clumsy rhetorician turned out to be writing some inspired cultural sociology, all beginning with a single notable premise: that a corrective was badly needed to the conventional and simple-minded notion that the South was a three-class composed of planters, poor whites, and slaves. Rather, Hundley argued, Southern society was divisible into at least eight classes, seven of them white and one black: "the Southern Gentleman, the Middle Classes, the Southern Yankee, Cotton Snobs, the Southern Yeoman, the Southern Bully, Poor White Trash," and "the Negro Slaves";[4] and any understanding of the region had to be seen in the complex and more than occasionally difficult patterns of relationship necessarily arising therefrom. Now, not only was this certainly a more sophisticated set of classifications than the one it proposed to correct; from a standpoint of sociological inquiry, it was also much more empirically precise, with many of Hundley's categories of enduring analytic value and interest to historians and interpreters of Southern culture. To this day, for instance, one reads in Hundley anticipations of Bertram Wyatt-Brown on Southern honor; of Frank Owsley, Clement Eaton, and Ritchie Watson on the yeomanry; of Grady McWhiney on the Cracker.[5] Hundley's image of the Cotton Snob—newly arrived on the scene of wealth and power, flashy, loud-mouthed, truculent—now conditions historical understanding of the new breed of sectionalist fire-eater taking control of state politics across the South on the eve of secession; the Southern Yankee, grasping, mean, callous, summons up the familiar image of the slave trader, the overseer, the cruel master, frequently of Northern origins, or at the very least a Southern simulacrum of the Northern breed, a fixture of popular-culture representation in a lineage extending from Stowe's Simon Legree and William Wells Brown's Reverend John Peck to Margaret Mitchell's Jonas Wilkerson; the Southern Bully finds the backwoods buffoon and ring-tailed roarer of the earlier frontier humorists metamorphosed into the courthouse idler and inmate of the village groggery; and the poor white anticipates the now familiar depictions of an Erskine Caldwell, a William Faulkner, a Flannery O'Connor, a Harper Lee. Even Hundley's compendious defense of the slave system would be remarked upon by Kenneth Stampp for its unusual candor regarding physical cruelties.

Still, in the part or in the whole, one does not have to read far in Hundley to feel the strains of a structural fiction frequently yielding itself up to ideological myth. The planter-aristocrat, for instance, quickly becomes a figure of impossible perfections, a cultural cynosure "motivated by gentility and warmth of spirit" and never permitting "financial gain or garish display to corrupt his values"; cherishing "education for education's sake" while holding "a deep respect for religion and family" and an "abiding concern for slaves" (Cooper xxx–xxxi); and above all, living "according to his own code" and never allowing himself "to become 'the SLAVE OF PUBLIC OPINION'" (63). Of "faultless pedigree" and "equally faultless physical development" (28, 29), he was invariably a hunter, a fisher, and an accomplished horseman. (And so on and on it went, as Fred Hobson astutely observes, for "Daniel Hundley, who himself loved the outdoors, loved hunting and fishing and riding, was descended from Virginians, was convinced of his fine bloodlines, was six feet, two inches tall, and handsome" [67].) He even came with a complete racial genealogy, descended in the Atlantic regions from English Cavaliers and the better class of French Huguenots, Anglo-Catholics, and Scotch Jacobites, and in the South and West from Spanish dons and French Catholics (27).

Likewise lavishly, if much more briefly, Huntley apostrophized the well-born Southern woman, "simple and unaffected in thy manners, pure in speech as thou art in soul" (72). Here, in all her quiet dignity, stood the goddess of patrician virtue, spiritualized, worshipful, modest, chaste.

All of this turns out to be, as they say, a tough act to follow. Accordingly, the middle classes next appearing in Hundley's scheme of social description, if worthy and useful, still seem decidedly lesser beings on both the social and spiritual scale. "As in all other civilized communities," in the South, Hundley enthuses, they "constitute the greater proportion of her citizens, and are likewise the most useful members of her society" (77). Among them can be numbered "farmers, planters, traders, storekeepers, artisans, mechanics, a few manufacturers, a goodly number of country school-teachers, and a host of half-fledged country lawyers and doctors, parsons and the like" (80). The women, accordingly, prove "modest and virtuous, chaste in speech and manners, . . . very industrious house-keepers, kind-hearted mistresses, and the most devoted of wives and mothers" (98). On the other hand, much is again made of breeding, with the middle classes tracing their status not as descendants of Cavaliers and Huguenots but of Scottish, Irish, and "sturdy English" (84). As a result, in countless respects, male and female alike, the middle classes seem mildly debased imitations of their aristocratic betters. The middle-class planter, for instance, lacks "the lithe, airy, and graceful carriage, that compactness and delicacy of muscle" for which the aristocrat is renowned, running instead from "the most diminutive and bandy-legged runt, to the coarse, large-featured, awkward, and bony seven-footer," but with most specimens "above medium size, with broad shoulders, and angular outline in general" (84). Likewise, household matrons of the breed "are not unfrequently quite simple and unsophisticated, easily gulled or deceived, knowing at best but little of the world and its manifest follies, and caring even less for its empty vanities and trumpery shows" (98).

But even more telling here is Hundley's direct structural progression out of his discussion of the middle class to various categories of Southerners indicted as rough social coequals: the Southern Yankee, the Cotton Snob, and the Southern Bully. The first, he notes, including in their number specimens ranging from the "model storekeeper" to the "miserly Negro trader" (139-40), enjoy the prosperity of a callous greed—noted as their unmistakably *Northern* trait—that "invariably boasts but one armorial motto, and that is, *vincit omnia AURUM*" (131). The other two cut more closely to the Southern bone. Cotton Snobs are the newly rich and vulgar, the image of the upwardly mobile, vaunting parvenu, while the Bully—"a swearing, tobacco-chewing, brandy drinking" wastrel "whose chief delight is to hang about the doors of village groggeries and tavern taprooms, to fight chicken cocks, to play Old Sledge, or pitch-and-toss, chuck-a-luck, and the like, as well as to encourage dog-fights, and occasionally to get up a little raw-head and bloody-bones affair on his own account" (223-24)—is as frequently a figure on the way down. In neither case, however, on the social or the economic scale, are they to be confused with bottom-line poor whites, "the descendants of paupers, convicts, and indentured servants from England" (71) for which the South served frequently as a convenient dumping ground during the colonial era; and still recognizable as lineal, inbred descendants in the image of their forebears as "lank, lean, angular, and bony, with flaming red, or flaxen, or sandy, or carroty-colored hair" (264). Accordingly, as economic creatures, these, he asserts, are almost sublimely unconcerned with material advancement: "Dollars and dimes," he says, "they never bother their brains any great deal about" (262).

Along the way—tellingly interpolated between Cotton Snobs and the Southern Bully—has also come a short chapter on another of the middle classes, the yeomanry, in this case distinct from their middle-class fellows mixing commercial occupation with farming and planting by their election for a life exclusively rural, where they serve as "the staple of southern agricultural society" (Cooper xxxvi). And once more, given his admiration of the landed planter class, Hundley finds much to praise. Distinguished by their "physical heartiness and dogged perseverance" (198), they are also, like their middle-class townsmen, "hospitable, civil, God fearing, independent of mind" (Cooper xxxvii). Yet at the same time, if they are seldom slaveowners in any large degree, it also remains among their fondest wishes to achieve such status in imitation of their landed betters (197–98).[6]

Still, as with the middle classes, one's chief impression of Hundley's chapter on the yeomanry is its cursoriness. They may be the salt of the earth and the foundation of the society, even to the notable point of being more politically well versed and engaged than their Northern counterparts (Cooper xxxviii); but Hundley finally seems just not really very interested in them, compared with figures eliciting more colorful emotional response, be that response undying adoration for the gentleman, or equally vivid scorn for the Southern Yankee, the Cotton Snob, the Bully, or the poor white.

Nor, really, albeit in the longest chapter in the text, does Hundley find much more passion or room to depart from conventional ideology in an extended, interminably orthodox concluding discourse on the Negro slave in which he proves for long stretches less interested in the scrutiny of his putative class of subjects than in assembling as much information as there is available to warrant depiction of Negro slavery at the institutional level in the South as a positive good, if not a part of sheer providential design. Facts and figures on church membership are adduced to show how thoroughly Africans brought out of the savagery and paganism of their native Africa had embraced the cleansing doctrines of Christianity (297). And corresponding sets of numbers emphasize the bounteous health of the slavery economy, with dollar values of exports from free states shown as being vastly outstripped by those to the South (298–99). "The finger of God," Hundley asserts, is surely to be found in "so marvellous a development" (299). Along the way, customary comparison is also made, of course, of the happy lot of Southern slaves, enjoying ample rewards of their master's love, with the North's "toiling poor" (61); and extensive notation is also made of the more heinous depredations visited by various contemporary European colonial powers on the dark races in Africa and elsewhere.

And it is only in such elaborately developed institutional contexts that Hundley at last turns his attention to the actual lives of slaves in the plantation economy, their folkways, their domestic arrangements, their seasonal festivities, their songs, their endearing superstitiousness, their habits of merrymaking; their cultivation of their own cabin gardens, their fondness for the hunting of coon and possum, squirrels and rabbits, quail and ducks, and wild turkeys, etc., etc.—the gifts of an edenic Southern landscape, where, the author is so bold to assert, "*they annually throw away food enough to feed during an entire winter the thousands of half-starved white laborers thrown out of employment in all the Free States during the months from September to March*" (344).[7]

What wonder, Hundley concludes, unless goaded "by the secret emissaries of the abolitionists" (346), that the average "honest, industrious slave" seldom thinks to escape from a bounteous agrarian landscape presided over by a wise and indulgent planter class. For at its best, it is precisely this reciprocity of relationship, Hundley concludes, that ensures the system's essential benignity, with general happiness coexisting in direct proportion to the refinement of the slaveowner. Or, as Hundley puts it, "the old adage of 'like master like man'" surely "applies with as much truthfulness to the negroes in the South, as to the hired servants of other places" (351). So Hundley hoped to find closure in a formula reconnecting his opening paean to an enlightened planter aristocracy with corresponding class sentiments he felt surely to be held by Northern and English elites among his readers—that of "racial uplift through domination" (Cooper xliv). To use Fred Hobson's acute phrasings, thus the South was in fact a model, with the noble values of "an enlightened patriciate" uplifting the common existence of all the lower orders, of "civilization's last chance" (73).

"We contend there is a great deal in *blood*" (251), Hundley had written at one overheated point. One is tempted here and in other references to something like racial genealogy to zero in on him according to that convenient category given us by the nineteenth century under the name of ethnology. On the other hand, as to any firm ideas of racial descent, in the sense of the primitive discipline as practiced, for instance, by Hundley's fellow Alabamian and quasi-scientific theorist of Negro inferiority, Dr. Josiah Nott, whose work Hundley seems not to have been acquainted with (Cooper xxxiv), he seems at visible remove. Further, such cultivated vagaries of mythic vision might have been pre-dicted by anyone looking at a book with title page epigraphs, both on the question of judgment, from Sir Philip Sidney, the Elizabethan exemplar of the courtier as cultural mythmaker, and the biblical Solomon, the ruler as lawgiver and cultural sage. Hundley clearly saw himself as writing in appreciation of the spirit of both. As to prospective audience, his work seems to have summoned up the shade of neither. Even in Hundley's beloved South, for instance, it largely went unread and unremarked upon by contemporaries; of all major Southern journals, only *De Bow's* reviewed it; and even there, as Hobson observes, the reviewer spent most of the space developing his own class theories (73). Furthermore, even that reader's attitude might be said at the time to have comprised a logical model of response. To put it simply, even allowing the work a certain objective status as social analysis, Hundley's structural premises and the argument devised on the basis of his resultant categories of analysis proved far too complicated for Northerners *or* Southerners, who by 1860 could only see "North and South, black and white" (Hobson 73). Northern interpreters at this point, for instance, were no longer particularly interested in having it pointed out to them that nabobs swaggering and boasting and flaunting their wealth at Saratoga were Cotton Snobs parading as aristocrats; nor was any such excoriation of visible Southern types, here or elsewhere, any more effectual in allaying Southern misinterpretations, based on mistaking Hundley's criticisms of pretenders to aristocracy for criticisms of aristocrats themselves. In both cases, the subtleties of sociological discrimination and cross-cultural argument seemed mainly just irrelevant in a country on the verge of war.

Contemporary events in Hundley's own experience should have shown him that in life and letters alike this was no time for subtlety. While still in Chicago, as a Stephen A. Douglas Democrat, he had served as an election judge "to prevent," he wrote to a friend, "the Republicans from committing frauds upon the ballot-box." Returning to Alabama, he declaimed that the triumph of the Lincoln party had obliterated "the *fact*" of the Union. And then, returning once more to Chicago for fear of having certain properties confiscated, he suffered narrow escape from a threatening mob of anti-Southern vigilantes.[8] Accordingly, back home for good, he firmly committed to the Southern cause and helped to form the Thirty-first Alabama Infantry Regiment, being elected colonel and serving until his capture on 1 May 1864 near Kennesaw Mountain, Dalton, Georgia. He was imprisoned at Johnson's Island in Lake Erie, near Sandusky, Ohio, from where he briefly escaped on 2 January 1865. Upon his recapture several days later, near Fremont, Ohio, one of the items taken from him was a journal kept during imprisonment. Released on 25 July 1865, he returned to his home, Thorn Hill, near Mooresville, Alabama. In 1874, after the unexpected return of the lost diary, he published it, with minor emendations, as *Prison Echoes of the Great Rebellion*. He then lived on another quarter century, dying in Mooresville on 27 December 1899 (Cooper xxi–xxiii).

For all the visibility of Hundley's attempt, whether he fully understood it or not, to make explicit in *Social Relations* the relationship between literary production and social ideology, it would be reductive, if not downright melodramatic, to cast the fate of this final Alabama author and his Alabama book as some terminal allegory of the similar work of such early figures as Sewall and Hitchcock, or, closer to the point, that of more visible near-contemporaries including Pickett, Meek, Hooper, Baldwin, Hentz, and Evans. Yet especially in the case of the latter, to venture the structural proposition is at least to begin to see why also, even as read today, they succeed as literary-cultural mythmakers where Hundley fails at the synthesis so earnestly desired. In a word, unlike Hundley they were "literary," and they knew it. More importantly, in contrast to Hundley's looking backward into what increasingly became, in Fred Hobson's terms, a mythic "South of the mind," they were also literary with that very particular kind of forward-looking nineteenth-century literariness characteristic of other American worthies of the era with whom they are frequently grouped—Stowe, Hawthorne, Simms, Melville, Twain: the synthesizing or creative literariness, albeit itself frequently manifest in a deep wish to create "historical" literature, born in the awareness bred by life in a burgeoning democracy of the frequently profound distances separating the real from the ideal, the actual from the imaginary, the particular from the universal, and above all, the past from the future. To put this in Frank Kermode's eloquent formulation, they understood precisely the *creative* difference between myths and fictions, with myths the instruments of "stability" and fictions the agents of "change," the former proposing "total and adequate explanations of things as they are and were" and the latter "changing as the needs of sense making change" (39). And it is in their own peculiarly American sense of that kind of generative literariness and writerly function that, like so many of their great mid-nineteenth-century contemporaries, such figures as Pickett, Meek, Hooper, Baldwin, Hentz, and Evans told a truer truth. We read them today and know the world of their texts as one that they not only managed to document and preserve, but, in the deepest sense of the term, also helped to create.

Notes

INTRODUCTION

1. As will be seen below, for an understanding of the extent and importance of an ascendant print culture in Alabama from the earliest days of territorial settlement throughout the antebellum era, one remains indebted to the pioneering work of Rhoda Coleman Ellison. Most important for my work here has been her indispensable 1947 book, *Early Alabama Publications: A Study in Literary Interests.*

2. I am aware that anyone acquainted with Alabama history of the territorial and early statehood eras will find these paragraphs of summary to be rife with oversimplification and generalization. I can only respond with an apology for such a brief overview and a reminder that, here and elsewhere, I do not claim to be writing as a historian. While wishing I were a historical mythographer, most of the time I am probably a cultural journalist, and a literary one at that. Still, there is nothing here in the big historical view of shifting Whig-Democrat power relations; of the uneasy accommodations of the largely independent yeoman farmer citizenry of the northern regions of the state with the Black Belt plantation aristocracy; or of the increasingly untenable positionings of conservative Unionists in their relation to the rise of the fire-eaters such as Yancey. For all these matters, I can only refer the reader to the work of a long tradition of distinguished writers of Alabama history: Thomas McAdory Owen, Albert B. Moore, and, most recently, William Warren Rogers, Robert David Ward, Leah Rawls Atkins, and Wayne Flynt. From the standpoint of

political history, the definitive work on the period remains, of course, Mills Thornton's prizewinning *Politics and Power in a Slave Society: Alabama, 1800–1860.*

In the same moment, I should like to advance the claim that when, in the reading of a particular text or texts, relevant historical specifics are required, they are present. One cannot write of Albert J. Pickett's conception of history in the planter style, for instance, without reference to the ethos of Southern honor so famously developed in the works of Bertram Wyatt-Brown and others; of the flush times narratives of Hooper and Baldwin without reference to the banking and currency crises of the 1830s; of Caroline Lee Hentz's depiction of antislavery agitation in *The Planter's Northern Bride* without reference to very real Southern fears of abolitionist fifth-column activity in the fomenting of what was gingerly referred to as "servile insurrection." In the event, at least some directly relevant detail can be filled in by individual discussions. It will be of importance that Pickett, for instance, while allied with Black Belt planter interests, was a lifelong Democrat; that Augusta Jane Evans, for all the seemingly enlightened intellectual sympathies of her novels, was opposed to women's suffrage and a staunchly conservative Southern patriot; that the travel writing of her Mobile compatriot Octavia Walton Le Vert, published just before the war, revealed a correspondingly fervent loyalty to the Union; or that the 1854 Alabama Education Act described in the sentence ending with this footnote was authored by A. B. Meek.

3. As with Ellison's distinguished work, one cannot begin to discuss the state's early literature without acknowledging the importance of Benjamin Buford Williams's groundbreaking survey, *A Literary History of Alabama: The Nineteenth Century.* Also indispensable to this study for invaluable biographical and historical information about a number of the major literary figures discussed has been Johanna Nicol Shields's "A Social History of Antebellum Alabama Writers."

4. For the pioneering and still definitive study of the patterns of settlement, see Thomas P. Abernathy's *The Formative Period in Alabama, 1815–1828,* written in 1922 and reissued in revised and updated form in 1965.

5. As is well known, the early-nineteenth-century settlement of Demopolis by Bonapartist exiles, although providing a colorful store of Francophile legend, proved a failure. On the other hand, by the 1830s and 1840s, mirroring the two predominant arrival groups on the national scene, a visible number of Irish immigrants had begun to appear, and German Jews had settled in various commercial centers around the state.

6. Exceptions could be found, including Mobile, with its shipbuilding and naval stores industries; Prattville, growing up around the production of the single machine most necessary for the economy, Daniel Pratt's mass-produced cotton gin; and Selma, with an ironworks that proved of strategic value during the Civil War. Textile mills appeared in various localities; and at sites like the Shelby Iron Works and Tannehill Furnaces, one could locate the birth of the iron and steel industry that would reconfigure the post-1865 map of north-central Alabama with new urban

place names like Birmingham, Fairfield, Bessemer, and Ensley (Rogers et al. 106–7, 174–77).

7. The spread of nineteenth-century Protestant fundamentalism across the region, with emphasis on the Second Great Awakening and its role in social developments along the antebellum frontier, has been given recent reconsideration in Christine Leigh Heyrman's *Southern Cross: The Beginnings of the Bible Belt.* Particularly enlightening, and of relevance here, is Heyrman's persuasive demonstration that modern evangelical denominations for a great part of the era comprised a political minority struggling against entrenched Episcopalian elites who saw them, on matters of gender and race, as a threat to prevailing social hierarchies.

8. For a study of the struggle of a "Virginian" cultural ethos to survive amidst the flush times atmospherics of the 1830s, see, for instance, John Grammer's lively discussion of Joseph G. Baldwin in *Pastoral and Politics in the Old South* 128–58.

9. For one not acquainted with the demographics of the growth of such an elite culture in its relation to slavery in Alabama, 1820–60 census figures on the growth of numbers of slaves in their relation to growth of the white population in general and the slaveowning population in particular provide breathtaking demonstration of this thesis. Slaves in 1820 represented 32 percent of the state population. In 1830 the figure was 38 percent, showing that slave importation had more than kept pace with the tremendous influx of white settlers. By 1860 slaves constituted an imposing 45 percent of the state's population; but by now, as to distribution of land and slave wealth, surely the most revealing figures were those of ownership. Of the state's white citizens, numbering 526,271, only 6.9 percent owned any slaves at all; and those considered large planters—through ownership of 50 slaves or more—constituted a bare .32 percent of the total white population. For census data of the various decades, see Moore 352–54. For the breakdown of 1860 figures, see Hubbs 61, where the details are provided as part of the editorial apparatus for a story by the humorist John Gorman Barr entitled "How Tom Croghan Carved the Turkey."

10. In this connection, on the other hand, in *Types of Mankind,* published by the Philadelphia firm of Lippincott, Grambo in 1854, Alabama may claim the dubious honor in print of producing one of the chief scientific spokesmen and defenders of theories of racial superiority, Josiah Nott—himself, ironically, a pioneer in medical education and public health matters in the state; and, as will be seen in a concluding chapter, it would also be home to one of the last major slavery apologists to write from a viewpoint we would now describe as that of a sociologist or political scientist, Daniel Hundley, author of *Social Relations in Our Southern States.* Also, as noted by Johanna Nicol Shields in her introduction to a recent reissue of Hooper's *Adventures of Simon Suggs,* the Montgomery firm of Bates, Hooper and Company printed, during a brief foray into book publishing, *A Defense of Negro Slavery as It Exists, in the United States* by Dr. Matthew Estes of Columbus, Mississippi (xli–xlii).

Regarding the discussion of the topic as part of the vast body of antebellum critical writing on the prospects and possibilities of Southern letters as an expression of the region's unique cultural character, among Alabama writers one may point to A. B. Meek's rather extraordinary claim, in the "Epistle Salutatory" to the first issue of *The Southron*, that slavery presents itself as a fertile field of inquiry as yet little addressed by the literary imagination. Indeed, "in that portion of our population," he avers, "who may be said to be the peasantry of our country, native writers will find a peculiar and abundant theme for literary composition" (6). At the same time, he quickly passes on, giving little guidance on how this might be done or why it should add to the common literary benefit. (In fact, as usual, the bottom line is financial. The slave system and the South's "unmatched natural advantages" will provide limitless riches; and "letters and arts always follow in the train of wealth" [7].) Similar sentiments are expressed in his oration of the same period, "The Southwest; Its History, Character and Prospects," delivered before the Erosophic Society of the University of Alabama on 7 December 1839. In print version, included as part of a prose collection entitled *Romantic Passages in Southwestern History*, the speech runs to fifty-six pages of effusive recitation concerning the glories, past, present, and future, of Southwestern culture. Two are devoted to a brief intellectual defense of what he refers to as "our Peculiar Domestic Institution" (58–60). As notable for the absence of any mention of slavery, however, is his effusively patriotic "Americanism in Literature," appearing in the same collection, and first delivered before the Phi Kappa and Demosthenian Societies of the University of Georgia on 8 August 1844.

Further, as Meek seems to have given little thought to any idea of the actual depiction of slavery in his own writing practice, so the hint delivered in his "Epistle Salutatory" to *The Southron* seems not to have been taken by any of his contemporaries save Hentz, who did so on several occasions, but is surely most remembered for her anti-abolitionist reply to Stowe. If there is an antebellum literary memorial to slavery in early Alabama, it is the set of slave codes matter-of-factly included in Hitchcock's *Alabama Justice of the Peace*.

11. It is something of a commonplace that nineteenth-century figures of religious authority frequently pronounced on the threats of literature to morality, particularly in the popular domain, with special emphasis on mass-market fiction and the contemporary stage. On the other hand, as to the fostering of an elevated literary culture, the clergyman frequently played a prominent role as educator. It should be noted here, for instance, that both Alva Woods and Basil Manly, first and second presidents of the University of Alabama, were Baptist ministers.

CHAPTER 1

1. The figure would shortly enjoy literary renown, for instance, in James Kirke Paulding's popular comedy, actually bearing the title *Lion of the West* and featuring the antics of the irrepressible frontiersman Nimrod Wildfire. The exemplar in life, of course, would be the incomparable Jackson himself; but he had already been

preceded by Mad Anthony Wayne at Fallen Timbers, William Henry Harrison at Tippecanoe, and, most recently, the legendary hero-cum-scoundrel General James Wilkinson. To be sure, citizen-soldier heroism, from the Revolution onward, had proven one of the surest paths to national prominence and political viability, as evidenced by the great Washington. New political dangers, however, seemed to arise with the appearance of a succeeding generation of would-be military despots. Especially on the frontier, in the disturbing wake of the Burr conspiracy, the new nation suddenly seemed to bristle with militia officers coupling an ability to inspire the American citizen-soldier of the settlements with martial and political ambitions far less generously motivated.

2. The standard account of the war remains H. S. Halbert and T. H. Ball's *The Creek War of 1813 and 1814.* In 1995 the University of Alabama Press also issued a paperback reprint of Frank Owsley's 1969 edition. Chapter 8 is devoted to the Battle of Burnt Corn. More recent accounts leave unchanged the basic information about the engagement and Caller's role in it, before, during, and after. These include Owsley's own *Struggle for the Gulf Borderlands: The Creek War and the Battle of New Orleans, 1812–15,* and Rogers et al., *Alabama: The History of a Deep South State.*

Bearing directly on Caller's leadership and motives, the issue of excessive officership is particularly remarked upon in various accounts. George Cory Eggleston, for instance, tallying the results of ad hoc battlefield elections, deduces a ratio of about one officer for every two men (73). Halbert and Ball similarly remark with deadpan accuracy, "It is stated that this unusual number of field officers was made to satisfy military aspirations" (Owsley, ed., 130).

3. An original exists in the Chapin Collection of the Williams College Library. A photocopy was provided by University of Alabama Special Collections.

4. This would occur with the publication in Mobile of an 1833 volume, entitled *The Miscellaneous Poems of Lewis Sewall, Esq., Containing the Last Campaign of Col. J. Caller—Alias Sir John Falstaff the Second—Alias the Hero of the Burnt Corn Battle; The Birth, Progress, and Probable End of G. F. Mynheer Van Slaverchap's Grandson—Alias Doctor Furnace; The Battle for the Cow and Calf; The Canoe Fight; And Other Miscellaneous Matters.* As the title suggests, the leadoff selection was again the Burnt Corn saga, albeit now in a second, much expanded version. In form, it was divided into numbered cantos, with each headed by a paragraph of prose argument. In subject, it had also become much more comprehensive, beginning with Burnt Corn and the misadventures of the titular hero but also going into much fuller detail on the Fort Mims disaster and subsequent Creek War events. Finally, as noted below, it also seized on the intervening death of Caller to picture him in a new mock-Miltonic addendum conspiring in hell with fellow minions of the devil. As revised, however, the poem proved anything but an improvement on the original.

5. Indeed, all three rate long index citations in multiple volumes of the territorial records, with Sewall, as will be seen, although now largely remembered as a literary figure, every bit as notable historically for his various shady participations

in territorial affairs. See volumes 5 and 6 of Clarence E. Carter, ed., *Territorial Papers of the United States*.

6. For a description of the affair written by Sewall presumably after the publication of his satire, see the 8 March 1816 letter of Lewis Sewall to Josiah Meigs (Carter 6: 666–67).

7. The letter in the territorial records of 8 March 1816 from Sewall to Josiah Meigs complaining of the official accusations lodged against him promises an enclosure of some "printed Notice from James Caller; published here" (Carter 6: 667). It was apparently not included, however. Although barely described as to details of its content, it is the main subject of the 1815 preface. Also, a few teasing bits of it are noted at various points in the poem. Caller, for instance, in his own attempt at literary preening, seems to have signed himself as writing from Pandaemonium. In the expanded 1833 poem, the latter reference also serves as the basis for the strange mock-Miltonic addendum described above.

8. According to Rogers et al., "participants in the battle endured the ridicule of the populace for many years, and few would willingly admit having been present at Burnt Corn" (97).

9. Here, on the other hand, would also remain the singular feature of the poem distinguishing it from the main body of humor to come: the casting of the *miles gloriosus* as Falstaff. For the primary tendency of Southwestern humor in this vein would quickly become mock-quixotic and/or Hudibrastic: the depiction of succeeding soldier-buffoons would invariably conflate the roles of "knight" and picaro to achieve the debunking from an upper-class Whig perspective of the martial pretensions of a backwoods aspirant of distinctly inferior social status.

10. Throughout, working the Falstaff parallel through puns and sight gags on the inside, the poem has made much of the present hero's corpulence. Also, tied in with the scatology, is discussion of the odyssey undertaken by a bullet—alleged by Falstaff-Caller to have dropped into his capacious drawers after passing through his coat sleeve—but more likely to have passed instantly through his digestive system as a result of panic after he has bitten off the wrong end of a cartridge.

11. In more official literary accounting, Sewall is missed by Benjamin Williams in his standard *Literary History of Alabama: The Nineteenth Century*. He does receive mention, however, for both the 1815 and 1833 versions of the Falstaff poem in Rhoda Ellison's *Early Alabama Publications*.

12. Surely he would have relished, for instance, William H. Brantley's paired descriptions a century and a half later of himself and Caller as being "among the leading St. Stephens citizens of note" during its days as a capital. Sewall was noted as "Alabama's first poet," and Caller as "the military man who commanded at Burnt Corn" (*Three Capitals* 41).

13. In contrast to Sewall or John Caller, for instance, only James Caller rates an entry in the biographical section of Thomas McAdory Owen's compendious, four-volume *History of Alabama and Dictionary of Alabama Biography* (3: 291).

CHAPTER 2

1. Biographical information here is drawn from William H. Brantley's 1951 *Alabama Review* article, "Henry Hitchcock of Mobile, 1816–39."

2. To survey some of "the petty civil cases" an Alabama justice of the peace was likely to encounter in the first decades of state history is to see the phrasing as surely one of the most wishful ever recorded in the history of constitutional pronouncement. According to Jack K. Williams in his 1953 *Alabama Review* article, "Crime and Punishment in Early Alabama, 1819–40," the menu of misdoing was endless and specialized in heavy violence. A visitor to Mobile wrote, "hardly a night passes by without a riot or fight, or without furnishing occasion for a duel or a murder at some subsequent date" (15). Of Montgomery, another traveler observed, "the life of man has very little value in this recently erected place; the mixed composition of the population gives rise to many frightful deeds, which in other towns would be severely punished by the authorities, but are here perpetrated without any serious consequences." Huntsville, a town of two thousand, recorded five murders in 1825. Further, according to Williams, "two dozen horses were reported rustled, five pocketbooks were stolen, seven Negroes were said to have been kidnapped, and such miscellaneous items as saddles, bridles, coats, blankets, and watches were pilfered." He goes on: "One house was robbed. Two men absconded with their employer's funds. A counterfeiter was caught, jailed, and, through carelessness, allowed to escape. One forger was reported in the neighborhood, and one brazen attempt was made to rifle the incoming mail" (16).

Homicide was astonishingly frequent. Often it was a result of a simple quarrel or insult. Self-defense was a common plea. The defense of one's honor was also frequently advanced as a justification.

The most common crime was robbery, both on highways and in towns. Also part of the larceny scene were various forms of "the confidence-game" or "artful dodge" (20). Probably the most feared crime short of murder was arson.

Deaths and injury by violence were ascribed to various contributing causes, including heavy drinking, the agitation of political campaigns, and the proliferation of published insults. As Williams notes, surely no small part was played by "the practice of allowing each male to go about armed to the teeth" (25). As late as 1837, it was legal to carry weapons anywhere and in fact was deemed rather foolish not to.

Finally, there was the justice system itself. Jails were poor and escape remarkably easy; and for those miscreants not so resourceful, fairly uniform evidence suggests that jury convictions were relatively rare. Only after 1841, Williams concludes, would come any drastic reduction of lawlessness, in large part through "sensible revision of the state criminal code, the establishment of a state convict system, and the general improvement of the state constabulary" (30).

3. What kinds of public character were displayed by persons deemed worthy by the legislature of judicial appointment in early Alabama? By good fortune, we

have the published reminiscences from one of their number, Benjamin Faneuil Porter, who from roughly 1820 onward worked in every area of law from service as a private attorney to the official reportership of decisions of the supreme court. In his first year of practice, he was also appointed a county judge; later, he served with distinction on the circuit bench in both Mobile and Greenville. Intermittently, he was also a legislator, specializing in the development of statutory law, and a trustee of the University of Alabama, which attempted in 1845 to secure his services as a professor of law. Most importantly, in his thirty years of experience with bench and bar, he seems to have known virtually every person of note, including a majority of the most prominent members of the judiciary. Judge Abner I. Lipscomb of Mobile, for instance, he remembered as "a very dark man, highly respected by the Bar, and a good lawyer. He was social, kind, and generous, and never failed to treat the younger members of the Bar with consideration" (*Reminiscences* 37). He similarly described Justice Henry Goldthwaite as "a man of clear, deep intellect," whose "opinions have given great character to the decisions of the Supreme Court of Alabama" (38).

At the same time, "character" could be a flexible word. There was Reuben Saffold of the supreme court, for instance, "a large man, with a physiognomy of the Matthew Hale order," whose "opinions were prolix but well studied and full of authority." Notwithstanding, he was also accounted "a person of much goodness of heart, and exceedingly respectful to the bar" (43). Henry Minor had moved from a judgeship to clerk of the supreme court. "In person," wrote Porter, "he was small and thin. In disposition, he was said to be money loving, but he was a good man. He had some eccentricities of temper, but was full of quaint stories and odd expressions" (43–44).

With particular relish, Porter recalled circuit judge Sion L. Perry as "the quaintest specimen of Tennessee drollery ever met with." He went on: "He was lank of form, and drawled out his words with little regard to grammar or elocution. He was incorrect from habit, rather than from want of education. His expressions were inexpressibly droll." "On one occasion," Porter recalled, Perry "interrupted a member of the Bar in an argument by saying, 'Boys, the solemn bell are tolled. Let's go and fodder'" (57). He was also remembered for his handling of a lawyer of notorious prolixity, who offered him a large roll of paper containing the "abstract" of a case and then asked to be allowed time to fetch a more extensive "synopsis." When he returned, Perry was ready. "Hutch," he said, "I don't want your synopsis—I've decided the case against you, and barring an accident, I've decided right" (44). He was eventually affirmed by the supreme court.

And finally, "among the older members of the bar," there was Judge Kelly, who was described meaningfully as "talented, but convivial." "On one occasion," said Porter, "Bagby, who was quite dressy, appeared at the Supreme Court Bar in a light stone-colored frock coat. Kelly came in rather tight. Surveying Bagby intently, he said aloud, 'Neat but not gaudy, as the monkey said when he painted his tail sky blue.'" "The Bench," Porter somberly recorded, "lost its gravity for some time" (58).

CHAPTER 3

1. The Alabama text, held at the State Archives in Montgomery, has to date been the subject only of brief descriptive notation in works by historical scholars such as Rhoda Ellison and Benjamin Williams and in a short article by Williams, mentioned below, speculating rather inconclusively on its authorship. A microfilm of the first edition was made available on loan from the University of California at Berkeley. As noted, the second text reveals, along with a variety of incidental alterations, two major changes: the addition, through the newly interpolated "manuscripts" of Es Joebe and Cecilia, and by the rewriting of various scenes of reunion near the end, of a bizarre pirate subplot tied in with various strands of the main captivity plot; and a long, lavish prefacing and dedication of the second edition to Andrew Jackson. Nevertheless, the two texts are clearly the same novel.

2. See Benjamin B. Williams, "The Identity of Alabama's First Novelist." As I will later suggest, a study of the 1831 Tallahassee edition, which Williams did not consult and consequently hypothesized as being a hoax, coupled with fairly certain information concerning Conner's whereabouts and employment in eastern Alabama as late as the 1840s and 1850s, when he is listed as an overseer and farmer in Talladega County, casts doubt upon both his authorship and his later ministerial career. He is, nevertheless, named as the author in one anecdotal source, James E. Saunders's *Early Settlers of Alabama,* where he is described as having read frequently from a book of his, identified as "*The Lost Virgin of the South,*" to a captive audience of locals. Indeed, the account smacks so wonderfully of a backwoods imposture layered upon the already mysterious circumstances of the book's origins that it is worth quoting at some length. Recording the attribution of the text to Conner, and describing it as "a story of a young girl captured by the Indians," Saunders writes: "While it was in manuscript he would detain his friends, almost by force, to hear him read portions of it, when tears would be profusely shed—by the author. A second edition was never called for, and the work unfortunately has been lost. How do we know but that the 'Lost Virgin,' if found at some future time, may cause as great a revolution in that kind of literature as the Institutes of Justinian (after being lost a thousand years) did in jurisprudence" (224).

Remarking further on Conner's purported removal to Mississippi, the author notes, "we had some rumors, one of which was that he had become a traveling preacher. If this was really so, I judge that on his circuit chickens have become very scarce, and turkeys roosted very high!" (224).

On the basis of subsequent scholarship, I think one can conjecture that Conner may have written the new dedication to Jackson, which, in disagreement with the copyright page of the second edition, is dated 1833. Bibliographer Rhoda Ellison, in *History and Bibliography of Alabama Newspapers in the Nineteenth Century,* reproduces local speculation "that Editor Connor [sic] is or has been a preacher." Her source appears most certain, on the other hand, about the editor's politics: "Supported Jackson in 1828" (41). As to the Jackson panegyric of "1833" appearing in the "1832" volume, it is signed "the author and publisher." In this case, the expression may refer not to Smith, but to Conner.

Finally, as will be noted in further detail below, because of an odd linkage of specific historical and biographical source materials often used verbatim in the text, one must also intrude into speculative discussion of authorship the name of the Rev. Timothy Flint. As will be shown, *The Lost Virgin* frequently quotes Flint's well-known *Condensed Geography and History of the Western States, or the Mississippi Valley*. At times, it also seems to use verbatim a source used verbatim by Flint himself, Senator John Eaton's *Life of General A. Jackson* (New York: Lydia A. Bailey, 1817; republished 1824, 1827, 1828, etc.; text cited here is Philadelphia: McCarthy and Davis, 1828). To complicate matters further, "Smith's" plagiarisms of Eaton often slide in and out of the phrasings of Flint's plagiarisms.

Circumstantial evidence makes a Flint connection intriguing. At the time of *The Lost Virgin*'s appearance, Flint, who resided in Louisiana in the 1820s and again in the 1830s, was exactly amidst the 1827–33 flurry of publication marking the center of his career; his output included, along with his work as a historian and journalist, several bizarre gothic novels placed in early American settings. As will be shown, "Smith" was tremendously influenced by Cooper; Flint wrote important early criticism on the latter. Both "Smith" and Flint are further distinguished among writers of the period by their pragmatic attitudes toward the role of Catholicism in American settlement. On the other hand, the textual provenance of *The Lost Virgin* corresponds in no way to Flint's biography during the period and thus makes a connection impossible to validate.

3. One should continue to note, even in beginning to detail the complex literary hybridizations here, the crucial degree to which published "history" itself is a part of the mix, with passages quoted at length and at times verbatim from both Flint's *Geography and History* and Eaton's *Life of Jackson*. See, for instance, the heavy reliance by the novelist on Flint's descriptions of the Battles of Tohopeka (1: 91 ff.; Flint 380 ff.) and New Orleans (2: 32 ff.; Flint 435 ff.). For a sample of direct reliance on Eaton, see an early account of the Battle of Tallushetchee (1: 34; Eaton 55). For a lift from Eaton acknowledged in the first edition and then more covertly assimilated into the second, see another portion of the same passage used at the end of chapter 2 (1: 20; Eaton 55).

4. As will be noted later, while textual parallels make possible the identification of direct reliance on Cooper's historical fictions, the gothic stratagems involved in the Casender manuscript—and particularly the various "international" complications—are characteristic of myriad texts in popular circulation. For evidence of the bizarre ubiquity of such devices in text after popular text, see, for instance, the plot summaries that conclude Henri Petter's *The Early American Novel* (397–463). As with the "historical" borrowings from Flint and Eaton noted above, in the realm of colorful pirate-lore, at least one popular "nonfiction" adventure text of the era, pos-

sibly known to the author, may also have guided composition in some places. This was *The Memoirs of Lafitte; or, the Barritarian pirate. A narrative founded on fact* (Providence: Wm. M. Spear, 1826). There, the narrative-within-the-narrative framing of the pirate's lurid adventures (his actual name turns out to be Mortimer Wilson) suggests the autobiographical manuscripts of the pirates Es Joebe and Hosmer Sprouse, the first actually interpolated in the revised text and the second inexplicably forgotten. Also, the staged reunion of the wounded Lafitte and his wife-to-be Annette Hanson, friend of his lost angel Mary Morton, after the Battle of New Orleans suggests some of the complicated recognition plotting engineered by "Smith" at the same site. For further romantic "literary" parallels, see also the Lafitte story rendered in Joseph Holt Ingraham's contemporary *Lafitte: or the Baratarian Chief, a tale. Founded on facts* (New York: n.p., 1828), which evolved shortly into *Lafitte: Pirate of the Gulf*, a novel that proved immensely popular (New York: Harper & Brothers, 1836, 1840, 1842, etc.) and enjoyed further printings throughout the nineteenth century. That novel's Constanza-D'Oyly plot of kidnapping, pursuit, rescue, and final reunion of chaste heroine and noble lover parallels the relationship of Calista and Perendio Cevillo; and the Gertrude-Lafitte subplot, where the hero, after the Battle of New Orleans, is nursed back to health by a nun of the Charity Hospital who turns out to be his long-lost sister, would also suggest the Calista-Casender recognition subplot, which is resolved in similar circumstances.

5. Of all the 1832 revisions, surely one here suggests M. Smith's eye for an audience susceptible to the titillating detail. In the 1831 version, Calista exposes herself to the strike of Perendio's dagger, "bareing her beautiful bosom" (318). In 1832 is added, after "bosom," "over which the rays of the moon lingered" (2: 122).

6. These include the supposed death of the heroine's family, her return after a passage of years, and, in Cooper's text, her death of shock after return to her white identity. One also has to suspect that Jackson's reprieve of the noble Creek chieftain Weatherford from the death demanded by his conquerors, as depicted in Smith's novel, provokes a parallel, supported by actual history, with the merciless execution in Cooper's novel of the savage but noble Conanchet, who has at the last saved the heroine's parents from death and engineered her reunion with them.

7. In further confluence of history and popular literature, this personage would also become, as is known even today by most Alabama schoolchildren, the titular hero of Alexander Beaufort Meek's 1855 epic poem, *The Red Eagle*.

8. Again, however, proximity here also measures distance. As noted, Calista, unlike Mary Rowlandson, delights in her access to a Bible first to keep up with her reading skills, and only later to experience conversion.

9. One may protest that this early Southern text mentions virtually nothing of chattel slavery. As noted, with the great importations of slave labor into the low, fertile regions of the frontier South, this would come later in the form of its own hard facts; but it would also remain a singular feature of literary avoidance.

CHAPTER 4

1. During the postwar period, Mobile would be notable among cities of the state for maintaining a flourishing literary culture, unmatched save perhaps in this century by that of new urban centers such as Birmingham and, as a consequence of its tradition of a strong creative writing program developed by Hudson Strode and others, at the university in Tuscaloosa. At the same time, it would be no exaggeration to suggest that Mobile remains in many ways a literary world unto itself. "Sweet lunacy's county seat," the Mobile writer Eugene Walter has called it. And through the work of figures as diverse as Thomas Cooper De Leon, novelist, dramatist, and parodist, Walter himself, and more recently Mark Childress, and Winston Groom, author of *Forrest Gump*, it has often richly repaid the epithet.

2. Roughly contemporary analogues, not much noticed at the time and now generally forgotten, would have included Thomas Holley Chivers's *The Path of Sorrow* (1832) and *Conrad and Eudora* (1834); and Edward Coote Pinkney's *Rodolph* (1833) and *Poems* (1825). William Gilmore Simms in the 1820s had produced five volumes of verse, and in 1832 would publish the longer poem *Atlantis;* and Poe had published *Tamerlane and Other Poems* (1827), *Al Araaf, Tamerlane, and Minor Poems* (1829), and *Poems* (1831). But as Smith wrote, even these figures, finding little reception for their poetry, were beginning to turn to fiction and criticism.

3. As noted elsewhere, Meek's essay is one of the few literary documents of the era about the prospects and possibilities of a Southern literature that makes any mention of slavery as a literary topic. Here, in a strange yoking of conventional political apologetics with a kind of chamber-of-commerce promotionalism, the institution is somewhat hastily concluded to be both a promising literary topic and an important source of wealth ensuring the general advancement of culture.

4. The fate of Muller—the Episcopal rector of Christ Church, whose other contributions to local letters included "The Wedding Feast," published in the magazine's final issue—suggested that literary culture had become deep enough to accommodate a scandal. Shortly, he found himself banished from the state and dismissed from the ministry for offenses, as the bill of particulars styled it, involving "very scandalous lapses from religion and morality." He was last said to be heard from by letter asking one of his former townsmen for money.

5. The last, as was well known to nineteenth-century Alabamians, had produced his travel book, one of the most well known and popular of the era, as an account of his sojourn as a tutor on a Dallas County plantation. In this connection, it should also be noted that one of the groundbreaking accounts of domestic manners in early Alabama—a fact that could hardly have been lost on Le Vert—had been written by another socially well-connected female literary traveler of the early decades of the century, Anne Newport Royall, herself both a famous belletrist and a noted hostess.

6. The studies cited are Harold F. Smith's *American Travelers Abroad* and Mary-Suzanne Schriber's "Julia Ward Howe and the Travel Book." Schriber has also

more recently published a book-length study, *Writing Home: American Woman Abroad, 1830–1920*, in which she discusses many of the popular antebellum travel narratives by women mentioned here. Le Vert's, however, is not included.

7. For Evans, to be sure, the cultural cosmopolitanism was something she could turn on and off according to the demands of her Southern patriotism. As noted later, for instance, her 1864 novel *Macaria; or, Altars of Sacrifice* was regarded as a major literary contribution to the Confederate cause.

<h2 style="text-align:center">C H A P T E R 5</h2>

1. Levin's book, standing on what he called the unfortified boundary of history and literature, was a groundbreaking contribution to the field just beginning to define itself as American studies.

2. As it turns out, Hedges's concise summary derives from a study of Washington Irving in which he must attend to a discussion of such "mixed" historiography in Diedrich Knickerbocker's *History of New York*.

3. Pickett's enthusiasm for the vivid style of history practiced by Macaulay in particular is evidenced in his rousing, fan-letter conclusion to "The Origins and Progress of History in the Eastern Hemisphere," an address delivered to the Alabama Historical Society at its annual meeting on 12 July 1854 in Tuscaloosa. Further, throughout the lecture—a sweeping survey of historians and historiography extending from Moses and Herodotus, the eminent Greeks and Romans, and the authors of the four gospels, through the great historians of Italy, France, Germany, Spain, and, most recently, England—Pickett's sympathies clearly lie with those who have made history, in the fullest sense, "come alive." The Scotsman Robertson's two volumes of history on America, for instance, he praises as being "in a style now of tenderness and pathos, now of picturesque descriptions perfectly inimitable"; and Gibbon is similarly lauded for "his glittering sentences, his tournaments and battlepieces, his polished irony and masterly sketches of character." But Macaulay is clearly the model, the historian who "relates everything that is important, and omits nothing that interests or instructs" (typed transcript, Alabama State Archives).

For a more broadly focused discussion of the identifiable Anglo-European literary and philosophical "Lineaments," as the author calls them, "of Antebellum Southern Romanticism," see also Michael O'Brien's essay under that title in *Rethinking the South* 38–56.

4. Biographical information here and elsewhere is taken mainly from Frank L. Owsley, Jr., "Albert J. Pickett, Historian of Alabama." That essay derives in turn from Owsley's extensively biographical 1955 Ph.D. thesis at the University of Alabama.

5. Here, as in various places in the text where Pickett mentions leisure time expended or personal travel and financial outlay made in support of his labors, there is more to such references than simple bragging or complaining. As Michael O'Brien records, in taking Pickett as an early case study of the various daunting "practicali-

ties" faced by the self-appointed regional chronicler trying to write history from the ground up, the seeking of advice and leads on documents and other research materials from established worthies; extensive correspondence with historical participants and/or their descendants; the purchasing of locally unavailable books and pamphlets; and the visiting of sites and gathering of oral testimony from living persons at their places of residence all added up to a simple demographic verity. "However you looked at it," O'Brien concludes, "writing history was a very expensive business, confined to gentlemen of means" (145). See "On the Writing of History in the Old South" 141–66, esp. 144–46.

On the other hand, recurrent references to gentlemanly leisure and wealth as facilitating the work of the historian should also be further read here, I believe, as indices of a high-minded notion of civic duty and intended to give the impression that the author finds it only natural to have happily enlisted personal resources in the labor of historiographic fact-finding and truth-telling. Indeed, in nearly all such instances there seems to be a direct attempt to make evidence of gentlemanly status integral to readerly assumptions about his historiographic veracity and authority. For studies of the gentleman as a cultural type, and of honor defined in these various senses as a comprehensive cultural ethos of word and deed, and vice versa, see Bertram Wyatt-Brown, *Southern Honor,* and Ritchie Watson, *Yeoman versus Cavalier.* Wyatt-Brown's classic study most successfully integrates the features of the code. As regards Pickett's somewhat insecure sense of relationship between social and literary identity, Watson is helpful particularly on the cultural anxieties suffered by a "new" planter class, often arising out of the yeomanry, attempting to transplant older aristocratic values to the Old Southwest. In Richard Gray's *Writing the South,* a corresponding ambivalence of class identity as reflected in writerly styles is profitably explored as a conflict between what Gray calls "patriarchal and populist structures of feeling" (43).

6. Most notably, in 1849 he had attracted attention with a widely distributed newspaper piece entitled "The Invasion of the Territory of Alabama by One Thousand Spaniards under Firdinand [*sic*] De Soto in 1540." As Frank Owsley notes, "This was designed as a prospectus for his *History* and was to be its first chapter" ("Pickett" 34).

At the same time, however, as noted by O'Brien, in keeping the rumor pot bubbling with regard to his project, Pickett also incurred another vicissitude frequently faced by the regional historian attempting to get there first: the jealous backbiting of a local competitor. In this case, the rival was the well-placed Alabama man of letters Alexander Beaufort Meek. In an 1847 letter to his brother, for instance, Meek smugly discounted any possibility that Pickett might beat him into print. And both before and after publication of Pickett's work, he took pains to trumpet the author's shortcomings, personal and professional, in correspondence with Simms. See O'Brien, "On the Writing of History" 147–48. Meek's letter to his brother Samuel of 18 May 1847 may be found in the A. B. Meek Papers at the University of Alabama.

The letters to Simms of 18 May 1847 and 23 November 1951 are in the Alabama State Archives.

As things turned out, Meek's own magisterially conceived "History of Alabama" never got out of manuscript. Instead, his own reputation as a historian was allowed to rest on a compendious but somewhat disparate gathering of pieces, culled from the author's "miscellaneous orations, sketches, and essays," as he put it in a preface, and disposed under the umbrella title *Romantic Passages in Southwestern History* (1857).

7. That genealogy of authorship is itself a well-known feature of Alabama history and historiographic tradition. The main lineage includes Thomas McAdory Owen, Albert B. Moore, Charles Grayson Summersell, and Virginia Van der Veer Hamilton. As to Pickett's centrality as a source, one turn-of-the-century writer, William Garrott Brown, went so far as to entitle his educational text *A History of Alabama for Use in Schools; Based as to Its Early Parts on the Work of Albert J. Pickett*. Research in recent decades has increasingly passed Pickett by. See, for instance, Rogers et al., *Alabama: The History of a Deep South State*, published in 1994 by the University of Alabama Press and likely to remain the standard text for some time. There, while occasionally footnoting the text, Leah Atkins concludes a discussion of Pickett with a just assessment of his current status. "Although his account is dated," she writes, "neglects much of North Alabama, and is uneven in quality, it is still an invaluable work" (132).

8. See Harper Lee, "Romance and High Adventure." To give some sense of the immense cultural "authority" of Pickett's text in the case of this particular writer, one might add, as noted by an early reader of my essay, that Lee's remarks on Pickett, adapted from a symposium talk, constitute her only appearance in print besides *To Kill a Mockingbird*.

9. In the traditional study of antebellum Southern letters, the aristocratic style of the gentleman-narrator has most often been examined in its connection with Southwestern humor, where in many cases it serves as a framing device for Whig satire of the local Jacksonian rabble. On the other hand, as scholarship has revealed, the "Whig" perspective in humor was frequently as much a matter of professional or class outlook as of explicit party affiliation, with many members of the "Whig" elite having spent their early years or even longer as enthusiastic Jacksonians; and within individual texts, "Whig" narrators could frequently reveal considerable empathy with their low-life backwoods "originals." On these points, see such classic studies as Kenneth S. Lynn's *Mark Twain and Southwestern Humor* and Hennig Cohen and William B. Dillingham's *Humor of the Old Southwest*.

Here, on both accounts, the term is used in the more broadly socio-literary sense. For one thing, Pickett was a lifelong Democrat and personal admirer of Jackson, was received as a guest at the Hermitage, and later was presented by Jackson with a presidential oil portrait. He also gained early political notice in Alabama for an early speech against nullification. At the same time, he was the son of a wealthy planter; he married the daughter of another, basically doubling his assets; and he spent most of his mature years as a large Autauga County landholder and slave-owner, obviously considering himself a member of the planter elite. See Michael L. Wood, "Personal Reminiscences of A. J. Pickett" 604; and Johanna Nicol Shields, "A Social History of Antebellum Alabama Writers" 182. On the other hand, as to range of politico-literary enthusiasms, the gentleman-narrator of Pickett's *History* frequently reveals a fascination with and even an affection for the maverick and the social outsider.

In terms of general literary characteristics, as an elevated historiographic style in the contemporary American vein, Pickett's narration frequently seems not all that different from those of popular frontier chroniclers such as Timothy Flint or John Eaton. And in mining the Southern-man-of-letters vein of historical grandilo-quence, as noted by Frank Owsley ("Pickett" 36–37), surely he must have profited by frequent collegial interchange with esteemed regional compatriots similarly en-gaged, most notably J. W. Monette and Jared Sparks, but also William Gilmore Simms and J. F. H. Claiborne.

The twentieth-century model of outdoor pageant drama anticipated in Pickett's management of historical spectacle, although not a Southern invention, is frequently thought of now as a Southern cultural fixture, with classics of the genre—called by its greatest practitioner, Paul Green, "symphonic" drama—still presented at various historic sites across the region. Among the most prominent of Green's pro-ductions are *The Common Glory* and *The Founders,* about colonial Williamsburg and Jamestown; *The Lost Colony,* about the vanished Sir Walter Raleigh expedition at Roanoke Island, North Carolina; *Lone Star,* about the formative period in Texas history; and *Trumpet in the Land* and *Wilderness Road,* about early settlement in Ohio and Kentucky. Analogous works by a counterpart, Kermit Hunter, include *Unto These Hills,* a drama of the Cherokee Nation; *Horn in the West,* a celebration of patriot rebellion against the British in the North Carolina Piedmont; and *Bright-hope,* a pageant of early Alabama. For a vivid study of the rise of the historic festival and pageant drama as popular-culture phenomena, see David Glassberg, *American Historical Pageantry.*

10. With intermittent British incursions, the Spanish and French continued to vie for supremacy in the Gulf Coast region, with Louisiana changing hands sev-eral times. The most pronounced British presence in the region was during the War of Independence, when loyalist and revolutionary struggled for control of the fron-tier and for the allegiances of native tribes. During most of the period in question, Britain also coexisted uneasily with Spain as a colonial occupier in Florida; and, of course, it was a British army finally defeated by Andrew Jackson at the 1814 Battle of New Orleans.

11. For an illuminating discussion of correspondences between Cooper's tragic depictions of the passing of Native American culture and the contemporary dis-placements and removals of the great Southern tribes, see Philip Fisher's *Hard Facts.*

12. As was once taught with great cultural pride to generations of Alabama students, the latter historical pairing alone would prove sufficient to inspire A. B. Meek's epic poem, itself entitled *The Red Eagle*. By extraordinary literary coincidence, it appeared in 1855, the same year as Longfellow's epic celebration of native culture, *Song of Hiawatha*, and also Whitman's first edition of *Leaves of Grass*.

13. As it turns out, Pickett's printed "sources"—French, Spanish, English, loyalist and revolutionary, as well as territorial records and texts provided by fellow Southern historians—with few additions still generally comprise the basic corpus still relied on by historians. (Frank Owsley notes, for example, that Pickett had managed to assemble three out of the four standard firsthand accounts of the de Soto expedition ["Pickett" 38]). In innumerable instances, as noted, Pickett was wealthy enough to travel to particular locations and to consult standard references. In others, as Michael O'Brien notes of a 23 March 1848 letter in the Pickett Papers (Alabama State Archives), he "had to ship off his money to Bartlett & Welford in New York, and acquire old Spanish and French volumes" ("On the Writing of History" 145). In the case of French writings, he was also wealthy enough to have major texts translated for him.

14. I should also note here the comment of an outside reader who suggests, from a reading of the author's manuscript correspondence with many of the figures identified, that such name-dropping—with the count on the original *dedication page alone* coming to sixteen Alabamians and sixteen figures from outside the state— could also be seen as "a toadying gesture, intended to elevate Pickett's insecure sense of himself by associating his name with illuminati (some of them not very luminous)." Having reviewed the materials in question, I am inclined to confirm Pickett's tendency to be what we might call a "networker," in search of influential contacts. His papers contain a file of nearly a hundred "letters from various distinguished and well informed persons" responding to queries made of them by Pickett regarding the writing of the *History*. A short list of such correspondents includes Edmund P. Gaines, A. P. Bagby, J. F. H. Claiborne, William Gilmore Simms, A. B. Meek, Charles Gayarre, Thomas Hart Benton, J. D. B. De Bow, A. P. Hayne, and F. S. Lyon. On the other hand, various replies are clearly cast as responses to the questions of a man trying earnestly to learn the craft of the historian. A letter of Mississippian J. W. Monette of 9 June 1847, for instance, gives extremely concrete information on how to build raw data into a chronology, while "leaving blank spaces for any *desideratum* which may be subsequently obtained." Another, from Jared Sparks of 29 November 1847, rates the utility of early accounts of Spanish exploration, including those of Cabeza de Vaca, the Gentleman of Elva, and others. And a long one from William Gilmore Simms—among a number from that author in the file—dated 8 March of the same year responds point by point on what has clearly been a whole set of inquiries about particular matters of style and organization, including the propriety of the occasional romantic "effect." "Undoubtedly," Simms has replied, "the historian has the privilege of heightening the colors of his picture by the adjuncts of

magnetism and art, whenever he can do so without digressing too greatly or lessening the value or altering the character of his facts." Still, he emphasizes, "in history it is particularly important that your fancy shall be regulated severely by your tastes."

This impression is corroborated by a survey of the correspondence conducted by Michael O'Brien, in which replies from figures as diverse as Simms, J. D. B. De Bow, Charles Gayarre, Jared Sparks, and William Bacon Stevens are similarly noted as responding to very particular and well-informed inquiries about various documents and printed sources, as well as the content of specific historical collections ("On the Writing of History" 144–45).

15. The Pickett Papers contain many of his research files, carefully catalogued as to subject and material content. One is labeled, for instance, "Notes taken from the lips of Abram Mordecai an old Jew 92 years of age who had lived 60 years among the Creek Indians." Another cover reads, "Notes taken from the lips of Mr. George S. Gaines by A. J. Pickett, in relation to his early settlement in Alabama, the arrest of Aaron Burr in 1807, elaborate and interesting accounts of the Choctaw Indians, etc., etc."; another, "Notes furnished me by Judge Hawkins at my earnest request, relating to his civil and political services to this state"; and another—indicating a palpable lack of interest in its subject evident in the *History* as well—"Some notes in relation to North Alabama furnished me by Mr. Charles A. Jones of Jackson County, Alabama."

The paper collection also contains five volumes of manuscript notebooks for the *History* out of an original eight.

16. It should be added that in his Alabama Historical Society lecture of 1854, Pickett also explicitly affirms this view from a historiographic perspective. Making a necessary distinction between "pure narrative" and "perfect history," he avers, "the good historian has a wider field and is at liberty to glean from it and to give his opinions." He goes on to warn, however, that "he must not give them . . . unless they are based on the facts which he introduces."

17. As with much writing, North and South, of the early national period commonly considered nonfictional—history, autobiography, journal, diary, memoir, travel narration, humorous sketch—the profound literariness of Pickett's *History* cries out for stylistic analysis. One should not be surprised, then, that Lee—like many other Alabamians of her generation, an avid reader of the state's early literature, probably acquiring her first introduction to major texts in the schoolroom—should have felt so pronounced an appreciation. Further, to this day, the paper cited above, presented as part of a 1983 NEH symposium on Alabama literature and culture, remains the only serious writerly assessment of Pickett's historiographic art.

18. In virtually all national histories of the era, as well as in biographies of Jackson, the triumphant American commander, the Creek War is usually blended into the larger conflict known to Americans at large as the War of 1812. By contrast, in Alabama literary history, as noted below in fuller detail, the Creek War looms as the dominant, even obsessive theme of antebellum writing, both historical and literary. The only major literary work traditionally associated with early Alabama

to confront slavery head-on, for instance, was Caroline Lee Hentz's *The Planter's Northern Bride;* and, as is well known, that novel was intended as a Southern riposte to *Uncle Tom's Cabin.*

19. For a sharp assessment of Cooper's technique of alternating rhythms of narrative stasis and dramatic action, see, for instance, Henry Nash Smith's introduction to *The Prairie.*

20. Although one can only speculate, it would seem likely that Pickett, as a member of an elite comprised mainly of the wealthy planters of the Black Belt and, to a lesser degree, of the Tennessee Valley, also intended his remarks on "fierce party spirit" as a comment on the political rift rapidly developing between his own political class and a largely non-slaveowning and decidedly independent-spirited yeomanry concentrated in the northern sections of the state. As Mills Thornton points out in *Politics and Power in a Slave Society,* the "booming" 1850s had seen a new legislative ascendancy of large planters after an erosion of power to members of lower economic and social status (296–99). But equally a feature of the times was a distinct "cynicism becoming widespread among politicians," whereby "office seekers had become more and more consciously aware of how to obtain election by focusing popular uneasiness" (296). Surely, Pickett would have found this a lamentable development.

Whatever the problem, Pickett still felt strongly enough about it in 1854 to venture a pointed aside on the matter during his Alabama Historical Society lecture. "Sir," he exhorted, somewhere amidst Sallust, Livy, and Tacitus, "the fame, the memory of a great historian descends to posterity!" In contrast, he went on, "The fame and the memory of some politicians, their bitter political essays and worthless stump speeches, sink into oblivion when they themselves go down to their graves."

21. Apropos of Pickett's choice to end the *History* at around 1820, and thereby to eschew treatment of the era of the rapid expansion of the slavery system into the state, the census figures cited earlier showing the growth of numbers of slaves over the three decades in question in their relation to growth of white population are probably worth repeating. Slaves in 1820 represented 32 percent of the state population. In 1830 the figure was 38 percent, showing that slave importation had more than kept pace with the tremendous influx of white settlers. By 1860 slaves constituted an imposing 45 percent of the state's population; but by now, especially given Pickett's class affiliations and outlook, perhaps the most revealing figures were those of ownership. Of the state's white citizens, numbering 526,271, only 6.9 percent owned any slaves at all; and those considered large planters—through ownership of 50 slaves or more—constituted a bare .32 percent of the total white population. Again, for census data of the various decades, see Moore 352–54; and for the breakdown of 1860 figures, see Hubbs 61.

22. This proves the case in such diverse analogues of the era as an early fictional romance, variously attributed, entitled *The Lost Virgin of the South: A Historical Novel, Founded on Facts, Connected with the Indian War in the South, in 1812 to '15,* or A. B. Meek's epic poem, *The Red Eagle.* As Johanna Nicol Shields has pointed

out in "A Sadder Simon Suggs: Freedom and Slavery in the Humor of Johnson Jones Hooper," the subject was not totally ignored by antebellum literary figures. On the other hand, in Hooper, as in his Alabama contemporaries Joseph Glover Baldwin and John Gorman Barr, one notes how matter-of-factly slave figures become part of the rough-and-tumble humorous scene; but one is also struck by the relative paucity of their appearances in these overwhelmingly "white" texts. Further, in the Suggs connection, one should observe that Hooper's disreputable hero gains his "captaincy" as a militia politico during the 1836 Creek War.

CHAPTER 6

1. Newton Arvin's phrase "phenomenally popular" (155), applied offhandedly to *Song of Hiawatha* as if it were a simple adjective, remains correct. The poem sold 10,000 copies in the first four weeks, and 30,000 by the end of six months.

2. Although we may enjoy the bemused retailing of anecdotes about Whitman's writing at least three of his own early reviews, it should not obscure the known information that the 1855 *Leaves of Grass* attracted more attention than might have been expected from established contemporary critics and reviewers. An immediate review, "friendly and sympathetic" as described by Gay Wilson Allen, appeared from Charles A. Dana in Horace Greeley's *New York Tribune*. Also appearing, perhaps less favorable, but of similar visibility, was an anonymous account—subsequently revealed to have been written by Charles Eliot Norton of Harvard—in the September *Putnam's Magazine*.

The letter of praise sent to Whitman by Ralph Waldo Emerson is well known. Emerson also plumped the book vociferously to such associates as Bronson Alcott, Henry Thoreau, Frank Sanborn, and Moncure D. Conway. On Whitman's part, permitting Dana to publish Emerson's letter stirred up further publicity. New reviews followed, some of them likely a direct result, in the *Criterion,* the Boston *Christian Examiner,* and the Washington, D.C., *National Intelligencer.* Most important in the second wave was surely Edward Everett Hale's quite favorable notice in the *North American Review* (Allen 169–76).

Ironically, as Ezra Greenspan points out, the latter was immediately preceded by a favorable review of *Song of Hiawatha*, praising it as "the first poem which savors of the prairie or the mountain hunting trail" (274). As Greenspan observes, "one person's truthfulness to nature was apparently another's artificiality" (250). The same confusion of standards seems to have marked the reception of the two poems in the Whitman family household. According to Whitman, his brother George and his mother had leafed through *Song of Hiawatha* and the 1855 *Leaves of Grass* at roughly the same time, with George reporting that "the one seemed to us pretty much the same muddle as the other" (Reynolds 485).

3. Indeed, in poetry alone, as revealed by Roy Harvey Pearce, the era had seen a veritable flurry of such melancholy production, including such titles as M. M. Webster's *Pocahontas* (1840), Seba Smith's *Powhatan* (1841), George H. Colton's

Tecumseh (1842), and Elbert Smith's *Ma-Ka-Tai-Me-She-Kia-Kiak; or, Black Hawk and Scenes in the West* (1848). Most notably in relation to Meek, even the magisterial Henry Rowe Schoolcraft, author of the multivolume *Historical and Statistical Information Respecting the History, Condition, and Prospects of the Indian Tribes of the United States* (1851-57), had earlier weighed in with *Alhalla* (1843), a poetic romance of the Creek War (Pearce 189).

Longfellow, of course, wished to exploit such topical appeal in *Song of Hiawatha;* but by setting his work resolutely in the dimension of myth—his main historical source was Schoolcraft's deeply antiquarian *Algic Researches*—and thus, by Western terms, the prehistoric native past, he was forced to treat the advent of white civilization in the realm of prophecy.

4. In a related comment on his general intention, Longfellow also called *Hiawatha* his "Indian Edda."

5. Actually, in this respect, Meek was outstripping such contemporaries as Cooper and Simms, taking as his subject the great frontier clash of savage and civilized cultures, but finding it unnecessary to displace the struggle to a more romantic past—in Cooper's case the French and Indian War and in Simms's the pre-Revolutionary era in the South.

6. Attesting to his concern for the particulars of historical actuality, Meek elected to preface the text with an explanation of what he called "the leading incidents" of his poem and the major historical figures involved. He also appended several pages of explanatory notes of imposing scholarly density, at the same time having resisted an earlier, larger plan, he confided to the reader, of "copious 'Historic Illustrations'" (9).

7. To complicate matters of naming and actual historical association further, as would have been well known to Alabamians of the era, Daniel Beasley had also been the real name of the commander taxed with the neglect of defensive preparations at Fort Mims that made the bloodbath inevitable. A militia major in deeply over his head, he is described by Meek in the Fort Mims chapter of *Romantic Passages in Southwestern History* as "a vain, rash, inexperienced, and over-confident soldier,—although unflinchingly brave when in the presence of the foe" (250).

8. In the first scene we witness in the poem, for instance, a forest meeting of the lovers in which Weatherford seeks to warn Lilla of the impending attack on the fort, Beazeley lies in ambush and narrowly misses killing the young chief with a rifle shot; and again on the work's final page, presuming his daughter dead at Weatherford's hands, he bursts into Jackson's tent swearing revenge just as the commander has made his decision to spare his noble adversary. Accordingly, a somewhat incongruous last scene eschews an embrace by the young lovers and instead has the daughter fainting happily upon her father's breast.

9. To show the vagaries of poetic taste, on the other hand, at the time, even Southern admirers of *The Red Eagle* found specific occasion to quarrel on just these grounds with Meek's departures from the formal regularities traditionally associated with epic. In the dimension of musicality, for instance, Meek's friend and poetic

compatriot William Russell Smith expressed disappointment at the poem's tendency to act too often as a lyric piece. Losing the opportunity to have his heroic
merits expounded in blank verse, Smith said, "Weatherford is shorn of much of his
majestic proportions, being cut off at the knees by the lyrical sword" (Ellison, *Early
Alabama Publications* 153). And similarly, praise leveled by a fictionalized admirer of
the poem cited below from Scott's *The Mobilians* was prefaced by an expression of
disappointment in Meek's failure to maintain sufficiently his core of muscular tetrameter.

As to the premium placed on variation, one suspects here the primary influence of Meek's idol, William Gilmore Simms, who esteemed his own poetic talents
highly and worked in a variety of forms, including the extended narrative. Particularly as to the operatic set piece of rhetorical performance constituting the climax,
however, one should note Meek's probable awareness of a long literary-historical tradition in American letters of celebrating Indian oratory. In national memory there
were the well-known examples, for instance, of Seneca and Chief Logan; and locally, Alabama legend had enshrined the speech to the legislature by Chief Eufala in
the role of the noble, vanquished, savage adversary, wisely representing his doomed
people, their protector, their last advocate.

10. Ironically, it should be noted, the same issue devoted thrice the space to a
review of Longfellow's poem that mainly rehashed comments about its self-parodic
meter and *Kaelevala* connections.

11. In Charleston's *Southern and Western Magazine and Review* 2 (1845): 119–20.

12. The list comes, in fact, from Jay Hubbell's classic *The South in Modern Literature, 1607–1900* (359). With the addition and/or deletion of a name or two, however, it would also have been fairly accurate within the contemporary era.

13. The first was delivered in 1841 to the Literary Society of LaGrange College
in Alabama, and the second in 1844 to the assembled literary societies at the University of Georgia.

14. A set of cultural commentaries styled as the camphouse gathering of a literary club, and subtitled *Talks about the South,* the work is set in 1878. It was published in 1898 by Brown Brothers of Montgomery.

15. This is not to discount a thriving business in Confederate history and memoir, with emphasis on combat accounts and the lives of military and political leaders.
It was the heyday, for instance, of the popular periodical entitled *Confederate Veteran*
(1893–1932); and across the region, also gaining immense popularity at the turn of
the century, was at least one bitterly pro-Southern novel of Reconstruction, Thomas
Nelson Page's *Red Rock*. In Alabama, wartime divisions within the state had been
resurrected in acrimonious fictions, with one side taken up by Jeremiah Clemens in
Tobias Wilson: A Tale of the Great Rebellion, about anti-Confederate activity in the
northern counties, and the other by Thomas Cooper DeLeon and Irwin Ledyard in
John Holden, Unionist, with the loathsome appositive of the title presumed to speak
for itself. The work of plantation nostalgists was reserved for romance, sentimen-

tal literature, and the occasional attempt at patronizing humor, with Alabama contributing a children's classic of the genre in Sara Louise Pyrnelle's *Diddie Dumps and Tot*. Serious attempts to preserve and represent traditions of African-American narrative, on the other hand, were also made by Joel Chandler Harris in the *Uncle Remus* stories and analogously by Alabamian Robert Wilton Burton in the tales of Marengo Jake.

16. This search for some version of a usable past was hardly an isolated phenomenon. Virginia, for instance, while revering its Confederate saints, would also put new effort into celebrating Jamestown, Williamsburg, and the fathers of the Republic. North Carolina and Georgia would be at pains to represent their myths of origin as contrasting to the hierarchical ones of the aristocratic colonial and antebellum South. To be sure, one would find a certain proud recalcitrance on the part of South Carolina, with its continuing celebrations of Charleston, Fort Sumter, and the low country planter society. At the same time, as with Louisiana, there would also be a new emphasis on the architecture, the cultural pluralism of colonial life, the admixtures of English, French, Spanish, slave, and Creole. In Mississippi and Alabama the emphasis would become most pronounced on the legacy of the native tribes, with literary reverberations running as far forward as William Faulkner and Harper Lee.

17. To examine the volumes of proceedings produced in the period, for instance, is to be struck with the preponderance of interest in pre-Confederate Alabama history and culture.

18. As a period artifact, one should add, in design and layout, the volume seems to have much in common with a contemporary publishing enterprise by G. H. Putnam known as the "Mohawk Edition" of the novels of James Fenimore Cooper and making its appearance in 1912. As to the book's old competitor, *Hiawatha,* one should note, numerous deluxe, illustrated editions had also appeared around the turn of the century, with a most recent one of 1911 from Boston's Houghton Mifflin featuring art by Frederic Remington, N. C. Wyeth, *and* Maxwell Parrish.

19. In this, as a promoter of state history and historical culture, Sheehan was a well-known admirer of and frequent collaborator with Thomas McAdory Owen. In the introduction at hand, the editors concluded with special thanks to Owen for his work in providing rare archival engravings of early paintings. More generally, as editor of the Montgomery paper, Sheehan proved also in print a frequent promoter of Owen's historical service projects. In turn, Owen conferred in his 1921 history the favor of a biographical entry on Sheehan, crediting him with, among other things, a crucial role in the campaign to establish an Alabama Department of Archives and History.

20. At the time it was virtually obligatory, as to the massacre at Fort Mims, to attempt to absolve Weatherford of responsibility of direct command. Blame was also usually leveled at the English for stirring up the Red Sticks against the Lower Creeks representing a peace party. In later years this would be followed by the ten-

dency of historians to treat the abortive attack upon a Creek packtrain by James Caller and his militia at Burnt Corn Creek as a direct provocation of the Fort Mims disaster that shortly followed.

21. For all his efforts, even Sheehan, for instance, seemed to express disappointment in a 1919 column, reprinted in *Literary Digest,* lamenting the neglect of Alabama literature within the state's educational and civic culture. Along the way he tried to give some favorite texts one last puff. As he had in his editorial columns some years earlier, he praised his competitor the *Birmingham News* for reprinting Johnson Jones Hooper's *Simon Suggs* stories. More diffidently, he also averred that "In recent years there was a revival of interest in A. B. Meek's notable 'Red Eagle' poem when it was published" (35).

CHAPTER 7

1. A third Alabama figure of the era worth mentioning, although his work was never published in book form, would surely be Tuscaloosa's John Gorman Barr. Barely a boy during the flush times, he did not publish until the late 1850s when, in a two-year period, he contributed fifteen sketches to William T. Porter's *Spirit of the Times* and its successor, *Porter's Spirit of the Times.* For an edition of Barr's collected writings, with extremely informative historical annotation, see G. Ward Hubbs's *Rowdy Tales from Alabama.*

2. Three examples of the relatively new form, all devoted to Andrew Jackson, hero of the new Democratic Party, are usually cited as supplying Hooper, an ardent Whig loyalist, with major targets. As itemized by Winston Smith, these included John Henry Eaton's *Memoirs of Andrew Jackson, Late Major-General and Commander in Chief of the Southern Division of the Army of the United States* (1828); Philo A. Goodwin's *Biography of Andrew Jackson, President of the United States, Formerly Major General in the Army of the United States* (1832), and Amos Kendall's *Life of Andrew Jackson, Private, Military, and Civil* (1843–44). To be sure, as Smith notes, in his opening chapter Hooper also alluded to analogous recent puff jobs on Van Buren, Clay, and Polk (xxxvii). Still, in this newest hagiography of a candidate for sheriff clearly trying to trade on his reputation as a backwoods *miles gloriosus,* Jackson was the real mark; and, as Johanna Nicol Shields puts it acutely in the introduction to the recent University of Alabama Press edition, beyond the weighty title parallels, Whig readers could hardly have missed the various other salient connections. To the latter, she writes, "it was a national disgrace that Jackson's military record—his 1813 victory over the Creeks at Horseshoe Bend and his 1815 triumph over the British at New Orleans—had made him President" (xxxiv). Meanwhile, it was also well known that Jackson had made a fortune in land speculation in Tennessee (lxvi).

3. Indeed, precisely because of Baldwin's focus on the frontier judiciary, the usual riffraff are definitely there, usually as legal clients—bankrupts; drunkards; horse and pig thieves; prisoners at bar; participants in lawsuits and other parties under indictment. The most notable of such figures not in custody is Simon Suggs,

Jr., scion of the original genius, a venal illiterate in his father's image who has lit out for the territories to practice the family skills, albeit now self-promoted to the status of lawyer and colonel. Asked for his biography by the narrator, naturally he fakes it with ghostwritten copy, albeit decidedly ambiguous in some of its more flowery attempts at eulogy. Of the subject's origins, for instance, the biographer has offered that he "was not quite, either in a literal or metaphorical sense, a self-made man. He had ancestors" (121); and sufficient information is further provided for us to learn that he has removed himself to Rackinsack, Arkansas, where he has married the daughter of a Choctaw chief and serves as federal agent for the tribe. On the other hand, we have probably received all the biography we really need to know from Suggs Jr.'s own hand in the postscript to a first letter: "I rite from here where I am winding up my fust wife's estate," he informs us, "which they've filed a bill in chancery" (119).

4. The most notable buyer conflicts, as recorded by Mary Elizabeth Young in her study of dealings in Creek and Choctaw lands during the era, were between various groups of Alabama speculators and the Columbus Land Company, formed in 1832 as a competing Georgia cartel (75).

5. For detailed descriptions of what the author aptly terms the "Creek Frauds" and the "Choctaw Speculations," see Young 47–98.

6. As will be seen, Baldwin deems this event particularly crucial in bringing an end to the flush times (90).

7. Indeed, regarding the inept performance of the state's political leadership in unsuccessfully attempting to resolve the crisis, as Mills Thornton puts it, on both sides "the central political event of the early 1840s was to be the oratorial transmutation of this bumbling effort to help into a malevolent exercise in self-interest" (79).

8. Further, in the text this turns out to be no mere metaphor, with Simon Suggs, Jr., as noted earlier, having set himself up as Choctaw agent in the wilds of Arkansas.

9. Indeed, the only character in the whole flush times worthy of being called a true hero—the Honorable Francis Strother—is accorded so mainly for one reason: he has been the figure locally credited with resolving the bank crisis; and in so doing, he has thus earned the fame of being the "one more instrumental than any other in redeeming the State from the *Flush Times,* in the course of our hasty articles illustrative of that hell-carnival" (263).

10. In this degree, it thus becomes hard to accept totally, as regards the view of the bench and bar, John Grammer's claim, largely on the basis of the late sketch of Strother, that Baldwin supplies "his account of moral anarchy on the frontier with an incongruously sanguine ending"—as if to hold out against the ruins of economic fraud, from the perspective of an older "legal-republican worldview," the still available prospect of "Alabama's comfortable, nearly inevitable progress toward civilized order" (143).

11. For an extended discussion of this matter, centered on such depictions of slavery as do occur in Hooper, see Johanna Nicol Shields's 1990 essay, "A Sadder Simon Suggs: Freedom and Slavery in the Humor of Johnson Jones Hooper."

12. Further, such a depiction probably would have been rather accurate. As to landed status, among slaveowners, large planters with major slave holdings comprised a minuscule fraction of the total, with individual families frequently owning just one or two. In fact, the vast majority of Alabamians and Mississippians were not slaveowners at all. As to Simon's activities as a speculator, the message would have been equally clear. Real planters may buy and sell slaves in quantity, but they would never besmirch their political and economic status with speculation.

13. Hele's status in the text, one might add, is hardly helped by a footnote informing us that his victim has capitalized on her departure to make off with a good lump of severance pay, which she plans to put at interest while living off the profits.

14. Further, as Johanna Nicol Shields documents in her "Social History of Antebellum Alabama Writers," for both Hooper and Baldwin this would have been a matter of self-indictment as well, albeit on a rather small scale, relatively speaking. At the time of Hooper's marriage, his family owned three slaves and his wife's family sixteen. Mary Brantley Hooper also received a slave from her father as a wedding present. When Baldwin married Sidney White, his father owned five slaves and hers owned twenty-one. She, too, brought one slave to the marriage, and Baldwin acquired others.

15. Accordingly, as detailed by Lynn, the relish of such political energy would flower into its literary correlative. The voice of the clowns would ultimately break its way out of the Whig narrative frame, creating in works such as *Huckleberry Finn* the style of a new political realism out of the vernacular poetry of frontier speech.

CHAPTER 8

1. It is accounted so, for instance, in J. V. Ridgley's *Nineteenth-Century Southern Literature* 70–72; in Nina Baym's *Women's Fiction* 136; in Baym's "Rise of the Woman Author" 302; in Robert S. Levine's "Fiction and Reform I" in *The Columbia History of the Novel,* where it is paired with Simms's *Woodcraft* (145–46); in Mary Anne Wimsatt's "Antebellum Fiction," where the author tells us it "remains Hentz's best known book through its status as the answer to *Uncle Tom's Cabin*" (101–2); in Wimsatt's longer consideration, "Caroline Lee Hentz's Balancing Act" 161–62; and in Thadious Davis's "Women's Art and Authorship in the Southern Region" 26.

2. Certainly the current visibility of the text can be connected with developments in professional criticism of the last several decades. Chief among these has been the critical resurrection of *Uncle Tom's Cabin* and its reinstatement in the academic canon. It could only follow, then, that the body of fiction created in response would benefit from a corresponding upturn in interest. More generally, it has also surely benefited, through the work of Nina Baym, Cathy Davidson, Jane Tompkins, and others, from a broad awakening of critical interest in nineteenth-century American women's fiction that has led to revisionary assessment and, in many cases, canonical reinstatement of numerous works of major figures of the era, including Stowe and Hentz; going on to others as diverse as Catherine Maria

Sedgwick, Lydia Maria Child, and E.D.E.N. Southworth; Susan Warner, Maria Cummins, and Sara Parton Willis (Fanny Fern); and extending to such postwar popular favorites North and South as Louisa May Alcott and Augusta Jane Evans.

3. In 1852 alone, as detailed in Jane Gardiner's comprehensive survey, eight contenders had entered the lists, chief among them the eminent William Gilmore Simms, loftily billing his *The Sword and the Distaff*—a work of ostensibly rather indistinct relevance to Stowe's recycling itself back into the action in 1854 as the more familiar *Woodcraft*—as his personal response to the affront leveled by Stowe against the region.

Some titles made clear their intention to confront—Robert Criswell's *Uncle Tom's Cabin Contrasted with Buckingham Hall, the Planter's Home,* for instance; W. L. Smith's *Life at the South; or, Uncle Tom's Cabin As It Is;* or C. H. Wiley's work by the same name, subtitled *An Antidote to Uncle Tom's Cabin.* Others ranged from the semi-parodic, as in Mary H. Eastman's *Aunt Phillis's Cabin,* to the deflationary, as in *Frank Freeman's Barber Shop* by the Rev. Bayard R. Hall. In 1853 at least five more followed, again with ingenious anti-Stowe entitling at a premium. M. J. McIntosh, for instance, contributed *The Lofty and the Lowly; or, Good in All and None All Good,* and J. W. Page *Uncle Robin in His Cabin in Virginia, and Tom without One in Boston.*

Matters tailed off in 1854, with Hentz's novel finding its chief competition in the newly titled *Woodcraft* and Lucien Chase's *English Serfdom and American Slavery; or, As Others See Us.* On the other hand, the last half of the decade would record at least ten more efforts extending to the very eve of war. See Gardiner, "Pro-slavery Propaganda in Fiction Written in Answer to *Uncle Tom's Cabin,* 1852–61."

In conjunction with Simms's opportunistic 1852 attempt to pronounce "anti-Tom" authority upon a novel set in the Revolutionary era, one should add that Hentz in the same year was not above implying a claim to first-strike retaliatory status for her own *Marcus Warland.* This she attempted to accomplish in somewhat hasty, ad hoc fashion through a prefatory "Address to the Reader," where she expressed the hope that a "truthful picture of Southern life" such as she avowed her own to be might help correct Northern misconceptions and thereby dispel "prejudices that have been gradually building up a wall of separation between these two divisions of our land" (7). Especially in her depiction of life on the Bellamy plantation—the site of much of the story's action—she insisted on her preference for the "real" over the ideal. She then went on to preview several instances from the book of the self-sacrificing magnanimity frequently characteristic on both sides of the master-slave relationship. These, she concluded, she knew to have occurred in actual life.

The problem with Hentz's implied claim was the romantic plot emphasis of the novel itself, which focused almost exclusively on a complicated love story involving the rise of the titular protagonist to wealth, reputation, and eventual union with a lady of high estate. To be sure, both *Marcus Warland* and *The Sword and the Distaff* gave extensive depictions of master-slave relationships in a host of benign lights, with various characters given frequent opportunities to speak in vindication of the Southern way of life. And with Simms, especially, it could be persuasively argued, as Richard Gray has done, that the author's novels of the American Revolution in South Carolina were invariably "a mirror for his own times," with the partisan invariably a stand-in for the gentleman-planter and the loyalist for the dreaded Yankee. Still, in both of the present cases, it is hard to see how basic elements of construction—plot, character, setting, and the like—evidence direct address to *Uncle Tom's Cabin* in much depth of calculated fictional reply. On Gray's assessment of Simms, see *Writing the South* 47.

4. As Bertram Wyatt-Brown argues in *Yankee Saints and Southern Sinners*, "since radical idealisms are almost by nature beyond the comprehension and workaday interests of Everyman, antislavery had to be an unpopular cause not only in the South but in the North, too" (6). Even so influential a Northerner as Horace Greeley, he goes on, was forced to admit that the abolitionist as Yankee saint was not only a scarce cultural commodity, but for the most part an unpopular one as well. And one of the chief causes of unpopularity, he confirms, citing the classic work of Stanley M. Elkins, was likely the effect of the abolitionist's susceptibility to a "romantic antinomianism" in which the would-be saint is "often burdened with simple Manichean extravagances and suspicions, intolerance, and an abstract way of thinking" (22). It is difficult to read such phrasings and not call to mind immediately Hentz's depictions of Hastings, Grimby, and others of their righteous New England ilk.

A more directly institutional view of the causes of widespread popular antiabolitionist sentiment in the North is supplied by James Brewer Stewart in his aptly titled *Holy Warriors*: "Because slavery had become by the 1830's interwoven with nearly all American institutions, Northern politicians, ministers, and businessmen all could find ample motives for opposing the immediatists." Further, "race prejudice also continued to permeate white culture in the North. In the ever shifting-confusing circumstances of this rapidly expanding region, white skin became an increasingly compelling assurance of stable identity" (61–62).

5. In the South, a causal connection had long been assumed between abolitionist activism and slave insurrection, with widespread belief that the organization and encouragement of fifth-column activity on plantations by Northern infiltrators was a very real abolitionist project. As David M. Potter writes in *The Impending Crisis, 1848–1861*, there was even a legendary date accepted by many Southerners as conferring quasi-official status on the concept of dreadful collusion: 1831, in which occurred both Nat Turner's rebellion and publication of the first number of William Lloyd Garrison's *The Liberator*. And at the end of the decade, Southern hearts were no doubt further chilled by highly publicized abolitionist support in legal proceedings to secure the release from U.S. custody of Africans who, while in transit across the Atlantic, had successfully seized control of the Spanish slave ship *Amistad*.

By the time of Hentz's novel, active insurrectionists were on the prowl, especially in border states. And within five years, of course, one of them, John Brown, would persuade Southerners by a single act that such fears had never been simple paranoia. Bankrolled and actively supported by a cabal of influential abolitionists known as the Secret Six, the Harpers Ferry raid had one major objective beyond all others: to fulfill a "belief," as Potter phrases it, however delusional, "in the possibility of a vast, self-starting slave insurrection" (372–73).

For a classic monograph devoted to exploring the centrality of this theory of revolutionary fifth-column abolitionism to antebellum Southern thinking, see Richard Brion Davis, *The Slave Power Conspiracy and the Paranoid Style.*

6. An illustrated first edition of *The Planter's Northern Bride,* in the Special Collections Library at the University of Alabama, actually bears different publishers' imprints on the two volumes. The first lists "A. Hart, Late Carey and Hart." The second then lists "Parry & M'Millan, Successors to A. Hart, Late Carey and Hart." Page references are taken from this original edition.

7. As Baym points out, such magnanimity and nobility are the moderating features of a generally laudable impetuosity in Hentz's male heroes, "whose passions are held in check by respect for the woman and by an ideal of appropriate manly behavior as protective rather than exploitive" (*Women's Fiction* 127).

8. In her introduction to a 1970 reprint of the novel by the University of North Carolina Press (xiii). This edition, along with Professor Ellison's fine essay, is regrettably out of print.

9. According to Rhoda Coleman Ellison, the period of shared residence in the city for Stowe and Hentz extended from 1832 to 1834. Further, they may have both attended meetings of local literary club—a fellow member of which, it turns out, a physician, probably precipitated the Hentzes' departure on the basis of what the jealous Nicholas Hentz deemed improper attentions paid to his wife. We will never know, of course, if Hentz and Stowe were acquaintances in Cincinnati nearly two decades before either became famous. On the other hand, in the Cincinnati scenes here depicting the attractive Dr. Darley as physician to the dying Richard Laurens and later as romantic companion to the widowed Ildegerte, one might at least speculate that Caroline Hentz got her revenge on the violently jealous Nicholas. See Ellison, "Mrs. Hentz and the Green-eyed Monster."

10. As Baym points out, the integration into plot structure of elements of melodrama created by the operations of a dark, vivid, "antagonist woman" in relation to the heroine was a signature of Hentz's novelistic style (*Women's Fiction* 26).

11. To be sure, throughout the decades of the impending crisis of Union, Southern political leaders in the halls of national government had inveighed against antislavery propaganda as an incitement to slave insurrection. But, as in the case of John C. Calhoun, they tended to isolate it in condescending response as the work of "ferocious zealots" (R. Davis 37).

12. For women readers generally, excluded from formal debate, there would likely have been no small additional satisfaction here, one suspects, in seeing morally objectionable males—imaging Stowe's treatment of slaveholders like Mr. Shelby on one hand and Legree on the other—portrayed as canting fools and/or villains.

13. Much has been written about Hentz's difficulties with her brilliant, imperious, irascible husband. One should also give equal time, it could be proposed, to

the qualities of intellectual stimulation and companionship they found in each other. Mr. Hentz, to put it another way, was no academic slouch. He held some impressive appointments and by the time of his death had also published important titles in language study and natural history.

14. In this connection, Elizabeth Fox-Genovese is precise in saying that "*Beulah* is a classic *Bildungsroman*—a narrative of a young woman's education and successful search for identity and a place in the world." On the other hand, she unnecessarily qualifies the definition by going on to call the work "an allegory of Evans' own reflections on the role of women and the future of the South" (xii). Frequently, the literary and philosophical aspirations of the work seem to transcend either gender or place, suggesting Evans's primary interest in the bildungsroman itself as a novelistic mode.

15. For a description of the women's novel as vehicle of a curriculum paralleling that offered college- and university-educated males, see, for instance, Cathy Davidson's *Revolution and the Word* 73–74. For the broader notion of a female curriculum as the authorized cultural content of women's fiction, see both Davidson, who concentrates on the early national period, and Nina Baym, whose study of the golden age of nineteenth-century women's fiction devotes most of a concluding chapter to Evans. To be sure, in virtually all cases, exceptions could be found. On the subject of slavery, for instance, both Stowe's *Uncle Tom's Cabin* and Hentz's *The Planter's Northern Bride* addressed the central issue of antebellum politics head-on in ways eschewed by most of their white male counterparts. Fanny Fern, both in her periodical writings and in her novel *Ruth Hall,* frequently proved a notable example of a woman reading and a woman writing against conventional social constraints. Gender roles were explored in adventure feminism, including E.D.E.N. Southworth's cross-dressing, etc.

16. In a parodist's cruel refinement on the theme, the heroine of C. H. Webb's *St. Twel'mo* was described by the author as having seized upon a nurse's inattention to ingest an unabridged dictionary.

17. Given the frequent participation of women in such intellectual discussions with both male and female counterparts, one is tempted to suggest something of a feminist "dialogics" here in the sense of the term made fashionable in current theoretical study as "discursive interplay." The result of the various dialogues in *Beulah* certainly is something like a Bakhtinian intellectual polyphony. At the same time, however, it is to complicate a rather more simple idea here—with its brilliance in fact lying in its very obviousness and simplicity—of Evans's own simple but bold realization as a writer of domestic realism of the discursive possibilities of fictional dialogue as intellectual conversation.

18. Further, if fictionally suspect, such a pattern of confirmation regarding conventional domestic values certainly conformed to the pattern of Evans's own life. She, too, indisputably went through a severe crisis of faith on which she admitted her heroine's to have been modeled. And she, too, emerged. Also, as a reflection of private attitudes, it is certainly of a piece with her essential conservatism in public

matters. In the political sphere, she was adamantly pro-Southern and pro-slavery; later she argued against women's voting rights.

For enlarged readings of the examples of feminist critique cited see Beverly Voloshin, "The Limits of the Female Bildungsroman in America, 1820–1870," and pertinent sections of G. M. Goshgarian, *To Kiss the Chastening Rod,* esp. 12–13 and 121–55.

19. A classic example of this in Cooper would be the Wagnerian funeral *cum* marriage-in-death of Uncas and Cora Munro in *The Last of the Mohicans.* While attendant Indian maidens sing of the possibility of a union beyond, Natty Bumppo, a firm believer in "gifts," resolutely shakes his head in denial. Still, the "fact" of the novel is that the imaginative possibility of such a union has been broached.

20. For an extended comparison of the sexual politics of this relationship in *Beulah* with that of Ellen Montgomery with the equally stern but pious John Humphreys in Susan Warner's *The Wide Wide World,* see Goshgarian, *To Kiss the Chastening Rod,* esp. 123–26, 150.

21. For a definition of the mode in the context of the "gothicism" of its fore-most American practitioner—by no surprise, the reading of whom presently brings Beulah to her own moment of metaphysical crisis—see G. R. Thompson's *Poe's Fiction* 19–38.

22. An even more extensive bibliographic inventory on the basis of "deviant" writers either discussed or at least mentioned is supplied by Goshgarian: "Byron, Carlyle, Comte, Cousin, Cowper, De Quincey, Emerson ('grim'), Feuerback, Fourier, Goethe, Hegel, Hume, Jean-Paul, Kingsley, Lamb, Locke, More, Parker ('disgusting'), Plato, Poe, Pope, Reid, Sappho, Schelling, Shelley, Sophocles, Southey, and Spinoza" (231–32 n. 1).

23. Certainly it is not the first time a woman writer has suffered pejoratively by the institution of some dominant concept of point of view as a literary technology. Against the great romantics working in first-person authority, we see Stowe's artless distribution. Against the postwar realists we counter the preference for dramatization over narration, the Jamesian prejudice advanced by such admirers as T. S. Eliot and Arnold Kettle.

24. For a detailed notation of the remarkable parallels between the two texts, see Fox-Genovese: "Beulah, like Jane, begins as an orphan who is taken into the home of the older man she will ultimately marry; Hartwell bears a strong resemblance to Edward Rochester; Beulah, like Jane, addresses her suitor as 'sir,' and he addresses her as 'child'; Beulah, like Jane, is courted by an apparently suitable man, whom she rejects even though she has already rejected Hartwell. Both orphaned heroines struggle to earn their living, cope with the arrogant dismissals of fashionable society, and experience a difficult coming-of-age, including a search for personal independence" (xviii). To all this—characteristic of Evans's tendency to concentrate on convention and prediction—one may add pronounced parallels in the novel's opening scenes. Jane, like Beulah, is first found in an orphan asylum, where she finds comfort and tutelage from a kind superintendent. Similarly, Jane is deeply

traumatized by the loss of a beloved fellow inmate, who dies of consumption in her arms.

At the risk of committing an anachronism, one can also see the work as prophetic, in transatlantic literary-intellectual regard, of that great English novel of female education devoted to the woman as radical intellectual—*Middlemarch*. In fact, by contemporary notice, as observed by Fox-Genovese, *Beulah* was favorably compared at the time of its publication to Eliot's *Adam Bede*, which Evans is said to have disliked. At the same time, the intellectual appeal of Eliot for Evans must have been significant, especially given Eliot's work as a translator of Spinoza and Feuerbach.

25. In fact, as a feminist issue in the broadest sense, will in this definition—and a woman's will, specifically—may be said to assume its own metaphysical status in the text. After one of several brief, stormy reunions with Hartwell, in which he has abjured responsibility for the solitary misery into which she has been forced in her quest for spiritual independence, Beulah sits with Clara and reflects on what must be her more conventionally pious companion's analogous journey toward faith in the face of persistent rebukes to her happiness—not the least of which includes an unrequited passion for Hartwell. "How is it," the narrator asks "that when the human soul is called to pass through a fierce ordeal, and numbing despair seizes the faculties and energies in her sepulchral grasp, how is it, that superhuman strength is often suddenly infused into the sinking spirit?" The only answer can be "that miraculous bit of mechanism, the human will" (205). Yet what can explain it? "Truly there is no Oedipus for this vexing riddle. Many luckless theories have been devoured by the Sphinx; when will metaphysicals solve it?" She goes on: "One tells us vaguely enough, 'who knows the mysteries of will, with its vigor? Man does not yield himself to the angels, not unto death, utterly, save only through the weakness of his feeble will'" (205). The lines, of course, are Ligeia's favorite ones from Joseph Glanvill, repeated on her deathbed.

CHAPTER 9

1. See Cooper's introduction to the 1979 Louisiana State reprint edition of *Social Relations* and Hobson's essay on Hundley, along with related figures such as Edmund Ruffin and Hinton Rowan Helper, as part of his opening chapter in *Tell About the South: The Southern Rage to Explain*.

2. "The Evils of Commercial Supremacy," *Hunt's Merchants' Magazine* 36 (March 1857): 316-17; "The Traffic in Coolies," ibid. (May 1857): 570-73; *Work and Bread* (pamphlet).

3. *Social Relations in Our Southern States* (New York: Henry B. Price, 1860), 7-8. Rpt. with Introduction by William J. Cooper (Baton Rouge: Louisiana State UP, 1979). Subsequent references are parenthetical in the text.

4. As phrased, these are a redaction of chapter headings in the table of contents.

5. In fact, McWhiney gives explicit endorsement to Hundley's assertion that

the poor white—"Rag Tag and Bobtail" as Hundley scornfully titled the breed—was an essentially Southern phenomenon, and also expresses grateful admiration for the accuracy of Hundley's enumeration of characteristic traits: "courageous, lazy, lustful, quarrelsome, violent, ignorant, superstitious, drunkards, gamblers, and livestock thieves" (xvi).

6. Oddly, this flies in the face of frequent claims by their descendants to the contrary. In Alabama, especially, a cherished myth of the northern counties remains that of a proud, independent, non-slaveowning yeomanry dragooned by Black Belt aristocrats into fighting a slaveowners' civil war.

7. Here, amidst Hundley's charming depictions of the plantation system, one may wonder what happened to previous admissions of the horrors of slavery. Then one realizes that they have been judiciously placed in a foregoing section where such cruelties can be assigned to the Southern Yankee (132).

8. Hundley to William B. Figures, 1 December 1860, printed in *Huntsville Southern Advocate,* 12 December 1860 (qtd. in Cooper xx n. 15). His escape from the Chicago mob is noted in the "Hundley Manuscript Diary," 21–24 April 1861 (in the possession of Mrs. J. Dexter Nilsson, great-granddaughter of D. R. Hundley) (cf. Cooper xiv).

Works Cited

~

Abernathy, Thomas P. *The Formative Period in Alabama, 1815–28.* 1922. Rev. ed. Tuscaloosa: U of Alabama P, 1965. Rpt. 1990.

Allen, Gay Wilson. *The Solitary Singer: A Critical Biography of Walt Whitman.* New York: New York UP, 1967.

Arvin, Newton. *Longfellow: His Life and Work.* Boston: Little, Brown, 1962.

Baldwin, Joseph G. *The Flush Times of Alabama and Mississippi.* New York: D. Appleton and Company, 1853. Rpt., with Introduction by James Justus. Baton Rouge: Louisiana State UP, 1987.

Baym, Nina. "The Rise of the Woman Author." *The Columbia Literary History of the United States.* Ed. Emory Elliott. New York: Columbia UP, 1988. 289–305.

———. *Women's Fiction: A Guide to Novels by and about Women in America, 1820–70.* 2nd ed. Urbana: U of Illinois P, 1993.

Brantley, William H. "Henry Hitchcock of Mobile, 1816–1839." *Alabama Review* 4 (January 1951): 3–39.

———. *Three Capitals.* University: U of Alabama P, 1976.

Caesar, Terry. *Forgiving the Boundaries: Home as Abroad in American Travel Writing.* Athens: U of Georgia P, 1995.

Carter, Clarence E., ed. *Territorial Papers of the United States.* Vols. 5 and 6. Washington, D.C.: U.S. Government Printing Office, 1937.

Cohen, Hennig, and William B. Dillingham, eds. *Humor of the Old Southwest.* 2nd ed. Athens: U of Georgia P, 1975.

Cooper, William J. Introduction. *Social Relations in Our Southern States*. By Daniel R. Hundley. Baton Rouge: Louisiana State UP, 1979. xii–xlv.

Davidson, Cathy. *Revolution and the Word*. New York: Oxford UP, 1986.

Davis, Richard Brion. *The Slave Power Conspiracy and the Paranoid Style*. Baton Rouge: Louisiana State UP, 1969.

Davis, Thadious. "Women's Art and Authorship in the Southern Region: Connections." *The Female Tradition in Southern Literature*. Ed. Carol S. Manning. Urbana: U of Illinois P, 1993. 15–36.

Doster, James F. "Early Settlements on the Tombigbee and Tensaw Rivers." *Alabama Review* 12.2 (April 1959): 83–94.

Eaton, John Henry. *Life of General A. Jackson*. Philadelphia: McCarthy and Davis, 1828.

Eggleston, George Cory. *Red Eagle and the War with the Creek Indians of Alabama*. New York: Dodd, Mead, 1878.

Ellison, Rhoda. *Early Alabama Publications: A Study in Literary Interests*. University: U of Alabama P, 1947.

———. *History and Bibliography of Alabama Newspapers in the Nineteenth Century*. University: U of Alabama P, 1954.

———. Introduction. *The Planter's Northern Bride*. By Caroline Lee Hentz. Rpt. Chapel Hill: U of North Carolina P, 1970. vii–xxii.

———. "Mrs. Hentz and the Green-eyed Monster." *American Literature* 22 (November 1950): 345–50.

Emerson, Ralph Waldo. "Self-Reliance." *Selections from Ralph Waldo Emerson*. Ed. Stephen E. Whicher. Boston: Riverside Press, 1957. 147–68.

Evans, Augusta Jane. *Beulah*. New York: Federal Book Company, 1900. Rpt. Baton Rouge: Louisiana State UP, 1992.

Fidler, William T. *Augusta Evans Wilson, 1835–1909: A Biography*. University: U of Alabama P, 1951.

Fisher, Philip. *Hard Facts*. New York: Oxford UP, 1985.

Flint, Timothy. *Condensed Geography and History of the Western States, or the Mississippi Valley*. Cincinnati: E. H. Flint, 1828.

Fox-Genovese, Elizabeth. Introduction. *Beulah*. By Augusta Jane Evans. Rpt. Baton Rouge: Louisiana State UP, 1992. xi–xxxvi.

Gardiner, Jane. "Pro-slavery Propaganda in Fiction Written in Answer to *Uncle Tom's Cabin*, 1852–61: An Annotated Checklist." *Resources for American Literary Study* 7 (Autumn 1977): 201–9.

Glassberg, David. *American Historical Pageantry: The Uses of Tradition in the Early Twentieth Century*. Chapel Hill: U of North Carolina P, 1990.

Goshgarian, G. M. *To Kiss the Chastening Rod: Domestic Fiction and Sexual Ideology in the American Renaissance*. Ithaca: Cornell UP, 1992.

Grammer, John. *Pastoral and Politics in the Old South*. Baton Rouge: Louisiana State UP, 1996.

Gray, Richard. *Writing the South: Ideas of an American Region.* New York: Cambridge UP, 1986.

Greenspan, Ezra. *Walt Whitman and the American Reader.* New York: Cambridge UP, 1990.

Halbert, H. S., and T. H. Ball. *The Creek War of 1813 and 1814.* Montgomery: White, Woodruff, and Fowler, 1895. Rpt., ed. Frank L. Owsley. University: U of Alabama P, 1969.

Hedges, William L. *Washington Irving: An American Study, 1802–32.* Baltimore: Johns Hopkins UP, 1965.

Hentz, Caroline Lee. *Marcus Warland.* Philadelphia: T. B. Peterson, 1852.

———. *The Planter's Northern Bride.* 2 vols. Philadelphia: A. Hart, 1854.

Heyrman, Christine Leigh. *Southern Cross: The Beginnings of the Bible Belt.* New York: Knopf, 1997.

Hitchcock, Henry. *The Alabama Justice of the Peace.* Cahawba, AL: William B. Allen, 1822.

Hobson, Fred. *Tell About the South: The Southern Rage to Explain.* Baton Rouge: Louisiana State UP, 1983.

Hooper, Johnson J. *Adventures of Captain Simon Suggs, Late of the Tallapoosa Volunteers.* Philadelphia: Carey and Hart, 1845. Philadelphia: T. B. Peterson, 1858. Rpt., with Introduction by Johanna Nicol Shields. Tuscaloosa: U of Alabama P, 1993.

Hubbell, Jay R. *The South in American Literature, 1607–1900.* Durham: Duke UP, 1954.

Hubbs, G. Ward, Jr., ed. *Rowdy Tales from Alabama.* University: U of Alabama P, 1981.

Hundley, Daniel R. *Social Relations in Our Southern States.* 1860. Rpt. Baton Rouge: Louisiana State UP, 1979.

Ingraham, Joseph Holt. *Lafitte: or the Baratarian Chief, a tale. Founded on facts.* New York, 1828.

Justus, James. Introduction. *The Flush Times of Alabama and Mississippi.* By Joseph G. Baldwin. Baton Rouge: Louisiana State UP, 1987. xiii–l.

Kermode, Frank. *The Sense of an Ending.* New York: Oxford UP, 1967.

Lee, Harper. "Romance and High Adventure." *Clearings in the Thicket.* Ed. Jerry E. Brown. Macon, GA: Mercer UP, 1985. 13–20.

Le Vert, Octavia Walton. *Souvenirs of Travel.* Mobile: S. H. Goetzel and Company, 1857. New York: G. W. Carleton, 1866.

Levin, David. *History as Romantic Art.* Stanford: Stanford UP, 1959.

Levine, Robert. "Fiction and Reform I." *The Columbia History of the Novel.* Ed. Emory Elliott. New York: Columbia UP, 1991. 130–54.

Lynn, Kenneth S. *Mark Twain and Southwestern Humor.* Boston: Little, Brown, 1959.

McWhiney, Grady. *Cracker Culture: Celtic Ways in the Old South.* Tuscaloosa: U of Alabama P, 1988.

Meek, Alexander Beaufort. *The Red Eagle*. New York: D. Appleton and Company, 1855.

——. *The Red Eagle*. Ed. Will T. Sheehan and Geo. N. Bayzer. Montgomery, AL: Paragon Press, 1914.

——. *Romantic Passages in Southwestern History*. Mobile: S. H. Goetzel, 1857.

——. *Songs and Poems of the South*. New York and Mobile: S. H. Goetzel, 1857.

——, ed. *The Southron* 1.1-6 (1939).

The Memoirs of Lafitte; or, the Barritarian pirate. Providence: Wm. S. Spear, 1826.

Moore, Albert B. *History of Alabama*. 1934. Rpt. Tuscaloosa: U of Alabama Book Store, 1951.

Nott, Josiah C. *Types of Mankind*. Philadelphia: Lippincott, Grambo, 1854.

O'Brien, Michael. "On the Writing of History in the Old South." *Rewriting the South*. Ed. Lothar Honnighausen and Valeria Gennaro Lerda. Tübingen: Francke, 1993. 141–66.

——. *Rethinking the South: Essays in Intellectual History*. Baltimore: Johns Hopkins UP, 1988.

Owen, Thomas McAdory. *History of Alabama and Dictionary of Alabama Biography*. 4 vols. Chicago: S. J. Clarke, 1921.

Owsley, Frank L. "Albert J. Pickett, Historian of Alabama." *Alabama Review* 11 (January 1958): 31–43.

——. *Struggle for the Gulf Borderlands: The Creek War and the Battle of New Orleans, 1812–15*. Gainesville: University Presses of Florida, 1987.

Parks, Edd Winfield. *William Gilmore Simms as Literary Critic*. Athens: U of Georgia P, 1961.

Pearce, Roy Harvey. *Savagism and Civilization*. Berkeley: U of California P, 1988.

Petter, Henri. *The Early American Novel*. Columbus: Ohio State UP, 1970.

Pickett, Albert J. *History of Alabama, and Incidentally of Georgia and Mississippi, from the Earliest Period*. 2 vols. Charleston: Walker and James, 1851.

——. "The Origins and Progress of History in the Eastern Hemisphere." Alabama Archives. Montgomery.

Porter, Benjamin F. *Reminiscences of Men and Things in Alabama*. Tuscaloosa: Portals Press, 1983.

Potter, David M. *The Impending Crisis, 1848–1861*. New York: Harper and Row, 1976.

Rev. of *The Red Eagle*. *Harper's New Monthly Magazine* 57 (December 1855): 118.

Rev. of *The Red Eagle*. *Southern Literary Messenger* 20 (December 1855): 674.

Reynolds, David S. *Walt Whitman's America: A Cultural Biography*. New York: Knopf, 1995.

Ridgley, J. V. *Nineteenth-Century Southern Literature*. Lexington: UP of Kentucky, 1980.

Rogers, William Warren, Robert David Ward, Leah Rawls Atkins, and Wayne Flynt. *Alabama: The History of a Deep South State*. Tuscaloosa: U of Alabama P, 1994.

Royall, Anne Newport. *Letters from Alabama, 1817–1822*. 1824. Rpt. University: U of Alabama P, 1969.

Saunders, James E. *Early Settlers of Alabama.* New Orleans: L. Graham & Son, 1899.

Schriber, Mary-Suzanne. "Julia Ward Howe and the Travel Book." *New England Quarterly* 62 (1989): 264–79.

———. *Writing Home: American Women Abroad, 1830–1920.* Charlottesville: UP of Virginia, 1997.

Scott, Sutton S. *The Mobilians: Talks about the South.* Montgomery, AL: Brown Brothers, 1898.

Sewall, Lewis. *The Last Campaign of Sir John Falstaff The II; or, The Hero of the Burnt-Corn Battle. A Serio-Comic Poem by ***** *******.* St. Stephens, AL, 1815.

———. *The Miscellaneous Poems of Lewis Sewall, Esq., Containing the Last Campaign of Col J. Caller—Alias Sir John Falstaff the Second—Alias the Hero of the Burnt Corn Battle; The Birth Progress, and Probable End of G. F. Mynheer Van Slaverchap's Grandson—Alias Doctor Furnace; The Battle for the Cow and Calf; The Canoe Fight; And Other Miscellaneous Matters.* Mobile, 1833.

Sheehan, Will T. "Alabama's Neglected Literature." *Literary Digest* 22 March 1919: 35.

Shields, Johanna Nicol. Introduction. *Adventures of Captain Simon Suggs.* By Johnson Jones Hooper. Tuscaloosa: U of Alabama P, 1993. vii–lxix.

———. "A Sadder Simon Suggs: Freedom and Slavery in the Humor of Johnson Jones Hooper." *Journal of Southern History* 56 (November 1990): 641–64.

———. "A Social History of Antebellum Alabama Writers." *Alabama Review* 62 (July 1989): 163–91.

Smith, Harold F. *American Travelers Abroad.* Carbondale: Southern Illinois UP, 1969.

Smith, Henry Nash. Introduction. *The Prairie.* By James Fenimore Cooper. New York: Rinehart, 1950. v–xx.

Smith, M. (Don Pedro Casender) *The Lost Virgin of the South: An Historical Novel, Founded on Facts, Connected with the Indian War in the South, in 1812 to '15.* Tallahassee, 1831. Courtland, AL, 1832.

Smith, William R. *College Musings; or, Twigs from Parnassus.* Tuscaloosa, 1833.

Smith, Winston. *An Annotated Edition of Hooper's* Some Adventures of Captain Simon Suggs. Diss. Vanderbilt University. Ann Arbor: University Microfilms, 1965.

Stampp, Kenneth M. *The Peculiar Institution: Slavery in the Antebellum South.* New York: Vintage, 1989.

Stewart, James Brewer. *Holy Warriors: The Abolitionists and American Slavery.* New York: Hill and Wang, 1976.

Stowe, William W. *Going Abroad: European Travel in Nineteenth-Century American Culture.* Princeton: Princeton UP, 1994.

Thompson, G. R. *Poe's Fiction: Romantic Irony in the Gothic Tales.* Madison: U of Wisconsin P, 1973.

Thornton, Mills. *Politics and Power in a Slave Society: Alabama, 1800–1860.* Baton Rouge: Louisiana State UP, 1978.

Twain, Mark. *Adventures of Huckleberry Finn.* Boston: Riverside Press, 1958.

Voloshin, Beverly. "The Limits of the Female Bildungsroman in America, 1820–70."

Women's Studies 10 (1984): 283–302. Rpt. in *American Literature, Culture, and Ideology: Essays in Memory of Henry Nash Smith.* Ed. Beverly Voloshin. New York: Lang, 1990. 95–114.

Watson, Ritchie D., Jr. *Yeoman versus Cavalier: The Old Southwest's Fictional Road to Rebellion.* Baton Rouge: Louisiana State UP, 1993.

Welsh, Mary. "Reminiscences of St. Stephens." *Proceedings of the Alabama Historical Society, 1898–99.* Tuscaloosa: Alabama Historical Society, 1900. 222–23.

Williams, Benjamin B. "The Identity of Alabama's First Novelist." *Alabama Review* 27 (July 1964): 234–35.

———. *A Literary History of Alabama: The Nineteenth Century.* Rutherford, NJ: Fairleigh Dickinson UP, 1979.

Williams, Jack K. "Crime and Punishment in Early Alabama, 1819–40." *Alabama Review* 6 (January 1953): 14–30.

Wimsatt, Mary Anne. "Antebellum Fiction." *History of Southern Literature.* Ed. Louis D. Rubin, Jr. Baton Rouge: Louisiana State UP, 1986. 92–107.

———. "Caroline Lee Hentz's Balancing Act." *The Female Tradition in Southern Literature.* Ed. Carol S. Manning. Urbana: U of Illinois P, 1993. 161–75.

Wood, Michael L. "Personal Reminiscences of A. J. Pickett." *Transactions of the Alabama Historical Society, 1899–1903.* Montgomery: Alabama Historical Society, 1904. 597–611.

Wyatt-Brown, Bertram. *Southern Honor: Ethics and Behavior in the Old South.* New York: Oxford UP, 1982.

———. *Yankee Saints and Southern Sinners.* Baton Rouge: Louisiana State UP, 1985.

Young, Mary Elizabeth. *Redskins, Ruffleshirts, and Rednecks: Indian Allotments in Alabama and Mississippi, 1830–1860.* Norman: U of Oklahoma P, 1961.

Index

~

Abernathy, Thomas P., *The Formative Period in Alabama,* 138 (n. 4)
abolitionism and abolitionists, 100, 103–5, 107–14, 133, 138 (n. 2), 164–65 (nn. 4, 5, 11)
Adair, James, 68, 71
Alabama, capitals of, 3, 7, 73
Alabama, constitutional convention (Huntsville, 1819), 3, 23–25, 73
Alabama, court system and judiciary, 25, 30–31, 143–44 (nn. 2, 3), 160–61 (n. 3)
Alabama, The University of, 4, 8, 48, 49, 50, 52, 53, 140 (n. 11), 144 (n. 2), 148 (n. 1)
Alabama Department of Archives and History, 84, 159 (n. 19)
Alabama Education Act (1854), 85, 138 (n. 2)
Alabama Historical Society, 84, 149 (n. 3), 154 (n. 16), 155 (n. 20), 157 (n. 17)
Alabama Library Association, 84
Alabama state bank, 91–92, 94, 99

Alcott, Louisa May, 163 (n. 2)
Allen, Ethan, 24
Allen, Gay Wilson, 156 (n. 2)
Amistad mutiny, 164 (n. 5)
anti-abolitionist novel, 54, 104, 108, 111
"anti-Tom" novel, the, 102–4, 106–8, 110, 112, 162–64 (nn. 1, 2, 3)
Arvin, Newton, 156 (n. 1)
Atkins, Leah Rawls, 27, 29, 90, 91, 137 (n. 2), 151 (n. 7)

Bagby, George, 82
Bakhtin, Mikhail, 166 (n. 17)
Baldwin, Joseph G., 4, 11, 53, 54, 80, 98–99, 102, 135, 162 (n. 14); *Flush Times of Alabama and Mississippi,* 9, 87–101, 138 (n. 2), 139 (n. 8), 156 (n. 22), 160–61 (nn. 3, 5, 6, 8, 9, 10); *Party Leaders,* 99
Bancroft, George, 63
Bank of Mobile, 99
Bank of the United States, 91, 92
Baptist church, 4, 6, 140 (n. 11)

Barnard, F. A. P., 52, 82

Barr, John Gorman, 53, 156 (n. 22), 160 (n. 1)

Bartram, William, 68

Baym, Nina, 162 (nn. 1, 2), 165 (nn. 7, 10), 166 (n. 15)

Bay Psalm Book, 23

Bayzer, Geo. T., 84, 85

Beasley, Daniel, 71, 157 (n. 7)

Bibb, William Wyatt, 24, 73

Bible, the, 40, 123

Biddle, Nicholas, 24, 91

Bienville, Jean Baptiste LeMoyne, 71–72

bildungsroman, female, 166 (n. 14), 167 (n. 18)

Birmingham, 139 (n. 6), 148 (n. 1)

Birmingham News, 160 (n. 21)

Black Belt, 7, 89, 137 (n. 2), 138 (n. 2), 155 (n. 20), 169 (n. 6)

Bolingbroke, Viscount (Henry St. John), 63–64

Boykin, Burwell, 50, 69

Brantley, William H., 142 (n. 12)

Brontë, Charlotte, *Jane Eyre,* 123, 124, 167–68 (n. 24)

Brown, Charles Brockden, 33, 41, 63, 115

Brown, John, 164–65 (n. 5)

Brown, William Garrott, *A History of Alabama for Use in Schools,* 151 (n. 7)

Brown, William Wells, *Clotel,* 130

Bryant, William Cullen, 48

Bunyan, John, *Pilgrim's Progress,* 40, 119, 123

Burnt Corn Creek, Battle of, 16–19, 22, 47, 71, 141 (nn. 2, 4), 142 (n. 8), 160 (n. 20)

Burr, Aaron, 68, 73, 141 (n. 1), 154 (n. 15)

Burton, Robert Wilton, 159 (n. 15)

Butler, Samuel, *Hudibras,* 19, 142 (n. 9)

Byron, George Gordon, 50, 121, 167 (n. 22)

Cadillac, M. de la Mothe de, 68

Caesar, Terry, 56

Cahaba, Alabama, 3, 7, 23, 24, 73, 91

Caldwell, Erskine, 130

Calhoun, John C., 58, 60, 165 (n. 11)

Caller, James, 16–22, 47, 68, 71, 141 (nn. 2, 4, 5), 142 (nn. 7, 10, 12, 13), 159 (n. 20)

Caller, John, 16–17, 22, 141 (n. 5), 142 (n. 13)

campaign biography, 88, 160 (n. 2)

captivity narrative, 33, 41

Carlyle, Thomas, 120, 167 (n. 22); *Sartor Resartus,* 123

Catholicism, 40, 45, 146 (n. 2)

Cervantes, Miguel de, *Don Quixote,* 19, 142 (n. 9)

Cherokee Nation, 33, 67

Chickasaw Nation, 33, 67, 72

Child, Lydia Maria, 77, 115, 163 (n. 2)

Childress, Mark, 149 (n. 1)

Chivers, Thomas Holley, 70, 82; *The Path of Sorrow,* 148 (n. 2); *Conrad and Eudora,* 148 (n. 2)

Choctaw Nation, 18, 33, 67, 90–91, 154 (n. 15), 161 (nn. 3, 4, 5, 8)

Civil War, 114, 134–35, 138 (n. 6)

Claiborne, F. L., 78

Claiborne, John F. H., 69, 152 (n. 9), 153 (n. 14); *Mississippi as a Province, Territory, and State,* 66

Clay, Clement, 65, 69

Clay, Henry, 58, 60

Clemens, Jeremiah, *Tobias Wilson,* 158 (n. 15)

Clemens, Samuel L. (Mark Twain), 40, 42, 44, 51, 55, 57, 62, 98, 135; *Adventures of Huckleberry Finn,* 46, 97–98, 162 (n. 15); *Innocents Abroad,* 57

Clopton, Virginia Clay, *A Belle of the Fifties,* 53

Coffee, Gen. John, 18

Cohen, Hennig, 151 (n. 9)

Coleridge, S. T., 12, 50, 51, 120, 122; *Rime of the Ancient Mariner,* 123

Collier, Henry W., 66

Columbus Land Company, 161 (n. 4)

Confederacy, Southern, 127, 158 (n. 15)

Confederate Veteran, 158 (n. 15)

confidence man, the, 88, 89, 97, 143 (n. 2)

Conner, Wiley, 8, 11, 33, 44, 46, 145–46 (n. 2)

Cooke, John Esten, 82
Cooper, James F., 4, 8, 9, 12, 33, 39–41, 43, 44, 47, 55, 63, 66, 73, 77, 86, 115–17, 122, 146 (nn. 2, 4), 152 (n. 11), 157 (n. 6); *The Spy*, 36, 39; *Last of the Mohicans*, 36, 39, 167 (n. 19); *Notions of the Americans*, 39; *The Red Rover*, 39; *The Wept of Wish-ton-Wish*, 39, 147 (n. 6); *The Prairie*, 155 (n. 19); "Mohawk Edition," 159 (n. 18)
Cooper, William J., 127, 168 (n. 1)
Cotton Snob, the, 130, 131, 132, 134
Courtland, Alabama, 32, 33
Cousin, Victor, 121, 167 (n. 22)
Cowper, William, 121, 167 (n. 22)
Creek Nation, 6, 17–18, 20, 33, 39, 40, 65, 67, 68, 78, 90–91, 159 (n. 20), 161 (nn. 4, 5)
Creek Uprising of 1836, 65, 90, 93, 95
Creek War of 1813–14, 8, 17–18, 45, 47, 65, 73, 78, 141 (n. 4), 154 (n. 18), 157 (n. 3)
Crozat, Antoine, 68
Cummins, Maria, 12, 115, 163 (n. 2); *Lamplighter*, 123

Dale, Sam, and the Canoe Fight, 73, 78
Dana, Charles A., 156 (n. 2)
Davidson, Cathy, 162 (n. 2), 166 (n. 15)
Davis, Richard Brion, 165 (n. 5)
De Bow, J. D. B., 153–54 (n. 14)
De Bow's Review, 134
Decatur, 91
De Leon, Thomas Cooper, 148 (n. 1); *John Holden, Unionist*, 158 (n. 15)
Democratic party, 6, 11, 88, 92, 99, 100, 101, 134, 137 (n. 2), 138 (n. 2), 159 (n. 9), 160 (n. 2)
De Quincey, Thomas, 167 (n. 22); *Analects from Richter*, 120
de Soto, Hernando, 67, 71, 72, 73, 153 (n. 13)
Dickens, Charles, 55, 116
Dillingham, William B., 151 (n. 9)
D'Israeli, Benjamin, 60
Doster, James F., 17

Dostoevsky, Fyodor, 122
Douglas, Stephen A., 134

Eaton, Clement, 130
Eaton, John Henry, 12, 46, 152 (n. 9); *Life of General A. Jackson*, 146 (nn. 2, 3, 4); *Memoirs of Andrew Jackson*, 160 (n. 2)
Eggleston, George Cory, 141 (n. 2)
Eliot, George, 122, 168 (n. 24); *Middlemarch*, 124, 168 (n. 24); *Adam Bede*, 168 (n. 24)
Eliot, T. S., 167 (n. 23)
elites, literary and cultural, 7, 9–13, 64, 74, 81, 88, 96, 101, 112, 125–26, 130–31, 133, 139 (nn. 7, 9), 140 (n. 11), 142 (n. 9), 150 (n. 5), 151 (n. 9), 155 (n. 20), 159 (n. 16)
Ellison, Rhoda Coleman, 107, 137 (n. 1), 138 (n. 3), 145–46 (nn. 1, 2), 165 (nn. 8, 9); *Early Alabama Publications*, 137 (n. 1)
Emerson, R. W., 12, 55, 77, 120, 121, 156 (n. 2), 167 (n. 22); "Self-Reliance," 57; "Circles," 121
epic, 76–77, 79, 85, 86, 157–58 (n. 9)
Episcopal church, 4, 6, 139 (n. 7)
Estes, Matthew, *A Defense of Negro Slavery as it Exists, in the United States*, 139 (n. 10)
ethnology, racial, 133–34
Eufala, Chief, 158 (n. 9)
Evans, Augusta Jane, 5, 11, 47–48, 54, 57, 102, 135, 138 (n. 2), 149 (n. 7), 163 (n. 2), 166–67 (nn. 16, 18); *Beulah*, 9, 49, 114–26, 166–68 (nn. 14, 17, 20–25); *Inez, a Tale of the Alamo*, 48, 114; *Macaria; or, Altars of Sacrifice*, 114, 149 (n. 7); *St. Elmo*, 114, 126

Faulkner, William, 130, 159 (n. 16); Snopes Trilogy, 98
feminism, 114–16, 122, 126, 166–68 (nn. 15, 17, 18, 25)
Fern, Fanny (Sarah Willis Parton), 57, 163 (n. 2); *Ruth Hall*, 166 (n. 15)

Feuerbach, Ludwig, 167 (n. 22), 168 (n. 24)
Fidler, William T., 120
Fisher, Philip, 152 (n. 11)
Flag of the Union (Tuscaloosa), 13, 49, 52
Flaubert, Gustave, 122
Flint, Timothy, 12, 46, 146 (n. 2), 152 (n. 9); *Condensed Geography and History of the Western States,* 146 (nn. 2, 3, 4)
Flournoy, Thomas, 18
Flynt, Wayne, 137 (n. 2), 151 (n. 7)
Fort Jackson, Treaty of, 18
Fort Mims, Massacre of, 17–18, 71, 78, 141 (n. 4), 157 (n. 7), 159–60 (n. 20)
Fox-Genovese, Elizabeth, 117, 126, 166 (n. 14), 167–68 (n. 24)
Fuller, Margaret, *At Home and Abroad,* 57

Gaines, George S., 154 (n. 15)
Galvez, Bernardo, 68
Gardiner, Jane, 163 (n. 3)
Garrison, William Lloyd, 106; *Liberator,* 164 (n. 5)
Gayarre, Charles, 69, 153–54 (n. 14)
gentry, society of, 5–7, 10–11
Gibbon, Edward, 149 (n. 3)
Gilmer, Rodominick, 17
Goldthwaite, Henry, 144 (n. 2)
Goshgarian, G. M., 116, 167 (nn. 18, 20, 22)
Gosse, Philip, 55, 148 (n. 5)
gothic fiction, 33, 41, 45, 167 (n. 21)
Grammer, John, 139 (n. 8), 161 (n. 10)
Greeley, Horace, 156 (n. 2), 164 (n. 4)
Gray, Richard, 150 (n. 5), 163–64 (n. 3)
Green, Paul, 152 (n. 9)
Greenspan, Ezra, 156 (n. 2)
Greenwood, Grace (Sara Jane Lippincott), 57
Groom, Winston, *Forrest Gump,* 148 (n. 1)

Halbert, H. S., and T. H. Ball, *The Creek War of 1813 and 1814,* 141 (n. 2)
Hale, Edward Everett, 156 (n. 2)
Hall, Fanny W., *Rambles in Europe,* 56–57

Hamilton, William, *Philosophy of the Conditioned,* 120–21, 124
Harper's Magazine, 81
Harris, George Washington, 16
Harris, Joel Chandler, 159 (n. 15)
Harris, Sarah Smith, 64–65
Harrison, William Henry, 141 (n. 1)
Hawthorne, Nathaniel, 40, 44, 55, 63, 115, 135; "Rappaccini's Daughter," 120; *The Scarlet Letter,* 122; *The Marble Faun,* 122
Hayne, Arthur P., 69, 153 (n. 14)
Hayne, Thomas Hamilton, 80, 82
Hedges, William, 64, 149 (n. 2)
Hentz, Caroline Lee, 5, 10, 11, 12, 52, 53, 54, 102–3, 107, 112, 135, 140 (n. 10), 165–66 (nn. 7, 9, 10, 13); *Planter's Northern Bride,* 9, 12, 102–114, 138 (n. 2), 140 (n. 10), 154–55 (n. 18), 162–66 (nn. 1–6, 8, 9, 12, 15); *Aunt Patty's Scrap Bag,* 103; *Linda,* 103; *Rena,* 103; *Marcus Warland,* 103, 163–64 (n. 3); *Eoline,* 103; *Helen and Arthur,* 103; *Victim of Excitement,* 103; *Wild Jack,* 103
Hentz, Nicholas, 103, 112, 165–66 (nn. 9, 13)
Herodotus, 149 (n. 3)
Heyrman, Christine Leigh, 139 (n. 7)
Hilliard, Henry, 50, 52, 82
historical fiction, 33, 45
historiography, romantic, 63–64
Hitchcock, Henry, 3, 10, 23–26, 135; *Alabama Justice of the Peace,* 8, 23, 24–31, 140 (n. 10)
Hobson, Fred C., 127–28, 130, 133, 134, 135, 168 (n. 1)
Holy Ground, Battle of, 78
Homer, 50; *The Iliad,* 19
honor, 70, 71, 138 (n. 2), 143 (n. 2), 150 (n. 5)
Hooper, Johnson J., 4, 11, 16, 53, 54, 80, 98–99, 102, 135, 162 (n. 14); *Adventures of Simon Suggs,* 9, 87–101, 138 (n. 2), 156 (n. 22), 160 (nn. 21, 2), 161–62 (nn. 11, 12); "Taking the Census in Alabama," 98

Horseshoe Bend, Battle of (Tohopeka), 18, 36, 43, 75, 78, 87, 146 (n. 3), 160 (n. 2)
Hubbell, Jay, 158 (n. 12)
Hubbs, G. Ward., 160 (n. 1)
Humor, Southwestern, 4, 9, 15–16, 42–44, 53, 54, 70, 73, 87–88, 101, 102, 130, 142 (n. 9), 151 (n. 9)
Hundley, Daniel, 127–28; *Social Relations in Our Southern States,* 127–35, 139 (n. 10); *Prison Echoes of the Great Rebellion,* 135
Hunter, Kermit, 153 (n. 9)
Huntsville, 3, 7, 13, 73, 91, 143 (n. 2)

Iberville, Pierre LeMoyne, 68
immigrants, German-Jewish, 138 (n. 5)
immigrants, Irish, 138 (n. 5)
Ingraham, Joseph Holt, 12, 147 (n. 4)
iron industry, 138–39
Irving, Theodore, 12, 69
Irving, Washington, 48, 55, 58, 63; *History of New York,* 149 (n. 2)

Jackson, Andrew, 8, 18, 21, 34, 44–45, 67, 78, 91, 101, 140–41 (n. 1), 145–46 (n. 2), 151 (n. 9), 152 (n. 10), 153 (n. 12), 157 (n. 8), 160 (n. 2)
James, Henry, 44, 55, 167 (n. 23); *The Portrait of a Lady,* 61
Jones, Anne Goodwyn, 116
Justus, James, 89

Kaelevala, 77, 79, 158 (n. 10)
Kelly, Judge William, 144 (n. 2)
Kennedy, John Pendleton, 82
Kermode, Frank, 135
Kettle, Arnold, 167 (n. 23)

Lafayette, Marquis de, 58
Lafayette East Alabamian, 87, 98
Lanier, Sidney, 80
Lafitte, Jean, 42, 147 (n. 4)
Lamb, Charles, 121, 167 (n. 22)
lawyers, 93, 96, 97, 98, 161 (n. 3)
Ledyard, Irwin, 158 (n. 158)
Lee, Harper, 66, 72, 73, 75, 151 (n. 8), 154 (n. 17), 159 (n. 16); *To Kill a Mockingbird,* 98, 130, 151 (n. 8)
Le Vert, Henry Strachey, 58
Le Vert, Octavia Walton, 4, 8, 11, 48, 57–59, 138 (n. 2), 148 (n. 5); *Souvenirs of Travel,* 8, 12, 54–55, 57–62, 149 (n. 6)
Levin, David, 63, 66, 149 (n. 1)
Lewis, Matthew, *The Monk,* 41
Lincoln, Abraham, 128, 134
Lipscomb, Abner I., 144 (n. 2)
literary amateur, the, 4–5, 8, 10–13, 15–16, 19, 21–22, 33, 46, 48, 53–54, 56, 66, 69–70, 74, 80–81, 85, 150 (n. 5)
literary professionalism, 5, 11, 48, 56, 103
literary regionalism, southern, 4, 10, 11, 12, 34–35, 39–40, 42–43, 45, 48, 51–52, 57, 64, 68–70, 72, 74, 76, 80–83, 139–40 (n. 10), 148 (n. 2)
Longfellow, Henry W., 4, 12, 48, 55, 80; *Song of Hiawatha,* 8, 76–77, 79, 85, 153 (n. 12), 156–57 (nn. 1–4), 158 (n. 10), 159 (n. 18); "A Psalm of Life," 118
Longstreet, Augustus Baldwin, 16, 82
Lynn, Kenneth S., 101, 151 (n. 9), 162 (n. 15)

Macaulay, Thomas B., 149 (n. 3)
McGillivray, Alexander, 67, 72, 78
McIntosh, William, 78
McQueen, James, 78
McWhiney, Grady, 130, 168–69 (n. 5)
Manly, Basil, 69, 140 (n. 11)
man/woman of letters, the, 10–13, 47–49, 53–54, 68–69, 80–81
Martineau, Harriet, 55
Maubila, Battle of, 71
Maxwell, Thomas, *King Bee's Dream,* 53
Meek, A. B., 4, 8, 11–13, 47–50, 52, 53, 54, 69, 84–86, 135, 138 (n. 2), 150–51 (n. 6), 153 (n. 14); *The Southron,* 8, 12, 48, 49, 52–53, 82, 103, 140 (n. 10); *The Red Eagle,* 8, 47, 49, 76–86, 101, 147 (n. 7), 153 (n. 12), 155 (n. 22), 157–58 (nn. 5–9), 160 (n. 21); *Romantic Passages in Southwestern History,* 47, 49, 83, 140 (n. 10), 151 (n. 6), 157 (n. 7); *Songs and Poems*

of the South, 47, 49, 83; "Southern Literature," 82; "The Southwest, Its History, Character, and Prospects," 82, 140 (n. 10); "Jack Cadeism and Its Prospects," 82; "Americanism in Literature," 82, 140 (n. 10); "History of Alabama," 151 (n. 6)

Melville, Herman, 40, 44, 73, 115, 122, 135

Memoirs of Lafitte, 146–47 (n. 4)

Mercury (Charleston), 82

metafiction, 34, 43

Methodist church, 4, 6

middle classes, southern, 131

miles gloriosus, 16, 140–41 (n. 1), 142 (n. 9), 160 (n. 2)

Mill, John Stuart, 12

Milton, John, 40, 141 (n. 4), 142 (n. 7)

Minor, Henry, 144 (n. 2)

Mitchell, Margaret, *Gone with the Wind,* 130

Mobile, 7, 13, 24–25, 47–49, 54, 57–58, 61, 91, 125, 138 (n. 6), 143 (n. 2), 148 (n. 1)

Mobile Register, 49

Monette, John W., 69, 152 (n. 9), 153 (n. 14)

Montgomery, 3, 7, 54, 91, 143 (n. 2)

Montgomery Advertiser, 84, 159 (n. 19)

Moore, Albert B., 30, 84, 91–92, 100, 137 (n. 2), 151 (n. 7)

Moore, Thomas, *Lallah Rookh,* 80

Mordecai, Abraham, 68, 73, 154 (n. 15)

Moses, 149 (n. 3)

Motley, John Lothrop, 63

Muller, A. A., 148 (n. 4); "Sunset at Rome," 52–53; "The Wedding Feast," 148 (n. 4)

Native Americans: removals, 3, 9, 43, 64, 73, 74, 78, 90, 152 (n. 11); land cessions, 18–21; depictions of, 39–40, 45, 67, 75, 77, 83, 85–86, 101, 152 (n. 11), 157 (n. 6); renewal of public interest in, 84, 159 (n. 16)

New Orleans, Battle of, 43, 146 (n. 3), 152 (n. 10), 160 (n. 2)

non-fiction novel, 34

Norton, Charles Eliot, 156 (n. 2)

Nott, Josiah, 133–34; *Types of Mankind,* 139 (n. 10)

novel of ideas, 114, 115, 122

O'Brien, Michael, 149–50 (nn. 3, 4, 6), 153 (n. 13), 154 (n. 14)

O'Connor, Flannery, 130

Old Northwest, 2

Old Southwest, 2–3, 7, 15, 18, 21–22, 24, 25, 32, 33, 39, 40, 42–45, 52, 64, 66, 68, 77, 78, 86, 87, 94, 127, 128, 140 (n. 10), 141 (n. 1)

oratory, Indian, 158 (n. 9)

Osceola, 85

outdoor drama, 152 (n. 9)

Ovid, *Metamorphoses,* 23

Owen, Marie Bankhead, 84

Owen, Thomas McAdory, 84, 137 (n. 2), 142 (n. 13), 151 (n. 7), 159 (n. 19)

Owsley, Frank, 130, 141 (n. 2), 149 (n. 4), 150 (n. 6), 152 (n. 9), 153 (n. 13)

Page, Thomas Nelson, *Red Rock,* 158 (n. 15)

Panic of 1837, 3, 24, 89, 91, 92, 161 (n. 6)

Paragon Press, 84

Parkman, Francis, 63, 66

Paulding, James Kirke, *Lion of the West,* 140 (n. 1)

Pearce, Roy Harvey, 156–57 (n. 3)

Peck, Samuel Minturn, 84

Perry, Sion L., 144 (n. 2)

Petter, Henri, 41, 146 (n. 3)

Phillip, King (Metacomet), 85

picaresque fiction, 33, 42–43, 92

Pickens, Francis W., 69

Pickett, Albert J., 4, 49, 54, 63–75, 80, 135, 138 (n. 2), 149–52 (nn. 4, 5, 6, 9), 155 (n. 20); *History of Alabama,* 9, 30, 63–75, 82–83, 101, 151–52 (nn. 7, 8, 9), 153–54 (nn. 13, 14, 15, 17), 155 (n. 21); "Origins and Progress of History in the Eastern Hemisphere," 149 (n. 3), 154 (n. 16), 155 (n. 20); "Invasion of the Territory of Alabama," 150 (n. 6)

Pindar, 50

Pinkney, Edward Coote: *Rodolph,* 148 (n. 2); *Poems,* 148 (n. 2)

planter-aristocrat, the, 130, 132, 133, 134, 137 (n. 2), 138 (n. 2), 150 (n. 5), 151–52 (n. 9), 155 (nn. 20, 21), 164 (n. 3), 169 (n. 6)

Poe, Edgar Allan, 12, 42, 48, 80, 82, 120, 121, 123, 167 (nn. 21, 22); "Ligeia," 120, 123, 168 (n. 25); "William Wilson," 120; "Morella," 120; *Eureka,* 120; *Tamerlane and Other Poems,* 148 (n. 2); *Al Araaf, Tamerlane,* and *Minor Poems,* 148 (n. 2); *Poems,* 148 (n. 2)

poor white, southern, 130, 132, 168–69 (n. 5)

Porter, Benjamin Faneuil, 143–44 (n. 2)

Porter, David M., 164–65 (n. 5)

Porter, William T., 53, 87, 95, 98

Pratt, Daniel, 138 (n. 6)

Prattville, Alabama, 138 (n. 6)

Presbyterian church, 4, 6

Prescott, William Hickling, 63, 66

Prophet, The, 68

Pushmatawhaw, 68

Pyrnelle, Sara Louise, *Diddie Dumps and Tot,* 159 (n. 15)

realism, literary, 34, 43–44, 101, 102, 115–16, 122, 126

Republican party, 134

Richter, Jean Paul Friedrich (Jean Paul), 120, 167 (n. 22)

Robertson, William, 149 (n. 3)

Rogers, William Warren, 137 (n. 2); *Alabama: The History of a Deep South State,* 151 (n. 7)

Rowlandson, Mary, 147 (n. 8)

Royall, Anne Newport, 4, 148 (n. 5)

Ruskin, John, 12

Saffold, Reuben, 144 (n. 2)

St. Stephens, 7, 16, 24, 73, 142 (n. 12)

Sandys, George, 23

satire, 14–15

Saunders, James E., 145 (n. 2)

Schelling, Friedrich W., 121, 167 (n. 22)

Schoolcraft, Henry Rowe, 157 (n. 3); *Algic Researches,* 158 (n. 3)

Schriber, Mary-Suzanne, 148–49 (n. 6)

Scott, Sir Walter, 4, 8, 9, 12, 50–52, 80; *Lady of the Lake,* 85

Scott, Sutton S., *The Mobilians,* 83, 158 (nn. 9, 14)

Second Great Awakening, 139 (n. 7)

Secret Six, the, 164–65 (n. 5)

Sedgwick, Catherine Maria, 12, 77, 115, 162–63 (n. 2)

Sehoy, 68

Seminole Nation, 33, 35, 40, 67

sentimental/domestic fiction, 4–5, 9, 10, 33, 41–43, 45, 102, 105–6, 108–12, 118–20, 123–24, 165 (nn. 10, 12); as medium of female education, 114–16, 120–22, 126, 166–67 (nn. 15, 17, 18), 168 (n. 25)

Sewall, Lewis, 7, 10, 16, 47, 135, 141–42 (nn. 5, 6, 7, 11, 12, 13); *Last Campaign of Sir John Falstaff the II,* 7–8, 16, 19–21, 22, 47; *Miscellaneous Poems,* 21, 141 (n. 4)

Shakespeare, William, 4, 12, 19, 50, 51; *Henry IV,* Part I, 19, 20, 93, 96, 142 (nn. 9, 10); *The Tempest,* 40; *Romeo and Juliet,* 78, 106

Sheehan, Will T., 84, 85, 159 (n. 19), 160 (n. 21)

Shelley, Percy, 121–22, 167 (n. 22)

Shields, Johanna Nicol, 50, 89–90, 92, 139 (n. 10), 155–56 (n. 22), 160 (n. 2), 161 (n. 11); "A Social History of Alabama Writers," 138 (n. 3), 162 (n. 14)

Sidney, Sir Philip, 134

Sigourney, Lydia H., *Pleasant Memories of Pleasant Lands,* 57

Simms, William Gilmore, 4, 9, 12, 47, 48, 53, 63, 66, 69, 73, 77, 80–83, 86, 135, 150–51 (n. 6), 152 (n. 9), 153–54 (n. 14), 157 (n. 6), 158 (n. 9), 163–64 (n. 3); *Richard Hurdis,* 53; *History of South Carolina,* 66; *Atlantis,* 148 (n. 2); *Sword and the Distaff/Woodcraft,* 163–64 (n. 3)

Simon Magus, 95

slavery, 3, 9–10, 64, 72, 74–75, 77, 83, 86, 88–89, 100–101, 103–5, 126–30, 132–33, 140 (n. 10), 147 (n. 9), 148 (n. 2), 154–56 (nn. 18, 21, 22), 161–62 (nn. 11, 12, 14), 164 (n. 4), 166 (n. 15), 169 (nn. 6, 7); in legal codes, 29, 140 (n. 10); slave insurrection, white fear of, 104, 109, 111, 112, 138 (n. 2), 164–65 (n. 5); census figures, 139 (n. 9), 155 (n. 21)

Smith, Henry Nash, 155 (n. 19)

Smith, M. ("Don Pedro Casender"), 8, 10–12, 32–33, 44, 46, 145–46 (n. 2), 147 (n. 5); *Lost Virgin of the South*, 8, 9, 32–46, 47, 155 (n. 22)

Smith, William Russell, 4, 8, 10, 11, 13, 48, 52, 53, 82, 157–58 (n. 9); *College Musings*, 8, 12, 48, 50–52; *Bachelor's Button*, 49

Southern Literary Messenger, 11, 81, 87, 125

Solomon, King, 134

Southern Bully, the, 130–32

Southern Yankee, the, 130–32, 169 (n. 7)

Southey, Robert, 121

Southworth, E.D.E.N., 12, 103, 115, 163 (n. 2), 166 (n. 15)

Sparks, Jared, 12, 152 (n. 9), 153–54 (n. 14)

Specie Circular of 1836, 91

Spenser, Edmund, *The Faerie Queene*, 40–41

Spinoza, Baruch, 167 (n. 22), 168 (n. 24)

Spirit of the Times, 11, 53, 87, 98, 160 (n. 1)

Stampp, Kenneth, 130

Stewart, James Brewer, 164 (n. 4)

Stowe, Harriet Beecher, 40, 107, 135, 165 (n. 9); *Uncle Tom's Cabin*, 9, 12, 42, 102, 103, 107–9, 112, 128, 130, 155 (n. 18), 162–64 (nn. 1, 2, 3), 165 (n. 12), 166 (n. 15), 167 (n. 23); *Sunny Memories of Foreign Lands*, 57

Stowe, William, 56, 59

Strode, Hudson, 148 (n. 1)

Strother, Francis, 161 (n. 9)

Summersell, Charles Grayson, 151 (n. 7)

Tartt, Ruby Pickens, 84

Taylor, Bayard, 56, 57

Tecumseh, 17, 35, 68, 85

Tennyson, Alfred, *Palace of Art*, 120

Thompson, G. M., 167 (n. 21)

Thornton, Mills, 6, 88, 92, 99, 155 (n. 20), 161 (n. 7); *Politics and Power in a Slave Society*, 138 (n. 2)

Timrod, Henry, 82

Tocqueville, Alexis de, 55

Toulmin, Harry, 3, 16, 17, 25; *Digest of the Laws of Alabama*, 25

travel literature, 54–57, 59, 62

Trollope, Frances, 55

Turner, Nat, 164 (n. 5)

Tuscaloosa, Alabama, 3, 7, 13, 24, 48, 53, 91, 148 (n. 1), 149 (n. 3)

Tuskaloosa, Chief ("The Black Warrior"), 67, 71, 73

Tuskaloosa Bards, 52, 53

Tutwiler, Julia, 84

Unionists, 61, 128, 137 (n. 2), 138 (n. 2)

Van der Veer, Virginia, 151 (n. 7)

Vine and Olive Colony, 68, 73, 138 (n. 5)

Voloshin, Beverly, 116, 167 (n. 18)

Walter, Eugene, 148 (n. 1)

Ward, Robert David, 137 (n. 2)

Warner, Susan, 12, 115, 163 (n. 2); *Wide, Wide World*, 123, 167 (n. 19)

War of 1812, 45, 154 (n. 18)

Washington, George, 141 (n. 1)

Watson, Richie, 130, 150 (n. 5)

Wayne, Anthony, 141 (n. 1)

Weatherford, William ("The Red Eagle"), 8, 18, 35, 39, 44, 67, 78, 81, 84, 85, 147 (n. 7), 153 (n. 12), 157 (n. 8), 158 (n. 9)

Webb, C. H., *St. Twel'mo*, 166 (n. 16)

Webster, Daniel, 58, 60

Weems, Mason Locke, 92

Welsh, Mary, 21

Wesley, Charles, 68

Wesley, John, 68

Whig explanation of history, 86

Whig party, 6, 88, 92, 98–99, 101, 137 (n.

2), 142 (n. 9), 151 (n. 9), 160 (n. 2), 162 (n. 15)

Whitman, Walt, 79, 80; *Leaves of Grass*, 8, 76–78, 153 (n. 12), 156 (n. 2); "Song of Myself," 76, 78

Wilkinson, James, 68, 141 (n. 1)

Williams, Benjamin B., 83, 145–46 (nn. 1, 2); *A Literary History of Alabama*, 138 (n. 3), 141 (n. 11)

Williams, Jack K., 143 (n. 2)

Willis, N. P., 61

Wilson, Augusta Evans. *See* Evans, Augusta Jane

Woods, Alva, 140 (n. 11)

Wordsworth, William, 50, 51

Wyatt-Brown, Bertram, 130, 138 (n. 2), 150 (n. 5), 164 (n. 4)

Yancey, William Lowndes, 69, 137 (n. 2)

Yankee, the, 164 (nn. 3–4)

yeomanry, southern, 132, 137 (n. 2), 150 (n. 5), 155 (n. 20), 169 (n. 6)

About the Author

~

Philip D. Beidler is Professor of English at The University of Alabama, where he has taught American literature since receiving his Ph.D. from the University of Virginia in 1974. His recent books include *The Good War's Greatest Hits: World War II and American Remembering* and *Many Voices, Many Rooms: A New Anthology of Alabama Writers*, both published in 1998.